D0466361

Joe McCarthy and the Press

JOE McCARTHY and the Press

EDWIN R. BAYLEY

The University of Wisconsin Press

Published 1981

The University of Wisconsin Press
114 North Murray Street
Madison, Wisconsin 53715

The University of Wisconsin Press, Ltd.
1 Gower Street
London WC1E 6HA, England

Printings August 1981, December 1981

Printed in the United States of America

ISBN 0-299-08620-8 ; LC 81-50824

Contents

Preface

Most of the reporters who covered American politics from 1950 through 1954, and especially those of us who were fortunate enough to work for papers opposed to Wisconsin's Senator Joseph R. Mc-Carthy, regard the "McCarthy years" as the most dismal and the most exciting of our lives. As those years receded, however, I realized that my recollections were different from the recollections of many others and that my conception of the role of the press was not the prevailing one. That was the origin of my interest in the questions surrounding the press and Joe McCarthy. A sabbatical leave from the University of California, Berkeley, gave me the chance to look for answers to these questions.

It was being said that the press had "created" McCarthy, that McCarthy "used" the press, and even that the press in those days was "supine." Were these things true? Eliot Fremont-Smith, a New York literary critic writing in the *Columbia Journalism Review* in 1974 about I. F. Stone, said that in the early McCarthy years "the majority of even ostensibly liberal journalists and journals, and nearly all that counted, suffered a prolonged attack of *laryngitis intimidatus.*" Was that true? Did McCarthy take advantage of the press's adherence to the principle of objectivity—"straight" reporting—to spread his un-diluted charges of Communists in government? Did the press "smear" McCarthy, as his supporters charged? Was the press's opposition to McCarthy, where it existed, effective? Did it help him or hurt him?

Other questions arose. In what ways did McCarthy's relations with the press differ from those of other politicians? What effect did dealing with the McCarthy phenomenon have upon press practices and prin-ciples? Did the press (or television) finally bring him down? Could another McCarthy emerge today? Underlying all these was a fun-damental question that had to be answered before the others could be sensibly considered: What did the press actually do about Mc-Carthy? No one knew. The final question was my own—a standard for judgment on the press's performance in the McCarthy era: Did the press inform its readers fairly and fully?

I began my research in the morgues of the *Milwaukee Journal* and the *New York Times*, where I read every story those papers had published about McCarthy. At the Widener Library at Harvard, I tried to read everything that had been written about McCarthy in books, magazines, and academic journals. I had done this once before, in 1957, when I spent two weeks writing McCarthy's obituary—the "A-matter"—for the *Milwaukee Journal.* I found that a great deal had been written since then.

Next, I sought to interview as many of the reporters who had covered McCarthy as I could find, with special concentration on the Washington reporters for the wire services and the members of Washington bureau staffs. I had known many of these reporters for many years, which helped. As the story unfolded, I extended my interviews across the country. I interviewed more than 40 reporters in all, and corresponded with several others. Concurrently I studied newspapers in the microfilm rooms of the New York Public Library, the Boston Public Library, the Baltimore Public Library, Doe Library of the University of California, Berkeley, the Library of Congress, and the State Historical Society of Wisconsin. Other microfilms were obtained through the Inter-Library Loan service. I also studied papers and memoranda from several collections in the Library of Congress and the State Historical Society of Wisconsin.

For coverage during the first month after McCarthy's speech at Wheeling, West Virginia, on 9 February 1950, the period I considered most important for testing the national coverage of McCarthy, I read 129 newspapers ranging in daily circulation from 2,287,337 (*The New York Daily News*) to 1,902 (*The Willows Journal*, in California). My sample included morning, afternoon, and Sunday papers, papers from every major chain and from every region of the country. In a few states, I read every daily paper in the state, to be sure that no pattern of editorial handling of McCarthy news was overlooked. Some papers I chose because I knew their political allegiances, some because McCarthy had made significant speeches in their cities.

The sample included 40 papers from the East, 36 from the Midwest, 22 from the South, and 31 from the West. The combined circulation of the 56 morning papers was 11,474,057, more than 54 percent of the total morning circulation of newspapers in 1950. The combined circulation of the 73 afternoon papers in the study was 8,093,681, more than 25 percent of the total afternoon circulation. And the combined Sunday circulation was 23,300,475, more than 50 percent of the total Sunday circulation in the United States in 1950.

I counted the number and measured the length of news stories on McCarthy in each of these papers, and noted their placement. I recorded the number and length of syndicated and staff-produced columns. I recorded each headline and summarized each editorial and editorial cartoon. I noted the source of each story—Associated Press, United Press, International News Service, Washington bureau, or staff. In order to see how coverage of McCarthy had changed when news coverage reached its peak, I studied 60 of these papers published on one day, 11 March 1954. To see what papers were doing with news of McCarthy after his censure, I checked 29 papers for a three-day period, 8–10 March 1956. Examining the coverage of McCarthy and Thomas E. Fairchild, his Democratic opponent in the 1952 election, I read the stories carried during the last week of the campaign by the 39 daily newspapers in Wisconsin and the three out-of-state papers with significant circulations in the state, and the stories that appeared in 27 Wisconsin weeklies during the last month of the campaign. (The reader will find a complete list of sources at the back of the book: newspapers read, persons interviewed, collections consulted, and books and periodicals used.)

The book that has come out of my research and reflection deals with four critical and revealing points of contact between McCarthy and the press (or in one case, television) and is roughly chronological. The first chapter takes a look at McCarthy's background and the times in which he rose to power, and suggests the effect on him of his early newspaper reading and of local newspapermen who were his friends and perhaps mentors. The chapter then reports and appraises the news coverage and editorial reaction that resulted from the fateful series of Lincoln Day dinner speeches that began at Wheeling. The second chapter continues the study of news coverage from Washington, as McCarthy exchanges accusations with President Truman and the Tydings subcommittee begins its investigation of McCarthy's charges. The work of news editors, editorial writers, columnists, and cartoonists is analyzed in relation to its effect on public opinion.

The third chapter is concerned with the problems and attitudes of the wire service reporters covering McCarthy in Washington, with McCarthy's techniques for manipulating the wire services, and with the long argument among newspaper editors and publishers about the propriety and efficacy of "straight" reporting in the case of McCarthy. In chapter 4, I take up the question of whether newspaper opposition to McCarthy had a discernible effect upon voting in the 1952 Wisconsin senatorial election, and a subsidiary question of whether the press's interpretation of McCarthy's victory in the primary contributed to his subsequent reelection. I analyze a major speech of McCarthy's to show why covering him was so difficult for reporters, and I provide new examples of McCarthy's success in dominating the headlines, even in opposition papers.

Chapter 5 is an examination of the relations between McCarthy and the newspapers and magazines which he characterized as "the left-wing press." Included also is a review of his relations with his most important newspaper ally, the *Chicago Tribune*, and of those between the *Tribune* and the anti-McCarthy newspapers. Chapter 6 traces McCarthy's early success in bullying the fledgling television networks and in using television to outmaneuver the Eisenhower administration as his actions led to an open split with that administration. It examines four critical television events that were turning points in his career and led to his eventual loss of public esteem and his censure by the Senate. In chapter 7, I summarize the answers to the questions with which I began, and make a final evaluation of the press's discharge of its responsibility to the public.

I wish to thank my colleagues who covered McCarthy and were so generous in responding to my requests for interviews; the invariably helpful librarians; John D. Pomfret, who arranged my long stay in the *New York Times* morgue; Hale Champion, who did the same for me at the Widener Library; Jack Gould, who advised me on the television chapter, and Nelson Polsby and Thomas C. Leonard of the University of California, who read the manuscript and offered many valuable suggestions. I am grateful to Mary Maraniss of the University of Wisconsin Press for her careful editing and valuable editorial advice.

Annual faculty research grants from the University of California, Berkeley, paid the costs of professional typing, telephone calls, and travel.

I relied constantly on the information in the admirable book on McCarthy and the Senate by Robert Griffith of the University of Massachusetts, Amherst. Thomas C. Reeves of the University of Wisconsin, Parkside, gave me useful information from his research for a forthcoming biography of McCarthy. I am especially grateful to Paul Ringler of Solana Beach, California, for his ideas and encouragement and for the use of his private collection of McCarthy historical material.

My special thanks go to my wife, Monica Worsley Bayley, who spent six tedious months reading microfilm and many California evenings reading copy on the manuscript after her day's work as an editor.

E. R. B.

Berkeley, California
July 1980

Joe McCarthy and the Press

1.
When It All Started

NEWSPAPER HEADLINES in February 1950 depicted a nation on the verge of hysteria. A banner headline on the front page of the *New York Journal-American* on February 12 said "Plan Wartime Roundup of 4,000 Reds," and another story quoted a Catholic priest telling an American Legion group that "Communists and their dupes" had taken over our foreign policy, that Secretary of State Dean Acheson was "befuddled and weak," and that United States radio networks had been infiltrated by Communists. Another *Journal-American* story that week charged that "some mysterious political power" was shielding 100 American scientists who were Russian spies, and the front page of the paper on February 19 was given over to a five-column doctored photograph, an imaginary air view of New York City after it had been hit by a Russian atomic bomb. The *New York Post* reported on February 10 that Lt. Gen. Leslie R. Groves, wartime head of the U.S. atom bomb project, had said that the late President Roosevelt was responsible for Klaus Fuchs's access to America's atomic secrets. Another *Post* story said that six New York public school teachers were suspected of being Communists, and another told of a reporter's infiltration of a Communist-front school: "Ten Long Nights at a Communist University." A *Post* headline later that week said, "Einstein Red Faker, Should Be Deported, Rep. Rankin Screams." The *Atlanta Constitution* reported on February 13 that George M. Craig, the national commander of the American Legion, speaking at Springfield, Missouri, on the same platform as Gov. Adlai Stevenson of Illinois, had stated, "There are those in our highest offices today who are enemies of our way of life." The *Constitution* reported a few days later that the Grand Exalted Ruler of the Elks had warned Elks in Atlanta that Communism was "hanging over the world like an evil shadow."

Fear of this "evil shadow" was nearing its peak in 1950 when Senator Joseph R. McCarthy, Republican of Wisconsin, began his career as the scourge of "Communists in government." The Soviet Union loomed as a powerful and implacable aggressor as it consolidated its hold on the nations of Eastern Europe, and the news in September of 1949 that it had successfully detonated an atomic bomb made nuclear war seem almost inevitable. The administration of President Harry S Truman, taking an increasingly hard line against Communist aggression, had succeeded in holding back the advance of Communism in Western Europe and in Greece and Turkey through the foreign aid program, but this somehow seemed less significant than the triumph of the Chinese Communists over the demoralized forces of Chiang Kai-Shek. "Spies" were being arrested on both sides of the Iron Curtain, and in England, scientist Klaus Fuchs, who had worked on the joint Anglo-American nuclear projects during World War II, confessed that he had passed atomic information to the Russians. In the United States, Alger Hiss, a diplomat, was found guilty of lying when he denied passing secret government documents to Whittaker Chambers, a former Communist agent, a conviction that further weakened confidence in the little-respected State Department.

To the Republicans, denied executive power since 1932, the disarray seemed to present a political opportunity. Since the Democrats were in office when all these unfortunate things occurred, they could be blamed for them, a contention which might have contained some merit, although it would have been possible for a neutral viewer to observe that there was no way short of war that the United States could have controlled or even influenced the actions of the Russians or the Chinese. But the Republicans, led by the party's dominant isolationist wing, sought not only to place blame but to convince the American people that the motivation of the Democrats was treasonous. Since 1936, Republicans had been saying that liberals were Socialists and Socialists were Communists, and since the liberals dominated the Democratic party, Democrats were Communists. The Republicans persisted in this line of attack until the election of Richard Nixon in 1968, and it had the effect of limiting Democratic options in the conduct of foreign policy. No Democratic administration, for example, would have dared to establish friendly relations with Communist China, no matter how logical such a step might have seemed; only a Republican could do that.

The principal means by which the Republicans, aided by some right-wing Democrats, sought to impeach the loyalty and the reputations of liberals was to link them in some way to "Communist fronts," organizations ostensibly under the control of Communists, whose members, if not Communists, were at least "dupes" of Communism. Lists of front organizations, as well as out-and-out Communist organizations, were issued periodically by the attorney general, the House Committee on Un-American Activities, and several state legislative committees. In its 1951 report on subversive organizations, the House Committee (HUAC) defined a Communist front as "an organization or publication created or captured by the Communists to do the party's work in special fields. It is communism's greatest weapon in the country today."[1] The committee also quoted from the testimony of J. Edgar Hoover, director of the Federal Bureau of Investigation, before it on 26 March 1947: "For the most part, front organizations assumed the character of either a mass or membership organization or a paper organization. Both solicited and used names of prominent persons. Literally hundreds of groups and organizations have either been infiltrated or organized primarily to accomplish the purposes of promoting the interests of the Soviet Union in the United States, the promotion of Soviet war and peace aims, the exploitation of Negroes in the United States, work among foreign-language groups, and to secure a favorable viewpoint toward the Communists in domestic, political, social, and economic issues." Hoover listed 14 questions to ask in determining whether a group is a front, questions such as, Does it follow the Communist party line?[2] The California State Senate's Committee on Un-American Activities stated that fronts were "the chief business of the Communist Party in the United States, and the basic framework upon which has been created the entire Communist structure of sabotage, sedition, espionage and treachery against the American people and their government."[3] The committee said that "a Communist front organization is characterized by the fact that a majority of its members are non-Communists. If this were not true, it should be quite obvious that the organization would be actually a Communist organization, and not a front in any sense." It added that membership in a front does not necessarily mean that a person is a Communist; it may mean that he is "a good-intentioned 'sucker' for Communist deceit and deception."[4]

Many of the organizations listed as fronts were ostensibly concerned with such causes as peace, racial equality, education, or welfare, and often held rallies devoted to those causes. Membership in a "front," attendance at a meeting, or the signing of petitions circulated by such an organization were the basis for many of the citations of individuals by HUAC, Senator McCarthy, and the private organizations which employed the lists for profit.

The Truman administration reacted to these pressures in two ways. The first was to take an increasingly hard line against the Russians, and it was not uncommon that the front pages of newspapers displayed a story about Acheson warning the Soviets that the United States would resist further aggression, and another about some Republican charging Acheson with being "soft on Communism." This opened the administration to another familiar Republican charge, that Democrats were "warmongers," and this charge seemed to have been effective after the United States intervened to halt the Communists in Korea; the Democrats lost badly in the congressional elections of 1950. It was in these years, too, that the foundations were being laid for intervention in Vietnam. Peter Edson, a Washington columnist writing in 1950 about Ho Chi Minh (who had emerged as the leader of Vietnam) commented that "the whole struggle against world Communism now seems centered about this little-known oriental revolutionist."[5] (Murrey Marder of the *Washington Post*, writing in 1976, speculated that if the most knowledgeable experts on Asia had not been sacrificed by the government under pressure by McCarthy, active intervention by the United States in Viet Nam might have been avoided.[6] I think it unlikely; the Democrats were pushed inexorably into that confrontation by the need to prove that they were not "soft on Communism," another legacy of McCarthy.)

The second way in which President Truman reacted to anti-Communist pressure was to issue an executive order, on 21 March 1947, setting up "loyalty boards" to screen employees of executive departments—purportedly to protect employees against unfounded accusations of disloyalty as well as to prevent the infiltration of the disloyal.[7] Political commentators speculated that the action was intended to head off even more repressive legislation. As grounds for dismissal from the federal service, the order listed actions such as sabotage and treason, but it also listed another kind of evidence for loyalty boards to consider:

Membership in, affiliation with, or sympathetic association with, any foreign or domestic organization, association, movement, group or combination of persons, designated by the Attorney General as totalitarian, fascist, communist, or subversive, or as having adopted a policy of advocating or approving the commission of acts of force or violence to deny other persons their rights under the Constitution of the United States, or as seeking to alter the form of government of the United States by unconstitutional means.[8]

This was the legitimization of guilt by association, although Truman and his associates denied it.* For civil libertarians, the issuance of this order made Truman an oppressor of freedom of thought and speech. They argued that citizens should be held responsible for disloyal acts but should not be punished for political thought and speech, even pernicious thought and speech, and that association with a front group was an expression of political thought. Alan Barth, a *Washington Post* editorial writer and a leading spokesman for this position, blamed the Truman administration for creating a climate of opinion receptive to McCarthyism. He wrote:

It was a little thick to hear administration spokesmen denounce Senator McCarthy for imputing guilt by association when the loyalty boards, operating under a presidential order, had for two and a half years been condemning men on grounds of "sympathetic association" with organizations arbitrarily called "subversive" by the attorney general. No doubt Senator McCarthy deserved to be excoriated for calling as witnesses against reputable men discredited ex-Communists and professional informers; but the loyalty boards from the beginning used anonymous, unsworn testimony from just such sources.[9]

Many of the leading newspapers shared Barth's view, and it was difficult for them to defend Truman against McCarthy's attacks more than half-heartedly. A number of editorials said, in effect, that McCarthy was unfair in his attacks on the President but that Truman was pretty bad, too.

Joe McCarthy came five years late to this game, and many of the most celebrated excesses of "McCarthyism" had occurred before he entered the scene, but most of those earlier Red-baiters have been forgotten. What was it about McCarthy that enabled him to dominate the headlines, to incense the Democrats, to make McCarthyism a dictionary word, and to stamp the years from 1946 through 1954 "the

---

*Attorney General Tom Clark, in a letter enclosing the list of subversive organizations required by Truman's executive order and submitted to Seth W. Richardson, chairman, Loyalty Review Board, Civil Service Commission, 24 November 1947, wrote: "I wish to reiterate, as the President has pointed out, that it is entirely possible that many persons belonging to such organizations may be loyal to the United States; that membership in, affiliation with or sympathetic association with, any organization designated, is simply one piece of evidence which may or may not be helpful in arriving at a conclusion as to the action which is to be taken in a particular case. 'Guilt by association' has never been one of the principles of our American jurisprudence. We must be satisfied that reasonable grounds exist for concluding that an individual is disloyal. That must be the guide."

McCarthy decade"?* All of the answers to this question concern McCarthy's relations with the media. Roy Cohn, McCarthy's aide, acknowledged that the senator's primary goal was to influence public opinion through the press. "The basic problem, as seen by a small but informed group in and out of government, was the need to reach the public. Nobody, so far, had been able to make America listen," he wrote in his book *McCarthy*.[10] Both Cohn and McCarthy, ignoring the majority of newspapers that supported or tolerated McCarthy, saw this job as one that had to be done over the opposition of the newspapers that opposed his actions, and McCarthy alone among the Red-baiters directed his attack against the press itself, calling it a major instrument of the Communist conspiracy. Nevertheless, he was able to generate the massive publicity that made him the center of anti-Communism because he understood the press, its practices, and its values; he knew what made news. He liked the company of newspapermen and sought them out, and he never did understand why his attacks on newspapers, which he considered simply "political," should have affected his personal relationships with those whose papers he castigated.

The roots of his understanding of the press were planted in Wisconsin's Fox River Valley, where several newspapermen were significant early influences. One of these was the late John Riedl, managing editor and later general manager of the *Appleton Post-Crescent*, a newspaper which, with the jointly owned *Green Bay Press-Gazette*, furnished McCarthy's most important press support in Wisconsin. According to John Torinus, present editor of the *Post-Crescent*, Riedl was the one who persuaded McCarthy to enter national politics. The two had long talks about politics when McCarthy would stay at Riedl's house during his visits to Appleton from Washington. And according to Victor I. Minahan, Jr., publisher of the *Post-Crescent*, McCarthy spent a lot of time drinking with Riedl and went to church with him. "John was an old Republican," Minahan said when interviewed. "He had a lot of pals and cronies who were all Republicans and Roman Catholics, members of the same church. He liked smoke-filled rooms, and he liked to sponsor promising young guys entering politics. Joe was one of these."[11]

Nathan M. Pusey, president of Lawrence College in Appleton in

---

*As I write this on 16 November 1980, a *New York Times* story from Warsaw, carried in the *Richmond/Berkeley Independent and Gazette*, compares the efforts of the Polish Communist government to control dissidents to the work of McCarthy, and an Associated Press story from Washington invokes the name of McCarthy to describe a demand by a group called the Heritage Foundation that the new, more conservative Congress revive the internal security committees to investigate and crack down on domestic radicals.

the early 1950s and later president of Harvard, remembers that Riedl "more or less adopted Joe McCarthy in his youth." Riedl had told Pusey that he recognized talent in McCarthy, that he had tried to educate him, and that McCarthy came to regard him as a father. In Pusey's words, "Riedl knew more about Joe as a human being than anyone else." Riedl advised McCarthy to attack the American prosecutors in the Nuremburg trials of the 73 German SS men convicted of taking part in the massacre of unarmed American prisoners of war and Belgian civilians at Malmedy in the closing days of the war, Pusey said. He told McCarthy to get the information about Malmedy to the villages and rural areas of Wisconsin where farmers of German ancestry still sympathized with Germany, as a means of developing a statewide political base.[12]

McCarthy did make a lot of headlines with his Malmedy attacks, and it has been said that it was in these hearings that he practiced the techniques for using the press that he used later in his "Communists in government" days. Whether it was because of the Malmedy hearings or not, he established an enduring political base in Wisconsin's rural areas, particularly in those areas where the farmers were of German background.

he believed Communists were in Govt

John Wyngaard, who covered Wisconsin politics from a base in Madison for about 40 years, also remembers that Riedl was fond of McCarthy and considered him a protégé. Wyngaard's home papers were the *Press-Gazette* and the *Post-Crescent*, although he sold his news service and his column to several other Wisconsin newspapers. Wyngaard grew up just outside Appleton. "Riedl loved people he knew on their way up," he said. "Everyone came to see him about everything. He called himself a Democrat, but he was very conservative. He didn't go around with the high muckamucks in Appleton; he played five-cents-a-chip poker."[13]*

Wyngaard's reference to "muckamucks" was related to the sharp social and ethnic divisions in Appleton in the 1930s. The First Ward, on the east side, contained Lawrence College and was called, in other parts of the city, "the silk-stocking ward." It was populated by Anglo-Saxons, Protestants, professional people, and business executives, particularly from the paper industry, although the wealthiest of the mill owners lived in Neenah, 10 miles south. The Second Ward was downtown, with no particular social characteristic except that most

---

*When I talked to him, County Judge Urban Van Susteren dissented from the view that McCarthy had been a protégé of Riedl, and indicated that he rather than Riedl had been McCarthy's principal mentor. "I was with Joe when he called Riedl at the time of his election to the Senate," Van Susteren said. "He didn't know him well at that time. But John admired Joe, and usually agreed with him."

transients lived there. Wyngaard remembers that McCarthy often lived in the Appleton Hotel, in the Second Ward, across the street from the *Post-Crescent*. The Third Ward, on the west side, was the Irish ward, "the bloody Third," and it contained two Catholic churches—one Irish, one German—and the Outagamie County courthouse. The Fourth Ward, across the river, was isolated from the rest of the city; its dominant ethnic strain was Dutch Catholic, people who had moved in from the Dutch communities east of Appleton—Kaukauna, Kimberly, Little Chute, Combined Locks. The Fifth and Sixth wards, on the north side, were almost solidly German, and the churches were Lutheran.

At the grade school level, there was hostility between the wards, and a youngster from the First Ward did not venture easily into the Third. There was one grade school in each ward, and athletic contests between schools often produced fistfights. I am sure that this hostility among children was a reflection of similar, more restrained, attitudes among their elders. When McCarthy attacked Nathan Pusey in retaliation for Pusey's public stand against his re-election, he did it with a degree of ferocity that was more than political; it was the Third Ward against the First.*

In the summer of 1952 Pusey came out against McCarthy by becoming a member of a citizens' committee sponsoring publication of a 134-page booklet called *The McCarthy Record*—a critical examination of that record intended to bring McCarthy's shortcomings to public attention.† There were better-known people among the mem-

------

*I first encountered Joe McCarthy, whose obituary I was destined to write, one Saturday morning in 1929 or 1930 in front of the Appleton YMCA at the corner of Lawrence and Oneida streets. My friends and I spent most Saturday mornings at the YMCA, and we'd get on our bicycles just before noon to ride home for "dinner." That's when we'd see Joe. He was 10 years older than I. I suppose he came down from the town of Grand Chute to sell his eggs. He sold them to Sumnicht's, the grocery in my neighborhood. He was always alone. He was a hick—he wore bib overalls—and we were little smart-alecky kids from the First Ward. We'd yell at him and he'd yell back. The teasing was mostly good-natured, but we enjoyed it because there was something dangerous about Joe. He'd lunge at us, and we'd run. I can't remember how we knew his name, but we did. He remembered us, too, and later, when I'd cover him as a reporter, he'd remind me that we both came from Appleton, sort of a bond.

†The editor of *The McCarthy Record* was Morris Rubin, editor of the *Progressive* magazine; it was written by Miles McMillin, editorial writer for the *Capital Times* of Madison, and the author, on our own time and without the knowledge of our newspapers, at least in my case. It was published by Anglobooks, London, New York, and Toronto, and sold for one dollar. Carlisle P. Runge, a University of Wisconsin law professor, was president of the sponsoring committee of 70 members. About 26,000 copies were sold.

bers of the sponsoring committee—labor leaders and the Republican secretary of state—but Pusey's action drew special attention because he was in Appleton, he was known as a Republican, and it was the first time he had taken a stand on McCarthy. Most of the people on the committee were Democrats, independents, or well-known Republican mavericks. (Pusey calls himself an "Eastern" Republican.) In Pusey's opinion, if more people had done what he did in 1952 McCarthy might have been defeated that year at the polls. This came up when I asked him if he thought that Edward R. Murrow's televised documentary on McCarthy had been instrumental in bringing McCarthy down. "I don't give a damn what anybody said about McCarthy in 1954," Pusey said. "By 1954 McCarthy was finished. The time to fight him—the only time it mattered—was before the election in 1952, when you could do something about it."

Pusey's action is still resented in Appleton. On May 5, 1976, I talked with County Judge Urban Van Susteren, a close friend of McCarthy's, at the Outagamie County courthouse. The mention of Pusey's name, in another context, set him off. "He's spineless," Van Susteren said. "Pusey is weak and spineless. He lent his name to that thing—The McCarthy Record—because some industrialist on his board pressured him into it. He was unaware of its being a political propaganda thing. He never checked anything in it. He's a spineless personality."[14] (The industrialist Van Susteren was talking about was Elmer H. Jennings, chairman of the board of the Thilmany Pulp and Paper Company, a pillar of the Congregational Church in Appleton and a member of the Lawrence College board of trustees. He also was a sponsor of The McCarthy Record.)

In June 1953 when Pusey was appointed president of Harvard University, Neal O'Hara, a columnist for the Boston Traveler, asked McCarthy for a comment on the appointment. "I do not think Dr. Pusey is or has been a member of the Communist Party," McCarthy replied. ". . . What motivates Pusey, I have no way of knowing. He is what could best be described as a rabid anti-anti-Communist." McCarthy called Pusey "a man with considerable intellectual possibilities, but who has neither learned nor forgotten anything since he was a freshman in college," and one who "appears to hide a combination of bigotry and intolerance behind a cloak of phony hypocritical liberalism." He said this about Pusey's sponsorship of The McCarthy Record: "In Wisconsin Pusey endorsed and lent his support to libelous smear campaign material. His legacy to Wisconsin was to help bring campaigning in that state to an all-time low in dishonesty, mud-slinging and smear. . . . I am very happy that he has left my home town of Appleton. Regardless of who takes his place, it will be an

[handwritten margin note: ← McC. doesn't like Pusey]

improvement."[15] (Despite this assertion that *The McCarthy Record* was libelous, McCarthy never sued for libel, nor did he or any of his supporters challenge any statement in the booklet.)*

[handwritten margin note: McC. asks Pusey →]

In November 1953 McCarthy sent a telegram to Pusey asking his attitude toward retaining teachers "who refuse to state whether they are Communists." According to McCarthy, Prof. Wendell Furry, a Harvard physicist appearing before his committee, meeting in executive session (McCarthy was chairman of the Permanent Subcommittee on Investigations of the Senate Committee on Government Operations), had refused to answer questions about Communist affiliations before 1 March 1951. Pusey replied that Harvard would not tolerate a Communist on its faculty because a Communist would not have the necessary independence of thought and judgment, and that he knew of no Communist on the faculty. He said that it was his understanding that Furry had not been connected with the Communist party in recent years, but that he did not know what had been said in McCarthy's "private" committee session and that McCarthy had not made the testimony public.

In January 1954, in his fourth appearance before the investigating committee, Furry admitted that he had been a Communist before 1951 but refused to tell the names of five other Communists he had worked with on a secret radar project during World War II at the Massachusetts Institute of Technology. Another Harvard employe, a research assistant in the department of social relations, took a similar position. McCarthy said that he would "hate to decimate the Harvard faculty" by sending those two to jail for contempt, but that that might be the only way to deal with "Pusey's Fifth Amendment Communists."

Pusey still becomes emotional—which for him is to develop a quiet intensity—when he talks about that period. He is not so much angry with McCarthy as he is with those who supported him or gave in to him, and he is more troubled by what happened during the year in Appleton after he took his stand than by the attacks on him at Harvard. There was a time, Pusey said, when he rather liked McCarthy. "Many journalists and university faculty members did not understand

---

*Pusey's stand on McCarthy was a factor in his selection by Harvard. On a Saturday night before the Tuesday on which the appointment was announced, John Cowles, Sr., chairman of the Harvard Corporation, telephoned J. D. Ferguson, editor of the *Milwaukee Journal*, to ask a question. Ferguson called me to the phone. Cowles said that they had almost settled upon Pusey but that they were troubled by a report that Pusey was somehow "tied up with the CIO." After a moment's thought, the answer came to me. "It's not the CIO," I said. "It's the AFL-CIO. They put up most of the money to publish *The McCarthy Record*, the thing that Pusey sponsored." "Oh, we know all about that," Cowles said. "That's one of the points in his favor."

McCarthy," he said. "He was no fascist, no power-seeker. He was just
a country boy, ill-educated, insecure, always on the defensive." The
menace of McCarthy himself has been overrated, but the menace of
the forces he stirred up has been underrated, in Pusey's opinion. "That
was the terrifying thing about that period. There really was some kind
of a conspiracy in the small towns of Wisconsin and Illinois. After I
came out against McCarthy, the invitations to speak stopped all at
once. The Rotary Clubs, the PTAs, the Kiwanis Clubs, other colleges,
commencements—they all thought I was some kind of a Communist."
Pusey said that when McCarthy attacked him (Pusey) in June 1953,
Riedl told him that he was "all through" with McCarthy.

According to Minahan, the attack on Pusey hurt McCarthy in Appleton, offending the conservative business leadership, people who
were proud of Lawrence College and Pusey. This view was supported
by the *Post-Crescent*'s story on Appleton reaction to McCarthy's remarks. Cola Parker, chairman of the Lawrence board of trustees, said
that anyone familiar with Lawrence College and McCarthy's actions
"can only conclude that the senator has gone overboard with respect
to anyone who exercised his political right not to support McCarthy
or actively to support an opposing candidate." L. R. Watson, a Lawrence alumnus and former Eighth Congressional District Republican
chairman, said that "an honest difference of opinion does not call for
name-calling or vicious public attacks."[16]

Several newspapers that had supported McCarthy or remained
neutral in the 1952 election became critical of him on the Pusey issue.
The *Racine Journal Times*, for instance, wrote, "He has made it pretty
clear in public statements that he considers opposition to himself,
political and personal, or to his conduct in and out of the Senate, as
opposition to the whole cause of combatting Communism."[17] The *Stevens Point Journal*, seldom critical of McCarthy, called the attack
"another example of the kind of tactics for which Joe McCarthy is
widely known and which have made him so controversial a political
figure."[18]

Riedl also wrote an editorial for the *Appleton Post-Crescent* in
which he said that McCarthy had gone too far in attacking a respected
citizen simply for not voting for him. But Riedl made his peace with
McCarthy. About two months later he told a correspondent for a
Swedish newspaper that he had known McCarthy "since he was knee-
high to a grasshopper" and that he was "as harmless as an eight-year-
old." An account of this interview appeared in the *Dagens Nyheter*,
a leading Stockholm newspaper, on 30 August 1953. In that interview,
Riedl said that the Pusey incident was one in which McCarthy "didn't
think as hard as he ought to have done" but that the senator would

meet "no opposition worth mentioning" in Wisconsin if elections were to take place then. "He is fundamentally a nice, likeable fellow, not at all the noisy fire-eater people have tried to make him," Riedl said. "We don't want a group of New Yorkers and Easterners to tell us whom we are to send to the Senate. That is our business and it is none of theirs."

McCarthy undoubtedly appreciated Riedl's support and valued his political advice, but one from whom he first learned about the practical workings of the press was Donald Hickok, a reporter for the *Shawano Leader* (and later news editor of the *Green Bay Press-Gazette*) who traveled with McCarthy in his campaign for the circuit judgeship in 1939. One of Hickok's ideas was thought to have contributed to the success of that campaign: as they drove from farm to farm, McCarthy dictated a highly personal letter to the family they had just visited, a letter which was mailed a few days before the election, impressing recipients with his memory and concern. Although he later deplored McCarthy's excesses, Hickok remained fond of the man; he liked his mordant sense of humor.

Another newspaperman who was an early influence on McCarthy was V. I. Minahan, Sr., father of the present *Post-Crescent* publisher and the editor of both the Green Bay and Appleton papers.[19] Minahan had come to Green Bay after military service in World War I. He was a lawyer, but he thought there ought to be two newspapers in Green Bay and he founded the *Green Bay Free Press*. He began by losing money, but when he bought the opposition paper and merged the two, he prospered. In 1930 he left his law office to become editor. Minahan, according to Torinus, was greatly disturbed by Franklin D. Roosevelt's "chicanery" in getting the United States into World War II and became very antimilitary. He was especially disturbed about his children entering military service and was receptive to McCarthy because of that. Wyngaard remembered Minahan as "an old-fashioned isolationist" who liked McCarthy because he thought he shared his views on foreign policy and because they were both Irish. He wrote dozens of editorials defending McCarthy for both the Appleton and Green Bay newspapers. Torinus said, however, that Minahan became increasingly disturbed about McCarthy as time went on.

Victor Minahan, Jr., became editor of the *Post-Crescent* in August 1954, and Riedl moved from managing editor, where he had controlled the news department, to general manager, strictly concerned with business. "I had to be very careful," Minahan, Jr., told me. "My father was still editor of the *Press-Gazette,* and Riedl was still across the hall, but I began to edge away from 100 percent support of McCarthy as soon as I could." Even Riedl began to cool on McCarthy, Minahan said. "I remember him saying to me, 'Joe doesn't listen to us anymore.'" In Minahan's opinion, Appleton had always been a conservative Republican city, but no one there was part of the "radical right." "The John Birch Society never could get going here," he said. "Outside reporters thought that because this was Joe's home town, everybody here was for him. That was never the case. No one was scared to say what they thought about Joe here—you'd hear them saying all over, 'That son of a bitch. . . .' " Torinus, then an editor at the Green Bay paper, became increasingly embarrassed at having to defend or apologize for the *Press-Gazette*'s support of McCarthy. "It was such an emotional issue," he said. "Arguments about McCarthy could split families and friends, even husbands and wives. I remember at dinner parties we had to agree not to bring up the subject; it would just ruin the evening."

People not thoroughly familiar with McCarthy's background and the city of Appleton have wondered why the senator, a former Marine, had gone after the United States Army on the Malmedy issue and others later, and with such vigor. But antimilitary feeling was strong in the Fox River Valley. What most people read there was the *Chicago Tribune* in the morning and the *Post-Crescent* or *Press-Gazette* at night, a double dose of isolationism and antimilitarism, and McCarthy's line of attack never surprised me. Nor did it surprise Pusey. "People now tend to forget the all-pervading influence of the *Tribune* in the 1930s," Pusey said. "It dominated everything within a 500-mile radius of Chicago, something like the influence of William Loeb in New Hampshire or (John) Fox in Boston." (Loeb was publisher of the *Manchester Union*, Fox of the *Boston Post*.)*

The *Tribune*'s influence outside of Illinois began to wane in the postwar years. The *Milwaukee Journal* became stronger and stronger, and *Tribune* circulation in Wisconsin declined; one by one it closed its several Wisconsin news bureaus. But it was a dominant influence in the Fox River Valley during McCarthy's formative years, and its antimilitary and antiestablishment views were reinforced by those of

---

*The Vietnam War and the argument about whether the United States should have pursued it aroused such passion that people are apt to forget that there was a strong antiwar movement in the 1930s. I marched in a peace parade on the Lawrence campus in 1936; we called ourselves the Veterans of Future Wars. An Appleton policeman wielding a night club fractured the skull of the first person to step off the campus into the street, a football player named Al Haak. Many of us who expected to be drafted joined a loosely organized group called OHIO, standing for "over the hill in October," which was supposed to carry out a mass desertion from the army. It didn't seem unreasonable at the time.

the *Press-Gazette* and the *Post-Crescent*. At no time during Mc-
Carthy's career did his ideas deviate much from those of the *Tribune*,
and his personal connections with the paper began early. His campaign for the Senate in 1944 was aided by Maxwell Murphy, the
Tribune's Milwaukee correspondent, and in September 1946 he met
with Colonel Robert R. McCormick, the publisher, in Chicago, and
won the support of American Action, Inc., a McCormick-controlled
right-wing group built on the foundations of the old America First
Committee.[20] And when he embarked on his fateful trip to Wheeling,
West Virginia, on 9 February 1946, he took with him a briefcase full
of notes and clippings from a man who became his closest newspaper
friend in Washington, a *Chicago Tribune* reporter.

If Joe McCarthy was indeed created by the press, then, it could be
said with a good deal of merit that McCarthy was created, or at least
"formed," by the *Appleton Post-Crescent*, the *Green Bay Press-Gazette*, and the *Chicago Tribune*. But that is not what people usually
mean when they say that the press created McCarthy; they are thinking of the newspaper space, the headlines, and the thousands of
editorials that resulted from his campaign against "Communists in
government," and of the press's ineptness in coping with McCarthy's
tactics.

If the press, in *this* sense, created McCarthy, it did it in the beginning, during the month that followed the historic speech in Wheeling.
Much of what we remember most vividly about McCarthy's five years
in the spotlight occurred during that first month. The phrase "I have
in my hand ..." (usually recalled as "I hold in my hand ...") brings
it back, and the charge that there were 205 Communists in the State
Department.

What the press did that month was important because it created
first impressions—impressions that lasted years, perhaps still last, in
some minds. If the press had conspired somehow to ignore McCarthy's
charges about Communists in government, this is when it would have
had to be done. If the press, through superbly accurate and interpretive reporting, keen news judgments, and brilliant headlines, had been
able to show up McCarthy for the fraud that he was, this is when it
would have had to be done. If the press failed to do these things, this
is when it failed.

At least one newspaper did try to ignore the story, hoping that others
would follow suit. Melvin Wax, a San Francisco newsman, was acting
publisher of the *Claremont* (N.H.) *Daily Eagle* (circulation 9,054) when
McCarthy's campaign began in 1950. The *Eagle* published no stories
about McCarthy for eight to ten months, Wax told me. "Then I realized

it was the wrong thing to do," he said. "The people who depended on us for news were unaware of what was going on. It wasn't fair to them. A newspaper can't put its head in the sand."[21]

The news was not always obvious during that first month. Republicans had been making charges about Communists in government for years and had even found some, but McCarthy made his charges in a way that disconcerted the wire services and most newspapers. The press was accustomed to reporting general attacks—"the government is honeycombed with Reds"—worth, by that time, a paragraph. McCarthy was specific—205, 4, 57, 81. This posed a new kind of problem.

This is also the time when McCarthy's tactics should have been perceived and analyzed, when he was out in the open, without staff, feeling his way, developing the techniques that he employed later with more skill as he "used" the press. For a student of newspaper performance, this is the key month. Which papers—editors—were quickest to see what was going on and to decide how to cope with it? Which stumbled, wavered, demonstrated fear or naïvité? Which led, which followed?

McCarthy's speech on the evening of 9 February 1950 at the Lincoln Day dinner of the Ohio County Women's Republican Club at the McClure Hotel in Wheeling, West Virginia, has been the subject of more speculation, argument, and investigation than almost anything he said in the next five years. The statement that McCarthy made in that speech was described by Senator William Benton, Democrat of Connecticut, as "one of the most sensational in America's entire history," and Richard Rovere wrote that this charge was "the myth on which [McCarthy's] whole subsequent career was based."[22] On 13 February 1956, speaking at another Lincoln Day dinner in Milwaukee, J. B. Matthews, a one-time member of the staff of McCarthy's investigating committee, declared that there are three great anniversaries in February—Washington's birthday, Lincoln's birthday, and the anniversary of the speech in Wheeling at which McCarthy stated that there were 205 Communists in the State Department.[23]

McCarthy later denied having said what he was quoted as saying, but what was reported on Friday, 10 February, in the *Wheeling Intelligencer* in a story by staff reporter Frank Desmond, was this statement:

"While I cannot take the time to name all of the men in the State Department who have been named as members of the Communist party and members of a spy ring, I have here in my hand a list of 205 that were known to the Secretary of State as being members of the

Communist party and who nevertheless are still working and shaping the policy of the State Department."

The Associated Press's story of the handling of the Wheeling speech was told by reporter Bem Price in a special series on McCarthy in April 1954:

It was too late for the morning papers when Charles R. Lewis, night editor in the Associated Press bureau at Charlestown, W. Va., received a telephone call from Norman L. Yost, managing editor of the Wheeling Intelligencer. *Yost, part-time AP correspondent at Wheeling, dictated a paragraph or two from McCarthy's speech. As Lewis began writing the brief story, he came to a figure he questioned—205 Communists in the State Department? He called Yost back and asked him to verify it. Yost told him to hold on and he would have his reporter re-check with McCarthy. In a moment he came back on the wire and said the figure was accurate. Shortly after 2 A.M. the 110-word story clattered over the teletypes.*[24]

Of the 129 newspapers I surveyed, 18 carried the AP story on Friday, 10 February.* Ten other papers, dependent on the United Press for national news, used the story on Saturday, 11 February, their first opportunity, when George Reedy, a UP man in Washington, caught up with the story by eliciting a State Department denial. Only three newspapers of the 18 that used the AP story put it on page one, and two of these were small papers that carried most of their national news on that page. Headlines were matter-of-fact: "Charge 205 Reds in State Dept." (*Racine Journal-Times*), "State Department Has 205 Commies, Senator Says" (*Nashville Tennessean*). Probably many news editors were suspicious of the story. They might well have reasoned that if the AP had thought that it was important they would have provided a more comprehensive story with background. But it is most likely that they just failed to grasp its significance; all through this study of newspaper performance there were indications that news decisions were made carelessly; in this case one paper even put the wrong Wisconsin senator in the headline: "205 Reds in U.S. State Dept., Wiley Says," said the *La Crosse Tribune.*†

*Twelve of these 18 were in Wisconsin: the *Milwaukee Journal, Capital Times, Appleton Post-Crescent, Green Bay Press-Gazette, Sheboygan Press, Racine Journal-Times, La Crosse Tribune, Wausau Record-Herald, Oshkosh Northwestern, Manitowoc Herald-Times, Stevens Point Journal,* and *Marinette Eagle-Star.* Papers outside Wisconsin were the *Chicago Tribune, Buffalo News, Baltimore News-Post, Newark News, Lowell Sun,* and *Nashville Banner.*

†There are myths about many aspects of McCarthy's press coverage, and one is that

It has been customary to attribute the writing of the Wheeling speech to Willard Edwards, the *Chicago Tribune*'s specialist on Communists in government, but Edwards says that George Waters, McCarthy's press secretary and former city editor of the *Washington Times-Herald*, wrote the speech. Waters told Edwards that McCarthy had assigned him to write a speech about Communism for some Lincoln Day speeches and that he needed some material. Edwards gave Waters the clippings of a series he had written on Communists in government "and some other stuff." "That's all I knew about it until the furor started," Edwards said. "I was very indignant about it being attributed to me. It was full of errors."*

---

the charge made in Wheeling immediately produced flamboyant headlines that electrified the nation. In their book *McCarthy: The Man, the Senator, the "Ism,"* Jack Anderson and Ronald W. May wrote, "But the headline that capped all other McCarthy headlines exploded on the morning of February 10, 1950, across that nation's front pages—after his Wheeling, West Virginia, speech. It was just the kind of sensational charge that reporters had come to expect from the Wisconsin Senator; and they gave it full play" (pp. 267-68).

This was not true, but neither was it true that the press ignored the story, as some writers have contended. William F. Buckley, Jr., and L. Brent Bozell, for instance, in *McCarthy and His Enemies*, wrote, "Only the Wheeling paper, and the *Chicago Tribune*, as far as we were able to discover, reported McCarthy's speech of Thursday night on the following day. It was another two or three days before his Wheeling statements reached a national audience" (pp. 50-51). According to Richard H. Rovere, in *Senator Joe McCarthy*, "The speech was reported in the *Wheeling Intelligencer* and the *Chicago Tribune*; the Associated Press picked up a couple of paragraphs from Desmond's *Intelligencer* copy, but its bulletin got scarcely any attention" (p. 126). Fred J. Cook, in *The Nightmare Decade*, stated that those who heard the speech in Wheeling were not excited by it and that "the rest of the nation almost slept through the great speech, too. Days passed before the first obscure mentions of McCarthy began to creep into even the redbaiting newspapers. . . . Most news editors apparently put the item on the spike of discarded wire-copy chaff" (pp. 150-51). Roy Cohn's version, in his book *McCarthy*, was that "the *Chicago Tribune* printed only a few spare paragraphs on an inside page. No other newspaper reported McCarthy's Wheeling talk" (p. 2). And Lloyd Wendt, in the *Chicago Tribune*, an authorized history of the newspaper published in 1979, wrote, "Frank Desmond of the Wheeling Intelligencer covered the event, but not until two days later did the press services of the country pick up the senator's charges and send them around the country" (p. 694). These remarkably similar observations were as inaccurate as those of Anderson and May.

*Edwards interview, 27 June 1977. The sixth in Edwards's series ran in the same edition that carried the Wheeling story and was headed "Tells How FDR Shrugged Off Red Spy News." Most of the *Tribune*'s policy stories and editorials endeavored, six years after Roosevelt's death, to convince readers that the late President Roosevelt had been a tool of the Communists, or worse. Two days after the Edwards piece, the *Tribune* said editorially that the series had proved that Roosevelt was sympathetic to Communist aims because the Communists carried New York City for him in elections. "He wasn't gullible. He was the willing partner in a conspiracy directed against his own country."

One of McCarthy's documents was a letter, dated 26 July 1946, from Secretary of State James F. Byrnes to Representative Adolph Sabath of Illinois, which said that of 3,000 government employes transferred into the State Department from other agencies at the end of World War II, a screening board had recommended against permanent employment in 284 cases, and that 79 of these had been separated from government service. Without any further information and assuming that nothing had changed since 1946, this could be interpreted as saying that 205 of those whose employment had not been recommended were actually employed. The letter did not say, of course, that these were Communists.

Nor did McCarthy say that, after Wheeling. The next day, at an airport press conference in Denver, Colorado, he told reporters that he had a list of 207 "bad risks" and that he would be glad to show it to them but that it was in a suit that he'd left on the plane. (The *Denver Post* ran a page-one picture that day of McCarthy outside his plane, with the cut line "Left Commie List in Other Bag.") McCarthy said that if Dean Acheson would call him in Salt Lake City he would read the list to him. It was no more true, of course, that McCarthy had a list of 205 (or 207) "bad risks" in Denver than it was that he had a list of 205 Communists in Wheeling. All he had was that letter from Byrnes to Sabath, which contained no names.

The 207 apparently were the same as the 205, or almost. But McCarthy introduced a new figure in Salt Lake City—57—for the number of actual Communists in the State Department. He did this in the course of a radio interview with a local reporter named Dan Valentine, an interview, picked up by AP, that provided the lead for the McCarthy story that Saturday. This is part of the transcript:

McCarthy: Last night I discussed the "Communists in the State Department." I stated I had the names of 57 card-carrying members of the Communist party. I noticed today that the State Department has denied that. They say that they don't know of a single one in the State Department. Now I want to tell the Secretary of State this, if he wants to call me tonight at the Utah Hotel I will be glad to give him the names of those 57 card-carrying Communists. I might say this, however, Dan, the day that Alger Hiss was exposed the President signed an order to the effect that no one in the State Department could give any information as to the disloyalty or the Communistic activities of any State Department employee. Then later they went a step further. They said, in addition to that, no one in the Department can give any information as to the employment of any man in the State Department. Now, obviously, before we will give him the information, give him the names of the Communists whom we, names he should certainly

have himself (if I have them, he should have them) I want this: an
indication of his good faith. The best way to indicate that is to say that
at least as far as these 57 are concerned, when you give their names
then all information as to their Communistic activities, as to their
disloyalty, will be available to any proper Congressional investigating
committee. Have I made myself clear, Dan?

VALENTINE: *In other words, Senator, if Secretary of State Dean Ache-*
*son would call you at the Hotel Utah tonight in Salt Lake City (*SENATOR
MCCARTHY: *That's right) you could give him 57 names of actual card-*
carrying Communists in the State Department of the United States—
actual card-carrying Communists.

MCCARTHY: *Not only can, Dan, but I will, on condition (*VALENTINE:
I don't blame you for that) that they lift this veil of secrecy and allow
the Congressional Committee to know about the Communistic activ-
ities and disloyalty in that Department.[25]

Twenty-five more newspapers began McCarthy coverage with this
story, and nine other papers which had already carried the Wheeling
story used it too. Typical headlines produced by the story were these:
"McCarthy Charges 57 in State Dept. Hold Red Party Cards" (*Wash-*
ington Star); "57 Commies in State Dept., Says Senator" (*Boston Her-*
ald); "57 of Red Variety Claimed" (*Memphis Commercial Appeal*).
McCarthy, speaking to Valentine, made the point that the night before
he had said that he had the names of 57 card-carrying Communists
in the State Department. This was the beginning of his campaign to
correct the record, or to rewrite history.

When McCarthy arrived in Wheeling he had given Desmond, the
reporter, and two radio men in charge of the broadcast of his remarks
on station WWVA a text which he called a rough draft. This was his
basic text for the week's speaking tour, and the same phrases recurred
in each news account of his speeches or news conferences. The text
given newsmen in Wheeling did contain the 205 Communists charge
quoted by Desmond and the AP. In the version given reporters two
days later at Reno, Nevada, however, the "205" had been crossed out
and "57" written above it.[26] When he returned to Washington on February 20, McCarthy inserted in the *Congressional Record* what he
said was the text of his speech in Wheeling. It differed from the text
given newsmen in Wheeling in several small details and in one major
one. The key paragraph, in which the charges were made, now said,
"I have in my hand 57 cases of individuals who would appear to be
either card-carrying members or certainly loyal to the Communist
party, but who nevertheless are still helping to shape our foreign
policy."

The change in the number was less important than the change in the definition of the charge; "loyal to the Communist party" could mean anything, a subjective rather than specific charge. Neither did the new version mention a spy ring. But the most important change was the omission of the phrase "known to the secretary of state" which had made the first charge so damning. McCarthy played that theme all through his trip; when asked by reporters about the names on his list, he repeatedly told them that the secretary of state had them. His telegram to Truman from Reno advised the president to get the names from Mr. Acheson. In the Salt Lake City radio interview, where the number 57 first appeared, the charge was that these State Department employes were "card-carrying Communists," a point which McCarthy made with great emphasis. In the new version the 57 were individuals "who appear to be either card-carrying members or loyal to the Communist party," a milder charge.

As McCarthy read his version of the speech into the *Congressional Record* on February 20, he interrupted himself to say, "I might say for the benefit of the Senator from Illinois [Scott Lucas] that what I am reading was taken from a recording of the speech. I did not use a written text that night." This turned out to be false. The recording of the speech had been erased the next day by the Wheeling station, and no copy every turned up. The point came up again in the 7 September 1951 issue of *U.S. News and World Report* in a long interview with McCarthy. It read, in part:

QUESTION: *Senator, there was, we've heard, a great deal of talk about your changing your numbers. What is your explanation for that—205 charges in one speech up in West Virginia, and then 81 . . .*

ANSWER: *(by Senator McCarthy): Up in West Virginia we read to the audience a letter written by Jimmy Byrnes, the then Secretary of State, to Congressman Sabath, in which he said that out of the 3,000 employees screened—employees who were being transferred from other departments into the State Department—they found 284 unfit for government service. He said of the 284 we discharged 79, leaving a total of 205. That night I called upon [Secretary of State] Acheson and the President to tell us where those 205 were, why they kept them in if the President's own board says they were unfit for service. I sent to the President a wire the next day and asked that he call Acheson in and get the names of the 205, finding out where they are, what departments they are working in, and I said, I have the names of 57 . . .*

QUESTION: *This is in your speech?*

ANSWER: *This is in the speech. The names of 57 who are either members of the party—I may have used the word "card-carrying"—*

I don't know, I used the terms interchangeably—either members of the party or certainly loyal to the party. Now, a great to-do was made about that. You may recall, Tydings [Dem., Maryland] got on the Senate floor and made his final report, and said: "I have in my hand a recording of the West Virginia speech that shows McCarthy is a liar. It shows that he actually said that he had the names of 205." Then he said that "McCarthy changed it the next day."

These contradictions and inconsistencies were cited by Senator Benton of Connecticut on 28 September 1951 when, as part of his effort to expel McCarthy from the Senate, he argued that McCarthy had committed perjury when he denied using the figure 205. Benton submitted a certified committee record showing that McCarthy had made that denial under oath. Several months of investigation had gone into Benton's charge. He had obtained affidavits from the news editor of the radio station, from the program director, from Desmond, and from the general manager of the *Intelligencer*, all saying that there was no doubt that McCarthy had followed the text he had handed out and that he had made the charge as reported. They also swore that at no time did McCarthy use the figure 57 in any context.

William F. Buckley, Jr., and L. Brent Bozell, in their book *McCarthy and His Enemies*, devote 12 pages to the question of whether or not McCarthy made the "205 Communists" charge at Wheeling. Through further questioning of a Tydings committee investigator and the Wheeling witnesses, they try to show that it is not absolutely certain that McCarthy said what was reported. The authors were dismayed, however, as strategists for the forces of anti-Communism, by McCarthy's unquestioned use of the phrase "card-carrying Communists" in Salt Lake City.

Perhaps [they wrote] McCarthy deliberately sensationalized the evidence he possessed in order to draw attention to the gravity of the situation. Perhaps, again, the complexities of the Communist problem were lost on Joe McCarthy in the early days of his venture. ... McCarthy could have said: "I hold in my hand investigative reports on 57 members of the State Department. The evidence of pro-Communism on the part of these 57 is so substantial that, in my opinion, no loyalty-security board composed of conscientious men who know the score about Communism would, after weighing it, clear them for sensitive positions. The Communists don't often give us a break and expose themselves. But here we have 57 people whose activities and associations are ominous. Perhaps some of them, perhaps many of them, are not Communists. But none of them should be working in the State Department."[27]

If McCarthy had made that speech instead of the one he made, there would have been no story out of Wheeling on the AP wire that night. What might the lead have been? That McCarthy had some investigators' reports? That in his opinion no loyalty board would clear some of them for sensitive positions? That he had the names of 57 people whose associations were "ominous"? If McCarthy had made that kind of careful legalistic argument in Wheeling and in subsequent speeches there might be no word *McCarthyism* in our dictionaries today. Buckley and Bozell might have known more than McCarthy did about Communism—as they claim over and over in their book—but McCarthy knew more about journalism.

The evidence is not conclusive. Probably McCarthy followed his text and used the 205 figure, but it is possible that he did not and that Desmond followed the text rather than the spoken words. It is not important. Fifty-seven Communists in the State Department, the figure used and recorded the next day, would undoubtedly have been as startling as 205. It seems likely that McCarthy realized, when newspaper reporters questioned him about the 205, that this figure could be easily traced to the Byrnes letter and debunked. Such impetuous changes were characteristic of McCarthy; when he saw what his audience liked, he gave them more of it; if they were bored, he shifted to something more exciting. When he learned something he thought he could use, he used it as soon as possible, often without checking at all. He had the instinct, if not the discipline, of a newspaper reporter; when a reporter learns something interesting, he wants to get it into print right away. So did McCarthy.*

The Wheeling episode raises questions about newspaper practice of the day. Why didn't Desmond, apparently the only reporter there, ask McCarthy to let him see his list of 205 Communists? If he had done that, history might have been different, for as McCarthy said himself, what he held in his hand was the Byrnes's letter, not a list.† But if Desmond had reported that what McCarthy held in his hand was not a list but only a letter without names, newspaper use of the story would have been different. The papers suspicious of McCarthy

*Richard M. Fried, in *Men Against McCarthy*, reviewed the evidence in this numbers muddle and concluded that "no fully satisfactory account of the speech has emerged." Fried wrote that "only possibilities remain. McCarthy may have said 205, or he may have corrected this to 57 as he did in subsequent addresses. He might even have used both figures—either in confusion and inadvertence or perhaps, as he himself conjectured, with 57 as the key figure and 205 in a lesser role" (p. 46).

†Fred Cook, in his book *The Nightmare Decade*, writes that a friend of his, a journalist who was once a close friend of McCarthy, asked the senator on one occasion, "Joe, just what did you have in your hand down there in Wheeling?" McCarthy grinned, the friend said, and replied, "An old laundry list" (p. 149).

would have reported it with that note of skepticism, and most papers probably would not have published it at all. There seems to have been a singular lack of curiosity all through the process. Why didn't the AP ask Yost, their correspondent, to demand the list? Why didn't telegraph editors on the afternoon papers, who had all morning to consider this odd story, query the AP about the list? Why didn't Desmond or someone from the radio station even sneak a look at McCarthy's alleged list? The answer, I suppose, is that the people in Wheeling did not know they were dealing with history. They probably assumed that no politician in his right mind would choose Wheeling as the place to make a major political charge or even that the Republican national committee would never send to Wheeling for a Lincoln Day dinner a politician capable of making a charge that would make national news. They might have thought the charge was preposterous and that while it was their duty to report it, it wasn't necessary to do more than that.

Wire service coverage outside of metropolitan centers was often a matter of chance. Only one of the three services in 1950 had any arrangements for getting news out of Wheeling, and, as it was, the entire nation depended on the reporting of one man—Desmond. Politicians seldom choose such out-of-the-way places to make major pronouncements unless state or national political reporters are there. (Edwards, of the *Chicago Tribune*, commented, "Joe didn't know what he had when he went off on that Wheeling trip. If he had known, he'd have taken one of us along.") On the other hand, politicians sometimes say things that they would never say in the capital just because there are no national reporters present; they fail to qualify, they oversimplify. McCarthy often issued new charges back in Wisconsin. "He often saved his best stories for Wisconsin because he got better national coverage if the stories originated here rather than in Washington," I was told by Dion Henderson, who was an AP outdoors writer in the fifties in Milwaukee, and covered McCarthy extensively. He said that McCarthy especially liked to plant stories with Arthur Bystrom, the AP's state political reporter in Madison, because Bystrom, a cynical, old-school reporter, "always wrote whatever McCarthy wanted him to write."[28]

If the AP had difficulty in keeping up with McCarthy out in Middle America, its problem was slight compared to that of the United Press or the International News Service. Where the AP did not have a bureau but where the local paper was a member of the AP (a cooperative), the AP had exclusive access to reporters' carbons on any local story that appeared in the paper. United Press coverage of McCarthy's trip was originated in Washington and depended on the

ingenuity of reporters there, a little theft of AP material, and a few
strategic telephone calls. George Reedy did most of this for the UP
during McCarthy's western foray. He would call the State Department
to get a denial of whatever McCarthy had said most recently and then
append to this McCarthy's latest charges, for which there could be
no other source, at that point, than the AP.

According to Reedy, the UP had no stories from correspondents in
the West on that trip. "UP and INS hired young kids for western
bureaus, didn't pay them anything, and they could barely write their
names," he said. "We couldn't trust anything they sent in, so we tried
to figure it out in Washington. Trying to make sense of it was our
biggest mistake. One thing McCarthy did know, though, and it's a
weakness with newspapers and wire services to this day, is that a
speech in some out-of-the-way place can make more goddamn trouble."[29] The headlines that week in the *Beloit Daily News*, which had
only UP service, were the products of Reedy's work: "State Dept.
Denies 205 Reds on Its Payroll," February 10; "Acheson Aide Asks
McCarthy Name Reds," February 11; "McCarthy Gets New Demand
to Name Reds," February 14. INS provided no stories at all until
Tuesday, February 14, when the State Department held a formal news
conference.

One of the most significant stories in that first month was the speech
McCarthy made on Saturday night, February 11, at Reno, Nevada, a
speech that revealed to any attentive reader the paucity of McCarthy's
information and the recklessness of his attacks. But because it was
Saturday night, because of the AP's difficulty in deciding what the
story was, and because it was quickly buried under the inevitable
overnight lead, the story appeared in coherent form in only a few
newspapers. Even in those few, only a handful of editors caught its
significance. For that handful, though, already suspicious of Mc-
Carthy's jumping numbers, it was the signal to begin the editorial fight
against him. It seemed to demonstrate beyond reasonable doubt that
he was just "winging it," making it up as he went along. Had they
known the full story—the part that never did appear in newspapers—
they would have had no doubts about their decision to attack.

McCarthy had introduced Senator George Malone (Rep., Nev.) in
Salt Lake City at that dinner; in Reno, Malone was to introduce him.
McCarthy arrived in Reno on Saturday morning. Edward A. Olsen,
Associated Press correspondent, and Frank McCulloch, a reporter for
the *Reno Gazette*, tracked him down. Olsen said that they found
McCarthy in Malone's office in the Sierra Pacific Power Company
building. "We opened the door and walked in," Olsen recalled.

"McCarthy was talking on the phone, to his Washington headquarters or his staff. The gist of his questioning was, 'How's it going? Are we making an impact? Are we getting some publicity out of it?'" While McCarthy talked he pounded his fountain pen against his front teeth, occasionally hitting the phone mouthpiece. When asked why, he answered, "I'm breaking up the wiretap." "We tried to interview him about his allegations of Communists in the State Department, and asked him if he could name some names for us," Olsen said. "Well, he did. He named three or four eminent people. . . . I asked him would he name these names in his speech that night, because I didn't want to run them as an interview unless he was really on the record about it. His reply to that was, 'Young man, I know more about libel than you do. I'm a lawyer.' So I didn't run his interview at all, and New York agreed."[30]

McCarthy gave the reporters a copy of a telegram to President Truman in which he repeated his claim that he had "57 cases of individuals who would appear to be either card-carrying members or certainly loyal to the Communist party" and suggested that the president could get these names from Secretary of State Acheson. This telegram was released by McCarthy's Washington office, too, and most newspapers carried the story under either the Reno or the Washington dateline, resulting in such Sunday headlines as "Purge State Department Reds, Senator Urges" (*Atlanta Constitution*); "57 Reds in State Department, Sen. McCarthy Insists" (*New York Post*); or "Get Acheson's List of Commies on Staff, Senator Bids Truman" (*Rochester Democrat & Chronicle*).

The headline that night in the *Gazette*—a four-column banner—read "McCarthy Prepared to List Communists at GOP Session." Two long stories dropped from the banner. One, headed "Republicans Meet in Reno for Lincoln Day," reported local details. The other, based on the interview, was headed "Senator from Wisconsin to Speak Tonight," and its lead sentence was "Senator McCarthy said today he would name at least four 'known Communists' in the United States State Department when he addresses Nevada Republicans at a Lincoln Day dinner here tonight." McCarthy's telegram to Truman was reported next, with an explanation of why the Federal Bureau of Investigation did not act to oust the "57 Communists." The FBI, McCarthy said, cannot act until the Justice Department tells it to, and the Justice Department "won't move until it has been approved by the State Department." The story continued: "He gave reporters the names of four State Department workers he said were Communists and who he will name in his talk tonight. 'If you use them, however, you'll be doing it at your own risk,' he warned." "He never really called them

Communists in his speech, of course," Olsen said. "But we were warned, and we hired a stenographer, Sadie Jackson, to take it down verbatim." (Mrs. Jackson's husband, Joseph S., was the managing editor of the *Gazette*. He saw McCarthy that afternoon at a local bar called the Sky Room, drinking with an "old Marine Corps buddy" who lived in Reno.)

In his speech, as reported by McCulloch in the *Gazette* on Monday, February 13, McCarthy said that spies had "been planted in the State Department to shape the policy of our government and rob this nation of its potency."

It has not been the less fortunate, or the members of minority groups, who have been traitorous to this nation, but rather those who have had all the benefits that the wealthiest nation on earth has had to offer . . . the finest homes, the finest college educations, and the finest jobs in government we can give. The bright young men who were born with silver spoons in their mouths are the ones who have been most traitorous. I would now like to cite some specific cases.

The "specific cases" were John Stewart Service, whom he called John W. Service, a veteran State Department diplomat who was on his way to take up a post as consul at Calcutta; Mrs. Mary Jane Kenny, a former State Department employe working as an editor for the United Nations publications office; Gustavo Duran, a State Department employe until 1946; and Harlow Shapley, a Harvard astronomer and left-wing activist who never had worked for the State Department.

The story continued:

After the talk, a reporter asked McCarthy if, as the text of his speech indicated, he had called these four people traitors. "I did not," he said, "and you will notice I didn't call them Communists, either." He added: "I don't care if these people sue me. It might give me a platform from which to expose them."

This bravado obviously was an attempt to save face, since McCarthy's disavowal would have removed the ground for a slander suit. But if McCulloch had followed the cynical journalistic maxim "Don't ask questions, you'll spoil the story" and not asked whether McCarthy had called the four traitors, it would have been a proper interpretation of McCarthy's remarks to have written, "Senator McCarthy said Saturday night that four State Department aides were traitors." The *San Francisco Examiner*, on Monday, did so interpret the speech. Its page-one headline was "4 in State Department Named as Reds."

Although both Reno newspapers had been owned by the Speidel

group (now Gannett) since 1939, each had continued to perform its traditional role as advocate and spokesman for one of the two major political parties, the *Gazette* (evening) for the Republicans, the *Nevada State Journal* (morning and Sunday) for the Democrats. The *Journal* that Sunday tiptoed through the McCarthy story with care, wary of libel. McCarthy, it said, "cautiously referred to members of the State Department staff in the light of being out-and-out Communists but left no doubt in the minds of the audience as to their absolute loyalty to the U.S. government and democracy." It referred to Service, Duran, Mrs. Kenny, and Shapley, "none of whom he referred to as Communists but whose activities he questioned and all of whom were given a clean bill of lading by the Senator's chief target in last night's speech, Dean Acheson, Secretary of State." The *Journal* story also reported that the number 205 on the typed copy of McCarthy's speech had been scratched out and 57 substituted.

The *Nevada State Journal*, on Monday morning, became the first paper in the country to criticize McCarthy editorially since the start of his Communists-in-the-State-Department campaign the previous Thursday, accusing him of playing politics with an important issue. Olsen, the AP man, said of the news story that he had never had a harder time trying to write a story of a speech in his life. "The man just talked circles. Everything was by inference, allusion, never a concrete statement of fact. Most of it didn't make sense. I tried to get into my lead that he had named names but he didn't call them anything. AP New York didn't know what to do with it, and they asked me to file the whole text, which I did. But they couldn't do any better with it."

This sort of frustration, shared by almost every reporter who covered McCarthy in those days, was especially keen for Olsen and McCulloch because of something else they had seen and heard that day in Malone's office, as McCarthy talked to a member of his staff in Washington. McCulloch tells this story: " 'That's great, great,' McCarthy said, taking notes furiously. 'Give me some more names.' I looked over his shoulder and saw him write 'Howard Shipley' on his pad. That's the way he used it in the speech that night. He had no idea who it was. It turned out to be Harlow Shapley, of course, but it led to all kinds of confusion."[31] It was obvious to the reporters that McCarthy's only research on the four persons he nearly called traitors had been to write down the names that someone on his staff had given him over the phone that day.

After the speech, McCarthy and the two reporters continued their argument about his charges at the Mapes Hotel bar. "By three or four o'clock in the morning we were stony drunk, McCarthy worst of all,"

Olsen recalled. "He and McCulloch and I were hollering back and forth about what a phony he was, and what phonies we were. At the end he was screaming at us that one of us had stolen his list of Communists. He'd lost it, and he knew he'd made a fool of himself." "He lost his list," McCulloch said, "between his eighth and ninth bourbons."

McCulloch's story about "Howard Shipley" marks one of the differences between reporting in 1950 and now. That story should have been told then, when it might have had an effect. Readers were entitled to know that background; they should have been told about the offer of the "Communist" names and the source of the names. But reporters covered politics then as if it were a stage play; only what happened in public counted.

One other paper used the Reno story on Sunday, the *Oregon Statesman*, which headed it "Senator McCarthy Climaxes Lincoln Day Talk on 'Traitorous Actions in Government' with Names of Four Persons with 'Communistic Connections.' " None but West Coast papers had much of a chance at the story for Sunday, as the speech would have ended some time after 1 A.M. in the East and after midnight in the Midwest, and it was not the kind of story that would have tempted editors to extend deadlines, especially on Saturday night with the presses rolling out big profit-laden editions. Smaller papers did not have Sunday editions, of course.

Despite Olsen's qualms, the AP story serviced to the morning papers for Monday, February 13, was a good one. It made clear that McCarthy had hedged, and in 10 bracketed inserts it thoroughly identified each person attacked by McCarthy, both as to clearances and to his or her connection, or lack of connection, with the State Department. Fourteen morning papers carried the story, including the *Nevada State Journal*, *Oregon Statesman*, and *San Francisco Examiner*, already noted. Five of these papers saw the significance of the story and pointed it out in their headlines: The *Baltimore Sun*, "McCarthy Names Names in Four 'Cases'; Senator, However, Calls None 'Communist' or 'Traitor' "; The *Providence Journal*, "Sen. McCarthy Lists Four Persons in Connection with Red Charges; However, Wisconsin Legislator Says He's Not Labelling Them Traitors or Reds but 'Specific Cases' of People with Communist Links"; The *Washington Post*, "McCarthy Names Four, Hedges on Charges"; The *Chicago Sun-Times*, "Senator McCarthy Names 4 'Reds,' Then Backs Down"; The *Wisconsin State Journal* (Madison), "McCarthy Cites Four for Red Connections; Hedges on Communist Label after References to 'Traitorous Actions.' " (The *State Journal*, a staunchly Republican paper, showed a commendable lack of bias in this accurate headline. The paper became one of McCarthy's firmest supporters in the next four years.)

Other morning papers chose to adopt McCarthy's coverup phrase "Communist connections." They were the *Chicago Tribune, Boston Post, Boston Herald, Louisville Courier-Journal, Miami Herald, New Orleans Times-Picayune,* and *Manchester Union.*

For the afternoon papers that Monday, the AP served a roundup of old news and trivia which began, "Republicans Monday pressed new attacks on what they called Communist infiltration into the government," and went on to recap days-old charges starting with McCarthy at Wheeling, Senator Martin (Rep., Pa.) in a weekend radio talk, and Senator Wherry (Rep., Neb.) in a speech in California. It did include the hedge at Reno, down in the seventh paragraph, and a few sharp-eyed copy editors made it the basis of headlines: for instance, the *Milwaukee Journal's* headline read, "McCarthy List Down to Four; 'Not Reds or Traitors' "; and that of the *St. Louis Post-Dispatch,* "McCarthy Names Four in Red Charges and Then Hedges; Senator Lists Them as 'Specific Cases of People with Communist Connection.' "

About 20 other afternoon papers used the Republican roundup that day under such headlines as these: "GOP Presses Attacks on Reds in Government" (*LaCrosse Tribune*); "GOP Pressing Drives on Reds in U.S. Jobs" (*Capital Times*); "Republicans Renew Fight on Reds in Government" (*Oakland Tribune*). Some papers used the stories in sufficient length to include the Reno hedge; some did not. The *Atlanta Constitution* used three inches of this story.

About 80 papers of the 129 I surveyed—more than two-thirds—carried no story at all about McCarthy's blundering adventure in Reno. The *New York Times* picked up part of the story the next day in reporting the detailed reply to McCarthy's charges issued for the State Department by John Peurifoy, deputy undersecretary for security. But this story contained only the statement that McCarthy charged the four people with "Communist connections"; nothing about the hedge. No New York newspaper carried this important story.

In Madison, Wisconsin, the *Capital Times* published an uncharacteristic editorial. Its editor, William T. Evjue, almost the last of the practitioners of "personal journalism," complained repeatedly during the next four years that the wire services, particularly the Associated Press, were writing stories unfairly favorable to McCarthy and suppressing stories unfavorable to him. But on February 15, Evjue wrote an editorial headed "Responsible Reporting by the Associated Press." It praised the AP for catching McCarthy in the hedge at Reno and said, "If news services showed this same sense of responsibility more often, there would not be so many innocent people injured by the irresponsible charges of demagogs like McCarthy."

Seven other newspapers published critical editorials in the next two days. On Tuesday, February 14, the *Washington Post*, in an editorial entitled "Sewer Politics," charged McCarthy with employing evasion and "foul play" in hedging on his charges. "Rarely has a man in public life crawled and squirmed so abjectly," said the *Post*. The *St. Louis Post-Dispatch*, under the heading "McCarthy Does Some Backtrack-ing," pointed out that not only was McCarthy throwing out different numbers almost every day but he was also deflating his charges as he went. The *St. Louis Globe-Democrat*, under the head "McCarthy's 'Red List,'" said that in addition to not being Communists or traitors, three of the four named in Reno were not employed by the State Department; "The Senator should further back up his statements or back up himself." The *Raleigh News & Observer*, under the heading "Utterly Irresponsible," wrote that if McCarthy really had a list of Communists, he would turn it over to the president or the State De-partment. As it was, the paper said, he was just trying to make "po-litical capital" out of it. The *Milwaukee Journal*, in a widely reprinted editorial headed "Jumping Joe McCarthy," recited all the numbers and the hedges and challenged him to name names. Two other papers, in addition to the *Capital Times*, joined this chorus of criticism on Wednesday. The *Sheboygan Press*, under the line "Irresponsible Sen-ator McCarthy," said that the hedge at Reno seemed to be an "ad-mission by Senator McCarthy that he was just talking a lot of hot air." The other paper to react quickly was the *New Orleans Times-Pica-yune*, which wrote, "There may be card-carrying Communists in the State Department right now. But Senator McCarthy's naming of these four persons neither substantiates nor encourages belief in his sen-sational charges."

On Saturday night, when McCarthy made his speech in Reno, only 48 hours had elapsed since the beginning of his historic campaign. Already wire service stories were proliferating. The Associated Press by this time had produced seven "new leads," the United Press three. The first had been the AP story out of Wheeling, which appeared Friday in morning and evening newspapers. On Friday morning, Lin-coln White, a State Department spokesman, had denied the "205 Reds" charge; some papers used that as their lead that evening. The Denver airport stop, with "207 bad risks," made another new lead for Friday evening or Saturday morning newspapers (depending on time zones), and the Salt Lake City radio interview—"57 card-carrying Commu-nists"—made another, chiefly for Saturday papers. Stories on Mc-Carthy's telegram to President Truman from Reno and the similar "open letter" to Truman issued by McCarthy's Washington office, in which he told the president to ask Dean Acheson for the names of the "57 Reds," were carried on Sunday. The Reno speech made a Monday story for most of the papers which carried it. The UP offered the Lincoln White denial for Friday afternoon papers and the "open letter" and the State Department's denial of the "57 Communists" charge for Saturday and Sunday papers.

On Monday, February 13, McCarthy was in Las Vegas, Nevada, for another Lincoln Day dinner. Newspaper accounts of this appearance are meager; only three of the papers surveyed used it at all, probably because there was nothing new in what McCarthy said. The lead in all three stories was that "John W. Service" was one of 57 who had not been cleared by loyalty boards.

On Tuesday, McCarthy held a press conference at the Greater Los Angeles Press Club, repeating his offer to give the names of 57 Communists in the State Department to President Truman if the president would rescind his order barring congressional committees from access to State Department personnel records. "I have the names," he said, according to the *Los Angeles Daily News.* "There's nothing mysterious or secret about how I got them. They came from a variety of sources, including newspaper accounts. These are men who have been working 100% with the Communist party. They are men of the [Alger] Hiss class." McCarthy also repeated the charge that 205 had been declared "unfit for service" by the president's loyalty board, yet presumably were still employed by the State Department.

The *Los Angeles Times* account of that press conference ("Senator to Name 57 Aides of Acheson Listed as Reds") revealed McCarthy at his slippery best. On Monday, John Peurifoy, deputy undersecretary of state for security, had held a press conference in Washington in which he said, among other things, that only one of the four people attacked by McCarthy at Reno was an employe of the State Department. The *Times* story read: "Peurifoy referred in Washington dispatches to four names previously given out by the Senator. Senator McCarthy said they were not on his list of 57. At the time he had mentioned the names in a speech, he said, he had given the present connections of the quartet, stating that one was still in the State Department, and that the others were working elsewhere. He thought *Peurifoy was confused,* he said." A dozen papers used the Los Angeles story, most of them western papers for which this was the first report on McCarthy. For some papers the fact that he had said these things on the West Coast made it news, even though he had said the same things earlier in other places.

The final stop on McCarthy's Lincoln Day dinner tour of the West was not reported nationally. It was in Huron, South Dakota, where he spoke to an overflow crowd—300 people—in the First Presbyterian Church on Wednesday night, February 15. The content of his speech was like that of the Reno speech. He named the same names in Huron as he had at Reno, but it is not clear from the story that appeared the next day in the *Huronite and Daily Plainsman* whether he qualified his charges, as he had in Reno; the paper reported no hedge. The visit produced a barrage of supporting editorials and columns in the *Huronite and Daily Plainsman*. No other paper in the sample supported McCarthy more passionately during this first month.

The political climate in South Dakota was right for McCarthy. On February 8, a state senator, L. R. Houck, had introduced a concurrent resolution in the South Dakota legislature demanding that Congress and the president check on "the loyalties of the men employed in the State Department from Dean Acheson on down." It took only four days for adoption of this resolution by both houses of the legislature. No debate was reported.

The *Plainsman's* first McCarthy story appeared on the afternoon of the senator's visit, an AP story from Los Angeles based on an interview at McCarthy's hotel: "McCarthy Says Will Give Names; To Visit Huron." McCarthy's speech itself produced a banner headline in the *Plainsman* the next day: " 'Odds against U.S. in Communism Fight'—McCarthy," followed by, "Says Traitors Are Undermining Foreign Policy; Wisconsin Senator Repeats Charges Communists in State Department; Says Truman Action Unlikely." A two-column picture of McCarthy speaking appeared on page one.

The story began, "A grim picture of a United States that is in a 'showdown fight with Communism' while its foreign policy is shaped by 'traitorous actions' in the State Department was painted in a Lincoln Day address in Huron Wednesday by a fighting Irishman and ex-marine." It went on to say that McCarthy spoke with "an obvious sincerity of purpose" as he charged that the State Department and the Truman Administration were "infested with Communist spies and sympathizers of the Alger Hiss type who are selling the United States to Communism." As he had in Reno, McCarthy said that our impotence was "due to traitorous actions in the State Department by persons who were born with silver spoons in their mouths." The next paragraph of the story seems to say that McCarthy called some persons Communists: "The Senator named several names of ex–State Department employes as Communists, outside of the 57 he has not revealed, as he has done on his speaking tour on the West Coast. He dwelt particularly on 'John W. Service, who during the war on a state department mission in China urged torpedoing Chiang Kai-Shek and said that communization was China's only hope.' " McCarthy apparently hadn't read the AP's correction of Service's middle initial or he didn't care. The *Plainsman* reporter did not say who else McCarthy had named as Communists, and we are unable to tell whether "Howard Shipley" was among them.

On Friday, February 17, the *Plainsman* ran an approving editorial which read, "U.S. Senator McCarthy gave a powerful speech in Huron Wednesday and bluntly stated that the U.S. is right now in a show-down with Russian Communism and that it is handicapped by trai-torous spies and sympathizers in our own State Department, and he presented names to document his charge." There were many such editorials.

On Tuesday, March 7, the day before McCarthy opened the Senate hearings into his charges with the name of Dorothy Kenyon, the *Plainsman* ran an editorial entitled "World War III Isn't Coming; It's Here." We're losing this war, it said, through the operations of "fifth-columnists." With emotions at this pitch, it is possible that McCarthy's revelation at the first hearing of the Tydings investigation committee—that Judge Dorothy Kenyon might have been affiliated with 28 Communist "fronts"—seemed anticlimactic to the editors of the *Plainsman*. The paper carried no story about it. The next day it carried a short AP story headed "McCarthy May Enlarge Charge." He never did, of course.

On Thursday, February 16, McCarthy flew from South Dakota to Milwaukee. That was the day that President Truman told his news conference that there was "not a word of truth" in McCarthy's charges about Communists in the State Department, and the senator was ready with a reply when he saw reporters while changing planes at the Milwaukee airport on his way to Appleton. "President Truman should refresh his memory about certain things," McCarthy said. "I refer him to a letter written July 26, 1946, by the then Secretary of State Byrnes, to Representative Adolph Sabath of Illinois. Byrnes said that the loy-alty board's screening of the first 3,000 State Department employes had resulted in recommendations against the employment of 285 per-sons, and that of the 285, only 79 had been terminated."[32]

McCarthy repeated his offer to give the names of 57 Communists in the State Department to President Truman if the president would rescind the ban on giving loyalty file information to members of the Congress. He said that it might be a good idea to hold up all appro-priations to the State Department "until they decide to play ball with Congress on this loyalty business." He said that he might recommend that when he returned to Washington.

McCarthy returned to Milwaukee Saturday morning on his way back to the capital. He telephoned Paul Ringler, the *Milwaukee Jour-nal* editorial writer who had already written two severely critical ed-itorials about his charges, to suggest lunch. "Joe tried to maintain good relations with *Journal* people until the end," Ringler said. "Partly I suppose this was good political sense, but even more it was a total failure to understand why we were opposing and criticizing him. He was so totally amoral that he believed we should understand that this was all political gamesmanship—that no matter what he said, it shouldn't make any difference between friends."[33]

Ringler regarded the invitation to lunch as a chance to find out what kind of information McCarthy really had, and he wanted witnesses to whatever he learned. There were no other editorial writers on duty that day, so he pressed two *Journal* reporters into service, Robert H. Fleming and John Hoving, and they met McCarthy at Moy Toy's, a small Chinese restaurant on Third Street that was popular with *Journal* employes. "What a session that was!" Ringler recalled. "The three of us used everything but the third degree in trying to get some hard evidence. He was at his evasive best (or worst). We cajoled, we pleaded, we insulted. Finally I said, 'Joe, I don't believe you've got a goddamn thing to prove the things you've been saying. It's all a lot of political hogwash.'" McCarthy flushed, pounded the table and shouted, "Listen, you bastards. I'm not going to tell you anything. I just want you to know I've got a pailful of shit and I'm going to use it where it does me the most good." Ringler reported this to the *Journal*'s editorial conference the next morning. "It confirmed what everybody was thinking," he wrote me. "I told them what I proposed to write and there was no objection. The *Journal* crusade against Joe McCarthy was off and running."

On Monday morning, in Washington, two reporters (among others) went to McCarthy's office. They were William S. Fairfield, who wrote a weekly column for six medium-sized Wisconsin newspapers, and the late Joseph Dear, Washington correspondent and part owner of a chain of small dailies. Fairfield recalled the conversation in an interview:

"We'd like the names," Dear said. "The 205 Communists."

"Look, you guys," McCarthy said. "That was just a political speech to a bunch of Republicans. Don't take it seriously."

"Don't you have any names?" Dear asked.

"Oh, one was a college professor," McCarthy began.

"Where?" Dear asked.

"A professor of astronomy," McCarthy said. "Another was a professor of anthropology, a woman. But it was just a political talk."[34]

The column on McCarthy that Fairfield wrote was a roundup of McCarthy's shifting numbers, and it provided background on those who had been so far identified by McCarthy as "cases" of something. Fairfield did not report McCarthy's dismissal of his own charges as "just a political speech to Republicans." At least, it was not in the column that appeared in the *Janesville Gazette*. The Associated Press kept the story going that Monday by soliciting a statement from Senator

Hoey (Dem., N.C.) that his special investigating subcommittee would "take a look" at any charges about Communists in government that McCarthy presented. No charges ever were referred to this subcommittee, and this irrelevant story was published by only three newspapers in the sample.

McCarthy's near-six-hour speech on the night of February 20, in which he read details of not 57 but 81 "cases" of individuals he said were somehow subversive, made the biggest story of his new career, carried in 83 percent of the newspapers in the sample. These "cases" involved association with known Communists, failures to obtain security clearance, or membership in Communist front groups. He named no one, and his refusal to do so led to acrimonious exchanges with Senator Lucas, the Democratic floor leader, and other Democrats.

This was another difficult story for newspapers. McCarthy's charges were so wide-ranging and mysterious that seven different topics suggested themselves to the nation's news editors as the most important aspect of the speech. In addition, Senator Lucas issued a statement Tuesday morning that he would propose that McCarthy's charges be investigated by either the foreign relations committee or the Senate's special investigating subcommittee, thus stealing the lead in most of the afternoon newspapers on Tuesday.

The largest number of papers—43—chose the Lucas lead, taking this as an indicator of official Democratic policy and printing such headlines as "Senate Democrats to Sift Spy Charges" (Christian Science Monitor); "Full Probe Promised on McCarthy Charge of Subversive Ring" (Washington Star); "Democrats Push for Probe of Spy-Ring Charge" (Buffalo News). Thirty-two papers centered on McCarthy's charge that a White House speech writer, whom he did not name, had been refused security clearance by the State Department but had obtained a job in the Defense Department and then in the White House. "I am doing President Truman a favor by telling him this," McCarthy said. "He wouldn't have this individual there if he knew it."

On this story, a number of newspapers did McCarthy the kind of favor that the press was going to do for him many times in the future: they went further than he did, to the edge of libel, and said in their headlines that McCarthy had called the speech writer a Communist. These are examples: "Speech Writer in White House Is Branded Red" (Boston Globe); "Charge Red Is White House Speech Writer" (St. Louis Globe-Democrat); "Pins Red Tag on Truman Aid" (Indianapolis Star). Other papers were more cautious, referring to the aide as a "pink," a "pro-Red," a "subversive," "with Communists," and a "loyalty flunker."

Eleven papers, including several which later supported McCarthy vigorously, chose the "spy ring" charge as a lead. McCarthy had said that a spy ring headed by a "big three" was operating in the State Department, that he did not understand why the secretary of state could allow these three to continue working, and that if these three were ousted, it would "break the back" of the spy ring. Among the "spy ring" headlines were "Senator Asks Probe of Spy Ring in State Department" (*Honolulu Star-Bulletin*); "McCarthy Says 'Big Three' Head Spy Ring at Capital" (*Appleton Post-Crescent*); "3 State Aids Spy Leaders" (*Washington Times-Herald*).

Four papers, including the *New York Times*, selected a charge that "one of our foreign ministers" had passed secret information to a Soviet agent in Europe. McCarthy said that the major part of the diplomat's file now had been removed from its usual place and locked in the safe of a "high official" of the State Department. The *Times* headline was "McCarthy Charges Spy for Russia Has a High State Department Post."

Four papers seized upon the fact that McCarthy had still named no names. Two of the headlines read "Senator Refuses to Specify Reds" (*Raleigh News & Observer*) and "McCarthy Still Names No Names" (*Providence Journal*).

Three papers chose the new figure of 81 cases as the basis for headlines; two focused on a charge that President Truman was the prisoner of "a bunch of twisted intellectuals." The *Washington Post* picked the fact that McCarthy had forced a quorum call, the first in five years, that dragged unhappy senators back to the chamber from dinner parties, the kind of procedural matter that often seems important to reporters who are close to the news. Other papers equivocated with general heads, such as "McCarthy Airs New Charges."

McCarthy made no more speeches, in the Senate or anywhere else, between February 20 and March 8, when he began his testimony before the Tydings subcommittee. The story continued to build, however, as the Senate voted an investigation based on his charges, the investigating committee was appointed, and the date set for the first hearings. McCarthy's name did not disappear from newspapers, and by furnishing quick, bold reactions to other happenings, he scored points in the fight to convince the American public—the newspaper readers—that he was right about all those Communists in Harry Truman's government.

That was the way it was to be for the next five years as the running "McCarthy story" settled down in Washington, where the largest number of reporters worked and where the competition for news was keenest.

2.

The Floundering
Press

EVENTS MOVED swiftly in Washington in the month
following McCarthy's speech at Wheeling as President Truman and
the senator exchanged accusations, while Democrats in the Senate
maneuvered toward a strategy to silence McCarthy's intolerable attacks and Republicans schemed to exploit McCarthy without taking
responsibility for his unproved charges. Much of this positioning by
both parties took place behind closed doors, and newsmen often mis-
understood and misinterpreted the moves that took place in public.
A battle for publicity that would last for years had begun, and in this
month, as a result of McCarthy's quick reactions and the ineptness
of the press, the Republicans had put the Democrats in a position in
which they seemed to be covering up for Communists in the State
Department.

President Truman held three news conferences during this month,
and in each of them made one or more newsworthy comments on
McCarthy and his charges. Relatively little of this news trickled
through to the readers of newspapers. In the first conference, on February 16, Truman said that there was "not a word of truth" in
McCarthy's charges and that the State Department had already answered the charges in detail, a reference to the statement issued by
Peurifoy, the deputy undersecretary of state, on February 13. This was
Truman's first comment on the McCarthy affair. It was ignored by
about 90 percent of the press. Only 18 papers out of 129 carried the
story, and 11 of these were Wisconsin papers. In the *Milwaukee Journal* it was a top-line story with a five-column head on page one:
"McCarthy Red Charge a Lie, Retort of President Truman." It was
on page one in six other Wisconsin newspapers and in the *San Diego*

39

Union. McCarthy was in Milwaukee briefly that day and held a news conference at the airport. The *Milwaukee Sentinel's* page-one story was headed: "McCarthy Says 'You, Too,' to Truman's 'Liar.' " The *Journal* carried that report as a "follow" to the Truman story. The *Appleton Post-Crescent* also had a McCarthy lead on its story, attributed to its Washington bureau: "McCarthy Tells Truman Where To Find Proof." The *New York World-Telegram*, the *Newark News*, the *Reno Gazette* and the *Sacramento Bee* were among the papers outside Wisconsin that carried the story. It may have been a line or two near the bottom of another Truman story in some papers; it was used this way in the *Minneapolis Star*. All three wire services carried the story, which meant that it was available to every newspaper.

In his February 23 news conference, Truman said that he would not turn over State Department loyalty files to the Senate investigating committee and that he doubted whether it was legally possible to subpoena the president to get these files. This was recognized as news, since most papers had carried one or more stories about McCarthy's demands for access to loyalty files and the Senate's action in giving the investigating committee the power to subpoena records. Most of the morning newspapers carried this story under headlines such as these: "Truman Again Closes Loyalty Files to Senate" (*New York Herald-Tribune*); "Loyalty Files to Be Secret, Truman Says" (*Washington Post*). But the mid-day press conference ran late that Thursday, and since afternoon papers go to press about noon, only a few afternoon papers carried the story. Convention demanded a new story for the next day, and this made it possible for the Republicans to steal the headlines and obscure Truman's statements.

The AP's overnight lead was based on a statement by Senator Wherry (Rep., Nebr.) that Secretary of State Acheson might be prosecuted for contempt if he refused to turn over the files: "Republicans Friday threatened a court fight to get secret loyalty files in the hands of a Senate committee ordered to hunt down any Communists in the State Department." McCarthy got into it, too, with a comment that the president's statement was "an obvious attempt to cover up Communists in the State Department," and about half of the AP story was given over to McCarthy's reiteration of earlier charges. Truman's statement, in that version, merited only two paragraphs.

Examples of headlines produced by this dubious story were "Republicans Threaten Court Fight to Get Loyalty Files" (*Denver Post*); "Threaten Suit for Loyalty Files" (*Minneapolis Star*); "Wherry Said He'd Sue over State Department 'Reds'" (*Berkshire Eagle*). The Republicans obviously did not take the "threat" seriously; neither Wherry nor anyone else mentioned it again. Reporters in Washington and telegraph editors for newspapers should have known that such a threat—if it was a threat—was hollow. But it was a new lead on the McCarthy story, and a new lead, for most papers, took precedence over yesterday's real news. The choices made between the Truman lead and the trivial Wherry-McCarthy lead bore no relation to the newspapers' editorial positions. *The New York Post*, the *Berkshire Eagle*, the *Nevada State Journal*, and the *Milwaukee Journal*, all on record as critics of McCarthy, used the Republican lead, while the *Chicago Tribune*, the *Washington Times-Herald*, and the *Wisconsin State Journal*, all supporting McCarthy, used the Truman lead. A few newspapers, the *New York Times* among them, also reported on February 24 that Truman had said that he was ready to cooperate with the investigating committee "to disprove charges made by McCarthy," but on March 2 the president was less defiant. News stories reported that his Democratic friends in the Congress had advised him not to be so adamant, out of fear that the Republicans could convince the public that the Administration was "covering up." This time Truman said that he would cooperate with the committee without qualification and that he would make a decision on the matter of surrendering the loyalty files on individuals to the committee when that question came to him. In the *New York Times* on March 3, William S. White wrote that an accommodation had been reached between the administration and the investigating committee providing that when specific charges were made by Senator McCarthy against a person, members of the committee could go to the State Department to examine that person's files, on condition that the contents not be made public. No source was given for the story, portions of which had been surfacing all week—first in a dispatch by the United Press—and which later turned out to be accurate.

The president also said in his press conference that the only concrete action against subversives in government had been carried out by the executive departments under his direction, through the loyalty program. He said that anyone who had information about Communists in government should come to him with it and he would see that action was taken. Only one-third of the newspapers carried this story at all. Some papers picked Truman's claim of action against Communists as the most important statement: "Truman Says He Alone Has Fired Disloyal" (*Washington Post*); "Truman Cites Action Against Subversives" (*Washington Star*). Some chose Truman's invitation: " 'If Congress Really Believes Red Charge, It Should Tell Me' " (*San Francisco News*); "Truman Asks Foes of Reds to Come to Him" (*Beloit Daily News*). But most picked his promise of cooperation: "State Department Quiz OK'd by Truman" (*New York Journal-American*);

"Truman to Cooperate on Spy Probe" (*Milwaukee Sentinel*). The newspapers' emphasis on "cooperation" was misleading. Nothing else in Truman's comments indicated any change in attitude, nor did subsequent events demonstrate a change. Newspapers should have seen it for what it was—just a tactical move in the running political struggle. None of the people involved paid any attention to it.

McCarthy's response later that day became the AP's new lead. It was directed at the president's claim that he alone had acted to eliminate subversives. The senator said that Truman had "disregarded the known fact that almost every one of the Communists who have been convicted in this country, including Alger Hiss, were convicted as a result of Congressional action." Of the 24 papers that used this overnight lead on Friday, March 3, only eight had published the story of Truman's press conference. Truman's statements, in this AP story, were boiled down to part of one sentence, and it would have been difficult for a reader to know what had precipitated McCarthy's statement. In some papers the story was so abbreviated that all mention of Truman was dropped. The Republicans reaped such headlines as these: "GOP's Belittle Truman Boast in Commie Rout" (*Superior Telegram*); "Congress Led Red Drive, GOP Claims" (*Salt Lake City Deseret News*); "McCarthy Denies Truman Claim on Red Action" (*Riverside Press*). It was clearly a propaganda victory for McCarthy, especially since 13 of the 24 papers that used the overnight lead were in Wisconsin, where it counted most for him.

Many papers had headlined McCarthy's charge, in his Senate speech on February 20, that a man who failed to obtain security clearance for a State Department job was now a speech writer for President Truman, and some papers had described this person—"Case No. 9"— as a "Red." On Tuesday, February 28, the *Washington Post* carried a story saying that David Demarest Lloyd had identified himself as Case No. 9. Lloyd explained that his file had been included by mistake among files of those who had failed to get security clearances and that the State Department had apologized for the error; he did get security clearance from the FBI before he got the White House job in 1948. He went on to say that he had resigned from the Washington Book Shop and the National Lawyers Guild when he heard that they were Communist fronts, and that his relative with a financial interest in the *Daily Worker* was a great-aunt, Mrs. Caroline Lloyd Strobell, who had been one of three women who became owners of the Communist newspaper when it severed direct connections with the Communist party. Mrs. Strobell had died five years earlier. (The *Chicago Sun-Times*'s Washington bureau reported gleefully on March 5 that Mrs. Strobell's investment in the *Daily Worker* had been one dollar and that Mrs. Strobell had a larger financial interest in another newspaper—shares valued at $14 million, representing a 20 percent interest—in the *Chicago Tribune*.)

The wire services called Lloyd, who confirmed the *Post* story. The result was a few headlines that indicated that there was at least some doubt about the absolute truth of McCarthy's charge—headlines such as "Truman Aide Hurls Denial" (*Nevada State Journal*); "Truman Aide Says He Quit Left Links" (*New York Times*); "McCarthy White House 'Red Writer' Revealed as Scarcely Even Pink" (*Capital Times*). Headlines in many more newspapers simply reported that Lloyd had identified himself as Case No. 9. McCarthy was ready. He said quickly that he doubted the extent of Lloyd's "reform." He said that Lloyd had once prepared a document entitled "President Truman's Loyalty Program" which "vigorously extolled the virtues of Alger Hiss, one of Russia's top espionage agents, after Hiss was exposed," and that Lloyd had written the Oklahoma City speech for President Truman in which Truman had defended his stand on Communists in government in 1948. (The AP story that day did not say whether the document cited by McCarthy actually did praise Hiss; it did not say for whom the document was prepared or when it was written. It did not say why writing a speech defending Truman's stand on Communists in government was subversive, even in McCarthy's eyes. It did not say whether Communists in government really were the subject of the president's speech in Oklahoma City.)

Once again, the nation's news editors played the game McCarthy knew so well. This was a new lead on the Lloyd story, so the headlines in many papers read like these: "McCarthy Calls Lloyd Backer of Alger Hiss" (*Wausau Record-Herald*); "McCarthy Doubts Loyalty of White House Aide" (*Salt Lake City Tribune*); "Reform of 'Case No. 9' Doubted by McCarthy" (*Kansas City Star*). In the stories, Lloyd's defense and his voluntary self-identification were pushed farther down by McCarthy's new charges and were usually abbreviated. A casual reader would not have noticed Lloyd's statements. Sometimes the McCarthy lead served to reinforce a larger headline of a week earlier, as in the *New York Daily News*, the nation's largest newspaper, in which readers got this succession: "A Loyalty Risk Now Truman's Aid: McCarthy" (February 21), and "McCarthy Doubts Red Suspect's 'Reform' " (February 28). The *Los Angeles Times* had these headlines: "Loyalty Flunker at White House, Senator Charges" (February 21), and "Senator Insists on Loyalty Quiz of Truman Aid" (March 1); the *Boston Post*, "Says White House Man with Reds" (February 21), and "Questions Reform of Case No. 9" (March 1); and the *St. Louis Globe-Democrat*: "Charge Red Is White House Speech Writer"

(February 21), and "McCarthy Calls Lloyd Backer of Alger Hiss" (March 1). Lloyd got a bad deal from the newspapers on a charge that even McCarthy seemed to regard as frivolous.

Why did it take a week for any newspaper to identify Lloyd? There were only a few members of the White House staff who could have been described as speech writers, and McCarthy offered plenty of clues in his Monday night speech. Why didn't investigative reporters try to identify other of McCarthy's 81 "cases"? As McCarthy himself said, their names had appeared in the *Congressional Record* and even in newspapers, and the remarks of Democratic senators trying to force McCarthy into naming names showed that they knew who some of the people were; certainly they could have helped reporters make the identifications. News staffs in Washington seemed to show a singular lack of initiative, even those on papers which had already taken a position of vigorous editorial criticism of McCarthy's doings.

Lloyd was defended effectively in a syndicated column by Peter Edson of the Newspaper Enterprise Association, a column which appeared during the first week of March. Edson wrote that Lloyd had been investigated by the House Appropriations Committee in 1947 and 1948 and cleared of any suspicion of disloyalty. He also refuted McCarthy's second-round charges, reporting that Lloyd had not written the Oklahoma City speech and that the 55-page report on the government's loyalty program which he had written as a researcher for the Democratic national committee did say that no evidence had yet turned up to indicate that Hiss was disloyal, but that it had been written before the discovery of Whittaker Chambers's "pumpkin papers," the turning point in the Hiss case. Edson predicted (correctly) that McCarthy would not bring up this case again. The column was run under headlines such as "McCarthy's Case No. 9 Backfires." Its impact was not great, however, since only three of the 18 papers which used it had circulations greater than 37,000.

Only two stories distributed by the Associated Press during this month were better than ordinary. One was the account of McCarthy's speech in Reno, already discussed. The other was a story by Jack Bell, the AP's senior political writer, on February 27, which provided some political explanation for McCarthy's attack. The story, under such headlines as "GOP Will Use Red Issue in Fall Campaign" (*Santa Barbara News-Press*), said that the Republicans intended to attack the Democrats on the basis of President Truman's dismissal of the Hiss case as a "red herring," Secretary of State Acheson's remark that he would not turn his back on Hiss, and Truman's refusal to turn over the loyalty files to the Senate in response to McCarthy's charges. The Republicans can say it is a "coverup" if they don't get the files, Bell said, and if they do get them and can find a Communist, they will "trumpet that until the last vote in November." On the other hand, if they don't find any, that will make McCarthy look ridiculous, he wrote. "As a political sideshow, the investigation may become Washington's best offering to this year's campaign."

His analysis was not particularly profound, but it was at least an expression of common sense; it agreed with McCarthy's offhand remarks to reporters about the whole thing being "just politics." Very few papers used it, only 10 out of the 129 surveyed. And of those 10, only 3—the Santa Barbara paper, the *Tulsa Tribune*, and the *Washington Star*—used more than three or four inches, and Bell's point did not come through in that short form.

Bert Andrews of the *New York Herald-Tribune* wrote a sound political analysis of the McCarthy affair; it appeared only in the *Tribune* and the *Boston Globe*.

On February 27, the same day that the Jack Bell story appeared, the United Press serviced a curious story that raised more questions than it answered. It ran under headlines such as these: "GOP Demand for Red Hunt Turned Down" (*Berkshire Eagle*); "GOP Not to Press State Department Probe" (*Stockton Record*); "McCarthy's Red Claims Toned Down" (*Sheboygan Press*). What the story said was that McCarthy had "hinted" that Republicans might not insist on looking at loyalty files and that it might be just as expedient to claim a coverup. The story speculated that senior Republicans, worried about the validity of McCarthy's charges, had cautioned him to confine his charges to "cases he can prove," perhaps the "big three" rather than all 81. This might have been a significant story if the reporters had gone a little deeper. Surely someone in the press corps had access to these senior Republicans. But nothing further was written about it. That story, too, ran in only one large paper, the *Milwaukee Journal*, in the three mentioned above, and in the *Lowell Sun*, the *Kenosha News*, the *Eugene Register-Guard*, the *Bakersfield Californian*, and the *Richmond Independent*.

Peter Edson wrote another story in the first week of March which summarized each of McCarthy's 81 cases, a tremendous job of condensation and analysis, running six newspaper columns. It was carried only in the *Racine Journal-Times*, the *Haverhill Gazette*, and the *Capital Times*.

On February 21, the day after McCarthy's "81 cases" speech, the Democrats introduced a resolution calling for an investigation of McCarthy's charges by the Senate Foreign Relations Committee. The Republicans, led by Senator Brewster (Rep., Maine), blocked immediate action; Brewster said the resolution ought to demand access to

State Department loyalty files. This was reported matter-of-factly and misleadingly under such headlines as these: "GOP Blocks Probe of Spy Ring" (*Montgomery Advertiser*); "Brewster Blocks Action on Red-Spy Ring Charge" (*Louisville Courier-Journal*). On February 22, the Senate adopted the resolution after Senator Lucas, the majority leader, "accepted" three Republican amendments that directed the investigating committee to procure loyalty files by subpoena, to hold open hearings, and to extend the probe to past as well as present employes of the State Department. Why did the Democrats, in the majority, meekly accept these amendments? One paper, the *Detroit News*, explained this, in an interpretive story by Martin Hayden. Hayden wrote that "unhappy Democrats argued against Republican amendments, but accepted them rather than face a roll call vote which [might] loom large in Congressional elections." This told a good deal about the mood of the times; even though Democrats were virtually certain that McCarthy could not back up his charges, they were too fearful of the effect of the "Communist" charge to risk a roll call vote, and they gave in.

On February 27 the *Milwaukee Sentinel*, a Hearst paper, carried a story under McCarthy's byline—"Written Expressly for INS"—in which McCarthy said that he got all his information from agencies "such as" the Federal Bureau of Investigation.

It was obvious, during the first week in March, that the wire services were turning out many more stories than any single paper was using. Sometimes one or two papers would have a certain wire story; sometimes papers would work five or six wire stories into a single report; the *Milwaukee Journal* did this regularly, combining AP and UP and *New York Times* material under the heading "From Wire Dispatches." The wire services were beginning to write advance stories, and there were two of these during that week, both saying that McCarthy would be the first witness when the hearings before the Tydings subcommittee opened on March 8.

Newspapers reported two court cases in March 1950—one in Ohio and one in New York—in which judges held that it was libelous to falsely call a person a Communist, but many newspapers continued to play carelessly with that epithet, even when McCarthy was careful to avoid making the direct charge. The first person the senator named in the March 8 hearing was Dorothy Kenyon, a former New York municipal justice who had been a delegate to the United Nations. McCarthy stated that Miss Kenyon had been affiliated with 28 Communist front organizations. Miss Kenyon promptly retorted that McCarthy was an "unmitigated liar" and that she had never belonged to a Communist front group. Belonging to 28 "fronts," even if true, is obviously something less than being a Communist, but the difference was not perceived by many of the nation's editors. Consider these headlines, typical of many others: "Senator Names Woman as 'Red' " (*New Orleans Times-Picayune*); "McCarthy Names 'Red,' Called 'Liar' " (*Miami Herald*); "State Employe Is Communist, Says Mc-Carthy" (*Superior Telegram*); "McCarthy Pins 'Red' Label on Woman" (*St. Petersburg Times*). Miss Kenyon was not a State Department employe, of course, and there is some question whether a delegate to the UN, which she had been until the previous December, was a State Department employe. Miss Kenyon had been a member of the U.S. Mission to the UN, serving on the UN Commission on the Status of Women. Some newspapers were careful about this part of her identification in their headlines—"UN Ex-Delegate Linked to Reds" (*Louisville Courier-Journal*); "McCarthy Slaps Red Label on Woman Ex-UN Delegate" (*Atlanta Constitution*). The *New York Times* was precise: "McCarthy Says Miss Kenyon Helped 28 Red Front Groups." So was the *Newark News*: "Ex-U.S. Aide in UN Called Red Fronter."

McCarthy's charge and Miss Kenyon's reply were all that most afternoon papers were able to publish on March 8, but McCarthy went on to charge that Philip C. Jessup, United States ambassador-at-large, had "an affinity for Communist causes." Only one paper translated this into a direct Communist charge, the *Eau Claire Leader*: "Probers Hear McCarthy Call State Department Envoy 'Red.' " Other Jessup headlines were these: "Senator Links Jessup to Communist Groups" (*San Francisco Examiner*); "Ambassador Accused as Sponsor of Reds" (*Seattle Post-Intelligencer*).

Miss Kenyon stole some headlines from McCarthy: "Woman Says Senator Lies" (*Detroit News*); "Terms Senator Cowardly Liar" (*Wichita Eagle*). Many papers ran two stories, one on the charge and another on the reply. In the battle for publicity, however, McCarthy clearly won the round, thanks to the newspapers' propensity for exaggerating his charges. Ninety-three percent of the newspapers surveyed used this story, a new peak of coverage. (It was almost saturation, for three of the newspapers carried no McCarthy stories at all the first month, and two other small newspapers carried only one story each. Only two papers that regularly carried stories about McCarthy failed to report the Kenyon charge.) This was to be the pattern for the next five years—daily stories, usually on page one, and often several a day, reaching a peak in 1954, when it was not unusual for a paper to carry 15 to 20 stories a day in which McCarthy was the central figure.

Newspapers in Washington, D.C., and those that maintained large Washington bureaus gave readers more information and more interpretation than those that had to rely solely on the wire services for news. A few stories stood out.

In the *New York Times*, there were informative stories by Cabell Phillips (February 19), in which he recited the history of the government's loyalty program and assayed the effect of McCarthy's campaign on these programs, and by James Reston (March 9), in which he examined the effort of Senator Tydings to question each charge by McCarthy at the time it was made. Coverage in the *Baltimore Sun* by Philip Potter and Gerald Griffin was particularly thorough, although neither reporter did much interpreting. They wrote lively stories, however, and the skillful use of direct quotes gave the reader the flavor of the squabble. There were good stories in the *Washington Post* by Robert C. Albright and Alfred Friendly, detailed and interpretive, with proper attention to partisan aspects of the fight. There was a similarly comprehensive story in the *Chicago Daily News* ("Has McCarthy Struck Red Gold? Commie Charges Stir Political Row") by Peter Lisagor. The best coverage of all was in the *Christian Science Monitor*—three stories by Richard L. Strout—highly descriptive, interpretive, and lively. "There could be no doubt," Strout wrote, "that this would be one of the bitterest Senatorial investigations in years. ... The Tydings committee is close to the breaking point. ... Keeping his temper under close check, Senator McCarthy admonished, lectured and reproved the committee.... Some of the difficulty in getting to the bottom of charges that the State Department is infiltrated by Communists is illustrated in trying to pin down what the charges are. ... The Republican party is assuming a hands-off and wait-and-see attitude on the McCarthy charges. If he can make only one case stick, in another 'Hiss case,' for example, it will be a major blow to the Truman administration."

Readers of these stories knew not only what was being said but why it was said and what the consequences might be. The reports were particularly valuable because they were spot news stories which got the information to the reader at the time of his highest interest.

Newspaper editorials in the 1950s were a more important part of the information process than they are now, when the role of the interpretive reporter is well established, when opinion writing and alternative news outlets have proliferated, and when many are willing to glean their understanding of the issues of the day from the tone of a television anchorman's voice. In those days the editorial page was the place where most readers sought help in trying to make sense of the puzzling, sometimes contradictory news reports.

Never were news reports more confusing nor citizens more in need of guidance than in the first days of Joe McCarthy's wild charges about Communists in government. And with a few exceptions, editorial writers in the nation's newspapers failed as badly in meeting their responsibilities to the readers as did the widely excoriated wire services. Most of the editorial writers and the editors and publishers who took part in making judgments about the McCarthy issue seemed as timid as the bureaucrats who sought to appease McCarthy or as ill-informed as their unfortunate readers.

Between February 10, the time of the Wheeling speech, and February 20, the date of the six-hour Senate speech by McCarthy, only 10 of the 129 papers surveyed found reason to criticize McCarthy's excesses and only eight attempted to defend him. After the February 20 speech, another 11 joined the McCarthy critics and 22 more took McCarthy's side. One paper switched from McCarthy's side to that of his critics in the last half of the month. Another 13 published observations to the effect that the matter was serious and that they ought to find out the truth. The majority of the newspapers did nothing at all editorially.

Some, but not all, of the papers that took stands against McCarthy were traditionally Democratic; the group included several independents and at least three traditionally Republican papers. Most of those that sided with McCarthy were traditionally Republican; others, if not aligned with a party, were devoted to right-wing ideas. Oddly, some newspapers that later became McCarthy's most vigorous tub-thumpers—notably the Hearst papers—carried no McCarthy editorials during this first month. The Hearst papers, in fact, carried very little news of the McCarthy controversy. Even though they came out each day, they looked almost as though they had been printed in an earlier time; their editorials and some of their columnists railed at the long-dead Roosevelt, while other columnists harried their own well-worn, favorite packs of Communists and fellow-travelers.

The newspapers that first criticized McCarthy based editorial judgments on the shifting numbers in his charges, the shifting identifications of the objects of his attacks, and upon his hedge at Reno, where he seemed to name four as traitors, then said he hadn't. The early McCarthy supporters argued that there must be something to the charges if a United States senator made them, that it was common knowledge that President Roosevelt welcomed Communists in government, and, most of all, that the conviction of Alger Hiss showed that there were Communists in government.

The papers that turned critical of McCarthy after February 20 cited many of the same reasons as the early critics, but they also said that they were finally moved to a decision because McCarthy, after all this time, had not mentioned names. Some were impelled to act by what they considered the absurdity of the charge against Dorothy Kenyon.

The surge of McCarthy support came as the Republicans centered on the State Department loyalty files as their point of attack, and editorials were less supportive of McCarthy than they were critical of President Truman; his refusal to turn over confidential personnel records to congressional committees proved, they declared, that he was covering up more Communists. Today, 30 years later, we have forgotten the scorn and hatred with which Truman was regarded by Republicans, Republican newspapers, and much of the populace; even normally Democratic newspapers were reluctant to defend him. In this instance, only a handful of papers approved his refusal to turn over loyalty files.

If we ranked newspapers on the quantity and vehemence of their criticism of McCarthy, first place would go to the *Capital Times* of Madison, Wisconsin. The *Capital Times* was an old enemy; it had opposed McCarthy in the 1946 primary contest for the Senate nomination in the election. McCarthy, in 1949, had charged that William T. Evjue, the paper's editor, had called his own city editor a Communist. The *Capital Times* published 10 editorials criticizing McCarthy that first month after Wheeling—five of its own and five reprinted from other papers—as well as four syndicated columns critical of McCarthy. The *Washington Post*, which would rank second, published five strong editorials, along with three editorial cartoons and four critical columns. Next would come the *Milwaukee Journal* and the *Raleigh News & Observer*, each with four strongly critical editorials, followed by the *St. Louis Post-Dispatch*, the *New York Post*, and the *New York Times*, with three each. Newspapers which produced two such editorials were the *Salt Lake City Tribune*, *St. Louis Globe-Democrat*, *Sheboygan Press*, *Berkshire Eagle*, *Worcester Telegram*, and *Tampa Tribune*. Those with a single critical editorial were the *New York Herald-Tribune*, *Washington Star*, *Arkansas Gazette*, *Sacramento Bee*, *Memphis Commercial Appeal*, *Nevada State Journal*, *Stockton Record*, and *Nashville Tennessean*.

The prize for the most fiercely anti-Truman, pro-McCarthy editorials would be divided between the *San Diego Union* and the *Huronite and Plainsman*. The *Union* carried five editorials of this kind, the *Plainsman* four editorials, a publisher's column, and a guest editorial. Next came the *Shreveport Times*, with four editorial attacks on Truman and Acheson, followed by the *Washington Times-Herald*, *Janesville Gazette*, *Miami Herald*, and *Cleveland Plain Dealer*, with three editorials each, and the *Indianapolis Star*, with two of its own and one guest editorial. (Guest editorials always agreed with the position of the paper reprinting them.) There were two pro-McCarthy editorials in the *Houston Post*, *New York Daily News*, *Los Angeles*

Times, Nashville Banner, Manchester Union, Chicago Daily News, Oakland Tribune, and Oshkosh Northwestern. Papers with single editorials backing McCarthy were the Chicago Tribune, Dallas News, Appleton Post-Crescent, La Crosse Tribune, Duluth News-Tribune, Columbus Dispatch, Wichita Eagle, Reno Gazette, Salinas Californian, San Jose Mercury-Herald, Wausau Record-Herald, Wisconsin State Journal, Jackson Clarion-Ledger, and Denver Post.

Some of the papers that straddled the issue wrote editorials on both sides, obviously troubled by the need to take a position. The New Orleans Times-Picayune, for example, had criticized McCarthy on February 15, after the Reno speech, but on March 9 it was less sure of its position. Its editorial said that it was "a pity that the probe started out on such a ridiculous note with Senator McCarthy making far-fetched accusations or insinuations," but that it would have been unwise and impolitic to ignore McCarthy's charges, "supported by the citation of 64 alleged instances of department hiring after investigation showed that they were national security risks." The Charlotte Observer went the other way. On February 14 an editorial headed "Red Spies in State?" asked, "Is the Wisconsin Republican telling the truth?" It said that McCarthy's charges were "too specific to be ignored," and continued, "It seems incredible, but let's have the facts." On February 25 the Observer agreed with the decision to investigate, saying that the public would have been satisfied with nothing less, in view of McCarthy's charge about 57 card-carrying Communists; "It is unbelievable that a United States Senator would publicly and repeatedly make such charges if he did not have any evidence to support them." But two days later the Observer decided that it was, after all, believable. "McCarthy has failed to make good his charge about 57 card-carrying Communists," the editorial said. "The public expected him to supply the names, but he did nothing of the kind. Nor did he provide any other concrete evidence to support his charge. He has been disappointing."

The inability of editors to believe that anyone could make such specific charges without the evidence to back them up was the basic reason for most of the hesitation. Typical was the response of the Philadelphia Bulletin: "McCarthy's charge that the State Department has 57 Communists on its payrolls seems incredible, but now that it has been made publicly it must be examined." The Worcester Telegram took the position that charges of this kind were serious, especially during the Cold War, and that McCarthy now had the chance to name names and prove the case or admit that he had made it all up; "The public is waiting to be shown." The Minneapolis Star wrote, "The State Department has had more than its share of undesirables and a responsible airing won't hurt. A quiet weeding-out process has been underway, but Senator McCarthy's charges of Communist infiltration and the Hiss affair have raised questions that need answering." In the opinion of the *Jackson Clarion-Ledger*, the conviction of Judy Coplon lent greater weight to McCarthy's 81 "case histories," and it wrote, "The public will certainly feel that the Administration should not dismiss McCarthy's charges without the most rigorous investigation." Other papers that took similar positions were the *Sacramento Bee* ("Should Get At the Facts"), the *Framingham News* ("Fight in the Making"), the *Des Moines Register* ("Let Committee Get the Facts"), the *Rhinelander Daily News* ("Get Facts"), and the *Humboldt Times* ("Red Spies in the State Department?").

In Appleton, Wisconsin, a confused woman wrote to Secretary of State Fred R. Zimmerman to demand that he get rid of all those Communists in his office in the state capitol, and editorial writers in Wisconsin had a lot of fun with this. Otherwise, there was nothing in the McCarthy affair to encourage humor. The *Oregon Statesman* on March 1 came closest to such an approach with a note of cynicism. "The inquiry," the *Statesman* said, "may turn up some dirt but the intradepartmental screening has been so severe that it is not probable that any 57 Reds will be flushed. The inquiry will make headlines and consume time which the Senate might otherwise spend in passing bad legislation. So the country should suffer it."

The *New York Times's* first editorial appeared on February 22, a summary of all the developments in the McCarthy story. The *Times* wrote that when McCarthy was asked to give names, he claimed that he could not because doing so might embarrass investigative agencies. This, according to the *Times*, was "not good enough to provide cover for the campaign of indiscriminate character-assassination" on which the Senator had embarked.

The most concentrated barrage of criticism of McCarthy came from the *Raleigh News & Observer*, whose editor, Jonathan Daniels, was a personal friend of Harry Truman. The paper published four editorials, two syndicated columns that criticized McCarthy, and two Herblock cartoons that ridiculed him, while running only six news stories. The *News & Observer's* first editorial on February 15—"Utterly Irresponsible"—said that if McCarthy really had a list of Communists he would turn it over to the authorities. The next day the *News & Observer* stated that the Senate must make McCarthy furnish proof, that so far he had just gone from one false charge to another. The last two editorials offered the opinion that the Senate as a body was on trial and that the country would "want to know if the Senate rebukes one of its own members if he is shown to be in need of rebuke." The last of these editorials said that hardly anyone believed McCarthy's charges, but that Senator Lodge (Rep., Mass.) seemed to be trying to protect McCarthy. "No one can 'protect' McCarthy without sharing in the irresponsibility of his charges," the *News & Observer* warned.

On the other side, the *San Diego Union* was equally forthright. In its first editorial, on February 25, it declared that the loyalty files were public property, that McCarthy was right in demanding them, and that the State Department needed "a good house-cleaning from top to bottom." On February 28 the *Union* charged President Truman with contempt of Congress for not turning over loyalty files and asked him what he was hiding. On March 1 the *Union* applauded Senator Wherry for suggesting going to court to force release of the loyalty files. On March 9 the paper again criticized Truman and wrote, "Fighting Communists in Europe and fighting them in the United States appear to have different meanings for Mr. Truman." On March 10 it argued that McCarthy had brought fresh charges and that these, too, could be proved true or false by the release of the loyalty files. The *Shreveport Times* of February 16 held that any government employe found to be sympathetic toward Communism or who had associated with Communists or "pro-Communists" should be fired. "In some instances," the *Times* said, "injustice might have been done. That is unfortunate, but could not have been avoided in any real house cleaning." On February 23 it wrote that Senate Democrats were not disturbed by the thought of a Communist sympathizer writing White House speeches. On February 25 it accused Truman and Acheson of trying to give McCarthy's charges "the quick brush-off," and on March 1 it charged Truman with hiding Communists and said that Congress should force him to give up the loyalty files. The *Los Angeles Times* on February 26 suggested that the President be impeached if he did not give up the loyalty files. "Truman shows no tendencies to ferret them [Communists] out," it said. The *Times* expressed a similar view on March 4, writing that Truman should "abandon this petulant attitude [on the files] and ferret out the Reds. . . ." An editorial comment that was expressed nowhere else in the country appeared in the *Appleton Post-Crescent* on March 6. Its language, its argument, and the fact that the paper's managing editor was a close friend of McCarthy invite the supposition that McCarthy might have had a hand in its composition. Headed "The Mouse Trap Play That Did Not Work," the editorial said that Senator Lucas had tried to get McCarthy to name names of those he accused. "That was a dried angleworm bait," the *Post-Crescent* said. "The administration is desperately trying to hide the shame . . . of the manner in which our policies were directed by the politbureau direct from the Kremlin.... It is startling that a President would hide the loyalty files ... that will show that supposedly responsible officials ... have performed acts or consented to policies which were wild and savage."

In 1950, the *Washington Times-Herald* had the largest circulation in the District of Columbia—275,954 daily. Its publisher was Colonel Robert R. McCormick, publisher of the *Chicago Tribune*, and its staff covering national affairs was the *Chicago Tribune*'s Washington bureau. Its editorials the month after Wheeling offered further evidence that the connection between McCarthy and the *Tribune* was close. In Wheeling, McCarthy had said that the 205 Communists were "working and shaping the policy of the State Department." That was the *Tribune* line, that the real Communists were the policymakers and that they were more important and more subversive than spies. Later McCarthy talked about "card-carrying Communists," which these "policymakers" obviously were not, and "spy rings," and it was such charges that made headlines. But if McCarthy forgot the "policy shapers" line for a while, the *Tribune* did not. On February 10 the *Times-Herald* ran the sixth of a series by Willard Edwards, headed "Reds Had White House Entry from '35, Official Papers Show." On February 11 Edwards wrote about Communists who had infiltrated the ranks of the army during World War II, and Raymond Moley was quoted as saying that Truman knew that there were Communists in government in 1945. The *Times-Herald*'s first editorial, on February 15, "The Spies' Best Friend," said that the point of Edwards's stories was that many spies were here not to spy but to infiltrate the Departments of State, Defense, and Labor and the world of communications. It said that President Roosevelt gave them whatever jobs they wanted in return for Communist support in New York City, which made it possible for him to win elections. It named, as part of the "pro-Soviet clique" in Washington, John Stewart Service, Owen Lattimore (a Johns Hopkins University lecturer on whom McCarthy later centered his attacks), and Dean Acheson. It said that Acheson had been "accused in Congress of leftist sympathies." This view was reiterated in an editorial on February 28—"Where Spies Hurt Us Most"—which argued that the spies who did the most damage were not those who gave away secrets but were those in policy positions where they had done such things as get the country into World War II, abandon Chiang Kai-Shek, and advocate turning Europe into a "goat pasture." "The State Department will never again command respect until it has come clean about the traitors it has harbored," the paper wrote.

The *Chicago Tribune* ran only one editorial that month, headed "Truman Is Against Reds—In Russia." It enunciated the isolationist line that everything that goes wrong in the world is the fault of someone in this country, a line that McCarthy followed in later speeches, almost in the words of the *Tribune*. "On the same day that President Truman, in his Alexandria speech, denounced the Reds in Russia," the editorial said, "his followers in the Senate were using every trick at their command to keep Congress from uncovering Reds in Mr. Truman's own State Department. Senator McCarthy's charges cannot be laughed down or pooh-poohed away. . . . Everything that the Administration forces could do to suppress the facts has been done. . . . What the people want to know now is who the Communist agents are and who has been protecting them. Obviously the protectors are in high places, or the investigation would not be opposed so vigorously." On March 6 the *Tribune* began a new series by Eugene Griffin about Harvard University and its connections with "left wingers." Its first story was headed "Harvard Ties to Red Groups Upset Alumni," and the first tie was to Dean Acheson. (Acheson was a graduate of Yale but attended the Harvard law school.) The second was "Harvard Men Help to Shape U.S. Policies; Accuse Many Law Grads of Aiding Reds." Harvard subsequently became the object of McCarthy's attacks, too.

Visual images tend to stick in our memories more tenaciously than words. Some of us recall the period most vividly in the memory of McCarthy glowering at witnesses in the televised hearings of 1954, of Attorney Joseph Welch registering shock at McCarthy's attack on a young member of his Boston law firm, or of the newspaper photograph of McCarthy grasping the reluctant hand of General Eisenhower in Milwaukee, after Eisenhower had capitulated to the senator and deleted praise of General George Marshall from his campaign speech. Others remember best the cartoons of the *Washington Post's* Herblock, whose work was a dramatic extension of the *Post's* editorial position. (Martin Agronsky, a radio and television commentator who was among the first broadcasters to criticize McCarthy, said recently that Herblock "had as much to do as anybody in our business with making people understand what Joe was; he really damaged him.")[1]

Herblock had not reached the peak of his artistry in 1950, and the four cartoons he produced in February were not among his best. His view of McCarthy as a fraud and a bully was already complete, though, and his cartoons were used regularly by more newspapers in the sample—eight—than those of any other cartoonist.* The first of the cartoons showed a transparent McCarthy labeled "Vague Charges" and two senators looking puzzled. The caption was, "Seem to You There's Something a Little Odd Here?"

A pro-McCarthy cartoon widely used (by seven small papers) was captioned "Loaded for Bear," and showed the Republican elephant looking at a shotgun labeled "McCarthy Charges" leaning against a hollow tree labeled "State Department." The elephant says, "No Tellin' What Might Be in Thar!" On the barn is nailed a bearskin labeled "Hiss." The cartoonist was Jesse Cargill of the King Features syndicate. Another carried by seven papers was by the *Chicago Daily News*'s Shoemaker: "Yes, Then We'll All Sleep Better." In a bed labeled "State Department" are three men—"Truman," "Public," and "Senate." Sticking out from beneath the bed are the shoes of a dozen spies. "Aw, go to sleep," says "Truman," but "Senate," waving a large revolver, says: "No, sir, not till I investigate!"† The *Chicago Tribune*'s cartoon, "Protecting Pets," by D. Holland, was also used in the *Washington Times-Herald*. It showed Truman standing in front of the "Loyalty Files," where mice played among papers tagged "Defense Secrets," "H-Bomb Files," "A-Bomb Files," and "American Security." In front of Truman was "Congress," holding a cat tagged "Investigation of Red Spies in the State Department." Truman says, "Now I'm telling you, keep that cat out of here!"

Cartoons by staff artists lampooning McCarthy appeared in the *St. Louis Post-Dispatch* (Daniel Fitzpatrick), *Milwaukee Journal* (Ross Lewis), *Louisville Courier-Journal* (Grover Page), *Stockton Record* (Ralph Yardley), and *Philadelphia Bulletin* (E. O. Alexander). The *Buffalo News* criticized Truman's "secrecy order" on loyalty files in a cartoon by William H. Summers. Other McCarthy cartoons during the month seemed to express no particular point of view.

Syndicated columnists furnished an impressive amount of information to the public during the first month after Wheeling. They not only supplied explanation and analysis that was missing from most of the news coverage, but also contributed a great deal of background and some news that did not appear in other columns of the news-

---

*The eight using Herblock cartoons were the *Washington Post*, *New York Post*, *Raleigh News & Observer*, *Chicago Sun-Times*, *Santa Barbara News-Press*, *Redding Record-Searchlight*, *Los Angeles Daily News*, and *Jackson Clarion-Ledger*. Many others reprinted them.

†The Shoemaker cartoon was used by the *Worcester Telegram*, *Appleton Post-Crecent*, *Houston Post*, *Reno Gazette*, *Richmond News-Leader*, and *Shreveport Times*.

papers. A few displayed a good deal of courage in offering views of McCarthy that must have been anathema to their clients, risking cancellation of their contracts. Because so many papers failed to offer any guidance through editorials, the syndicated columns were often the only source of interpretation available to readers. For a number of papers, Drew Pearson's column on February 18 was the first mention of the McCarthy story; news coverage began then, as if Pearson had awakened editors to the fact that something was going on. Where papers supported McCarthy editorially, the columnists supplied the only indication that there might be two sides to the story. Many newspapers that supported McCarthy continued to run columns that were damaging to him. The danger of losing readers who were devoted to certain columnists must have outweighed the desire to present an undiluted version of the controversy.

Pearson was the most influential of the columnists. His columns appeared in 34 of the papers surveyed. He was the first columnist to take on the subject of McCarthy, and the first reporter to expose the source of the discredited lists of possible security risks upon which McCarthy was basing his accusations. He wrote two columns on McCarthy during this month. In his February 18 column, Pearson reviewed the records of the four persons named by McCarthy in Reno, pointing out that Gustavo Duran and Mrs. Mary Jane Kenny had resigned from the State Department four years earlier, that Harlow Shapley, the Harvard astronomer, had never worked for the department, and that John S. Service, the only one still in the State Department, had been cleared and reinstated after a long and careful investigation. This column appeared in many papers that had overlooked the Reno story on February 13. Pearson's second column, a week later, began with an anecdote from which he concluded that McCarthy's telephone was being tapped by the Democrats. He traced McCarthy's list to old sources and said, "Every man on the McCarthy list has already been scrutinized by the House Un-American Activities Committee or by a House appropriations subcommittee. ... This writer, who has covered the State Department for about 20 years, has been considered the career boys' severest critic. However, knowing something about State Department personnel, it is my opinion that Sen. McCarthy is way off-base."

Marquis Childs, a member of the Washington bureau of the *St. Louis Post-Dispatch*, was the next columnist to criticize McCarthy. His column was used by 17 papers between February 22 and 24. He explained the backgrounds of the four persons named by McCarthy at Reno and lectured McCarthy: "To broadcast vague charges about the State Department without supporting names or facts is merely to

feed the atmosphere of suspicion and apprehension. It does not contribute to the security of the United States at home or abroad. . . . Any
authentic information about subversive individuals in government
should be given to the FBI."

A column by Stewart Alsop appearing the first week of March in
27 papers was sharply critical of McCarthy, and it carried weight.
Stewart and his brother Joseph, who alternated in writing the column,
consistently supported the Cold War against Russia and urged a strong
defense establishment; they were considered "conservatives" among
columnists, and many papers that would not have carried columns
by writers such as Childs or Thomas L. Stokes—"liberals"—did carry
the Alsop brothers. In many cases their column was the only note of
criticism of McCarthy that slipped into these papers. "The issue of
internal security in these times is a deadly serious issue, as the Hiss
trial and the Fuchs episode have clearly revealed. But blanket charges
like McCarthy's serve to obscure this issue, to destroy morale in the
government, and thus in fact to serve the interests of Communists."
If the State Department could prove McCarthy's charges to be just
"irresponsible headline-hunting," it would discourage others from
following his example, Alsop continued. "And if this is the outcome,
McCarthy will undoubtedly have done the country a service."

A surprising column by the most conservative of columnists, David
Lawrence, appeared on March 3 in 15 papers. (Lawrence later became
a staunch supporter of McCarthy.) Lawrence scolded the Republicans
for attempting to make Communists-in-government the 1950 campaign
issue. In order for such a campaign to be effective, he wrote, "the
President's complicity with Communist infiltration must be proved
and the responsibility of each Democratic candidate for the same
laxity must be established." He said he did not think this was possible,
and that if the Republicans thought they could win a campaign on
"charges and innuendoes about Communism" that produce headlines,
they were mistaken. A similar view was expressed, more explicitly,
by the liberal Thomas L. Stokes in a column published in 14 papers
during the first week in March. Stokes's point was that the beginning
of a new Communists-in-government campaign was a sure sign that
the election season was beginning. "Spreading gossip and rumor in
an irresponsible way is not the way to ferret out disloyalty and to
protect security in the United States," he wrote. "Such tactics infringe
on the Bill of Rights. It can, of course, produce sensational headlines
and attract attention to a publicity-hungry politician and maybe make
a temporary political issue."

Peter Edson's column defending David Demarest Lloyd has been
noted. Edson wrote another column that appeared March 10, in which

he said that all of McCarthy's cases that had been identified had come from the so-called Lee Report of 1947, a list compiled by Robert E. Lee, a former FBI agent who was made chief of the House Appropriations Committee investigative staff by Representative John Taber (Rep., N.Y.). Very little of McCarthy's information originated later than 1947, Edson wrote.

Columns by Fred Othman of the United Press on March 9 and 10 were feature stories describing the first two days of the hearings before the Tydings subcommittee. Othman treated the hearings as farce, and his descriptions of McCarthy and Tydings glaring at each other for the benefit of photographers, of McCarthy's files sliding off a chair, as he searched for documents, made a point about the fakery of the squabble and the hypocrisy of the participants. Othman's stories did in a way what television did later—gave the reader a real feeling for the event. The hearings were serious but they were also ridiculous, and Othman made this apparent. Most accounts of the hearings were deadly sober, and only a few reporters described the scene in a way that made it come alive visually. Othman's ending was prophetic: "There'll be more later about Commies. Much more. Much later."

Doris Fleeson's first column, on March 10 in the *New York Post*, was an interpretive account of the clash between McCarthy and Senator McMahon (Dem., Conn.) in the first hearings. In her opinion, McCarthy's assault on McMahon was "profoundly disturbing to thoughtful Senators."

Victor Riesel, a labor columnist, wrote one of the few columns that supported McCarthy, taking note of McCarthy's comment that he had received "many valuable tips" from newspapermen. Riesel said that he himself had given various senators much valuable information about Communists but that they hadn't believed him.[2] Another column that seemed to support McCarthy was that by Dorothy Thompson appearing February 24 in the *Holyoke Telegram-Transcript* under the heading "They Are Not Red Herrings." She was willing to name one diplomat she suspected of "left-wing sympathies," she said—John Carter Vincent. She said that Vincent had thought the Chinese were merely agrarian reformers and that Vincent had, in Switzerland, once employed a man who had been a Hungarian Nazi.

Arthur M. Schlesinger, Jr., writing March 5 in the *Chicago Sun-Times*, commented that so far the only person revealed as "what McCarthy regards as a Communist sympathizer" was David Demarest Lloyd, "who has been an anti-Communist for years. . . . If McCarthy's information is no better than this, his only success will be in making the country forget the name of Senator Hickenlooper." (Schlesinger's reference was to an accusation by Senator Bourke B. Hickenlooper

(Rep., Iowa) that David E. Lilienthal, chairman of the Atomic Energy Commission, was "soft on Communism.")

Local columnists often contributed significant comment. Gladstone Williams, on February 24 in the *Atlanta Constitution*, rounded up McCarthy's activities from Wheeling on, and said that unless the senator could produce better evidence, his charges would be "written off as another fizzle and a dud." "Little credit is reflected on the Senate by charges of this kind coming from one of its members," he wrote. "The Wisconsin Senator's behavior indicates that he is more interested in putting out sensational headlines than anything else." A pro-McCarthy column by Reed Blaine, identified as a columnist for the *Globe Syndicate* of Saugatuck, Connecticut, appeared in the *Frederick News* on March 4. Blaine asserted that the Tydings subcommittee really wanted the names of McCarthy's informants, not those of his targets. "The defense technique of 'put up or shut up' has been rubbed into his hair, and he is now glad of the opportunity to put his cards face up and let the committee do the rest," Blaine wrote.

Lowell Mellett, on March 2 in the *Washington Star*, criticized McCarthy for trying to force open the loyalty files. McCarthy wants to "burn down the house to get rid of the rats," Mellett said. On March 10, also in the *Star*, Constantine Brown wrote the first of many columns supporting McCarthy. He predicted that the investigation would be "the most sensational in recent years," and accused Senator Tydings of "bullying" McCarthy. Brown said that McCarthy wasn't claiming that the people he attacked were Communists; only that they were affiliated with subversive organizations.

Frederic W. Collins described McCarthy's techniques in a column March 9 in the *Providence Journal*. Collins said McCarthy shuffled documents to stall for time, kept changing the numbers of his "cases" to keep the Democrats from identifying his sources, and had disregarded senatorial courtesy; he defeated Tydings by talking when Tydings tried to talk, never stopping. McCarthy and Tydings were old enemies, Collins said, and McCarthy knew exactly how to infuriate him.

Joseph C. Harsch, in his March 10 column in the *Christian Science Monitor*, praised the subcommittee for interrupting McCarthy. If McCarthy had been permitted to read his cases straight through, the press would have had to report just that, he said. As it was, the defense came right along with the charges. "It's all the Democrats now against McCarthy," Harsch wrote. "Many of Senator McCarthy's own Republican colleagues are keeping themselves in a safe position, from which they can leap to his support if his case begins to look solid, or stand clear if it wobbles like the Hickenlooper case against David Lilienthal."

A light-hearted column by Carl W. McCardle in the *Philadelphia Bulletin* on February 25 reflected the lack of seriousness with which some of the Washington press regarded McCarthy's presentation. "McCarthy, 'the one-man sleuth of Congress,' is stirring up a big fuss over card-carrying Communists in the State Department," McCardle wrote. "It is unlikely that even he thinks there are real Communists in the State Department . . . but Joe feels he will be able to force two or three . . . of the personnel to resign. It will be a razzle-dazzle all right, and there are some who feel it will only serve to undermine confidence in the State Department. But Joe McCarthy will have some fun and satisfaction out of it, and soon he'll be working on some new 'cases.' "

Another column, one of a series by John Jarrell, the Washington correspondent of the *Omaha World-Herald*, is significant for its exposition of a strain of political thought in the Midwest, an attitude which helps to explain why McCarthy's campaign was so warmly received in places distant from Washington. The Jarrell piece on March 1 was headed "U.S. Commies Mostly Native; Few Are Foreign Born; Many Well Off," and read:

They are not dumb. They're plenty smart. Some of them hold good jobs in important posts. They have infiltrated into almost every industry. They've gotten into government, too.

Their methods are clever. They don't openly talk about revolution. . . . Their best weapons, however, are the preaching of class hatred, the foment of industrial disputes, the provoking of race struggles. You never hear a Communist express any concern about the national debt, or any fear of inflation. . . . A major depression is just what he's hoping for.

He's a shrewd customer. He's a far cry from the cartoonist's conception of a Red back in the '20's—invariably a bewhiskered individual labeled "Bolshie" carrying a bomb. Instead, he's a subtle, hard-working and plausible individual.

Twenty-three newspapers carried more than 200 column-inches of news on the McCarthy controversy that first month, as table 1 (p. 223) illustrates. The quantity of information is not a measure of a newspaper's success in properly reporting on McCarthy, but it was a prerequisite for success; the first thing that a reader needed in order to understand the affair was a certain amount of information. The paper that gave readers the most news was the *Baltimore Sun*. Its 417 column-inches were all news, straight reporting by the *Sun*'s Washington bureau. The paper did not, however, offer much in the way of guidance for the reader; there were no interpretive reports, no columns, no editorials. The *Washington Star*, on the other hand, was long on guidance, with an editorial and eight columns of opinion—two pro-McCarthy and six con. The quantity of news was large, too.

The *Washington Post* offered both quantity and interpretation, with 324 column-inches of news, along with four columns and five editorials. The *Capital Times* was most generous of all with opinion, with 10 anti-McCarthy editorials (five of them reprints from other papers) and four anti-McCarthy columns. Its news coverage was not as thorough as the figures seem to indicate; more than one-third of its total was the long story by Peter Edson, the detailed report on McCarthy's "81 cases." (The *Racine Journal-Times* was the only other paper that used this long story.) The space devoted to that single story by these two papers was more than that used for news of McCarthy during the entire month by 88 papers, about 70 percent of those surveyed, a group that included such well-regarded papers as the *Buffalo News*, the *Cleveland Plain Dealer*, the *Atlanta Constitution*, the *Boston Globe*, the *Denver Post*, and the *San Francisco Chronicle*. The only paper in the South to devote this much space to McCarthy news coverage that month was the *New Orleans Times-Picayune*.

There were a few other papers that carried less than 200 column-inches of news but that nevertheless provided a useful balance of news and interpretation. Among these were the *Christian Science Monitor*, the *Chicago Daily News*, the *Lowell Sun*, the *Berkshire Eagle*, and the *St. Louis Post-Dispatch*. Seven of this list had taken an editorial stand in opposition to McCarthy by the end of the month, and seven had taken a pro-McCarthy stand.

Coverage varied by region. It was heaviest in the Washington-Baltimore area, where national political news was a local story, and in Wisconsin and nearby midwestern states, where McCarthy was a local story both geographically and, for many of the readers, philosophically. The other area of heavy coverage was New York City, but concentrated coverage of McCarthy during the first month was provided only by two of the city's seven major newspapers. These areas account for all but four on the list of the twenty-three newspapers that carried the most news. Two western papers, those in Salt Lake City and Reno, printed as much as they did because McCarthy made controversial speeches in their cities during the first week after Wheeling. Coverage in Western newspapers generally was light.

Coverage of the McCarthy story was skimpy in New England, the South, and the Far West. Editorial comment, however, was offered in comparative quantity in the South; it was almost totally absent in New England. In the Far West, the only papers that devoted much space to the story were the *Stockton Record* and the *Oakland Tribune*, on opposite sides of the issue.

Newspapers that devoted the most space to the McCarthy story were those that approved of his actions most enthusiastically and those that most strongly disapproved. Editorial responses to news developments showed certain patterns, as noted earlier, but there was no evidence that newspapers in this month took any actions in concert. Editors sometimes made similar decisions—on news coverage or editorial position—at similar times, but that was because they were of like mind, on both sides of the controversy. More often they did not make similar decisions; the most impressive aspect of the month's coverage of McCarthy was its variety. No story was considered so important that every paper used it. Major stories were interpreted six different ways by editors who sought to extract the key fact for a headline. Some editorial reactions were predictable; others were surprising. Why did the *Chicago Tribune* comment editorially only once? Why did the *Louisville Courier-Journal* carry no editorial? Why were there no editorials in the *Chicago Sun-Times*?*

Readers of newspapers that first month after Wheeling were often uninformed and sometimes misinformed about McCarthy's attacks and the Democrats' counterattacks. There were failures of news judgment that resulted in the omission, or the downplay, of important developments in the chain of events. Newspapers failed to provide background or continuity in news stories, and the majority of newspapers provided no editorial guidance or analysis. Headline writers exaggerated McCarthy's charges to the point of libel, making McCarthy seem bolder than he was, and implanted the idea that McCarthy actually did call individuals Communists. The argument made in later years by McCarthy's opponents—that the senator had never exposed a single Communist in government—had no effect on McCarthy supporters, because the news during the first month left a lasting impression that McCarthy had named *many* Communists.

In September 1952 on the way to Kasson, Minnesota, Joseph Alsop, the columnist, stopped to sample political sentiment in Coon Valley, Wisconsin. In a bar, Alsop sat down next to the owner of the Coon Valley Ford automobile agency. Alsop asked him who he intended to vote for in the Republican senatorial primary, in which McCarthy was being challenged by Leonard Schmitt, an attorney. The Ford dealer said that he would vote for McCarthy. "Why?" asked Alsop.

"He exposed all those Communists," said the dealer.

"What Communists?" asked Alsop, his voice rising. "Name one."

"Dean Acheson," the man said.

---

*See table 1, p. 223, for an analysis of the first-month coverage of each of the newspapers surveyed.

"Dean Acheson?" shouted Alsop. "How do you figure *he's* a Communist?"

"If he isn't a Communist," said the Ford dealer, "how come he's in jail?"

Most responsible for implanting this kind of misinformation was the assumption that underlay most of the headlines written that month—that McCarthy's charges were founded in fact and that there really were Communists in the State Department—headlines that *stipulated* that the Communists were there. How else could headlines like these be interpreted: "Senate to Probe Department Reds" (*Washington Times-Herald*); "Reds in High Places Face Senate Quiz" (*Oakland Tribune*); "Probers to Check State Department Reds" (*Stockton Record*)? There were dozens more like them, even though the stories which followed said that the Senate was investigating McCarthy's *charges* that there were Communists in the State Department.

There were many like the following, too: "Senator Asks Ouster of Reds in State Department" (*Dallas News*); "McCarthy Urges Cleanup of Reds" (*Wisconsin State Journal*); "McCarthy Insists Truman Oust Reds" (*New York Times*). These are perfectly reasonable demands— if you accept the assumption that the Reds are there in the State Department.

There were flat statements in the headlines where the fact in the story was merely a charge or an allegation: "McCarthy Has New Evidence" (*Baltimore Sun*); "Knows Names of 57 Reds" (*Kansas City Star*); "McCarthy Has Names of Reds in U.S. Employ" (*Manitowoc Herald-Times*). None of these things were true, it turned out.

Other headlines also promoted inaccurate views of the quarrel in the Senate. Most prevalent was the kind of headline that said that the object of the investigation was to find Communists or spies in the State Department. What the Democrats voted to do, and what the Tydings subcommittee did, was merely to investigate McCarthy's charges that there were spies. But this was too complex an idea for the writers of headlines, and it took too many words. They wrote: "Senate Votes Probe of Reds in State Department" (*Chicago Tribune*); "Senate to Hunt State Department Spies" (*Cleveland Plain Dealer*); "State Department Spy Hunt Ordered" (*Los Angeles Times*). The erroneous concept in these heads was furthered by the repeated use of the phrases *Red hunt* or *spy hunt* to describe the investigation. Headlines gave the impression that the dispute was between the president and a monolithic Senate, although news stories made it clear that it was in fact between Senate Democrats and a faction of the Senate Republicans.

Inaccurate headlines—and there are hundreds of examples of each kind described above—helped McCarthy convince the public that there were Communists and spies in the State Department.

The performance of the press as a whole during this important month was poor. Most of the wire service reporting was inadequate, flat, unimaginative, devoid of interpretation or analysis, lacking even description. Bad as this was, the use that local editors made of wire service news was worse. In the papers where there were signs of intelligent editing and where sufficient space was allocated, even the wire service stories made more sense. But in most papers the stories were short and confusing; overnight leads obscured the real news; stories with hoked-up leads or those invented for the sake of having a McCarthy story on a day when nothing had happened were selected by news editors for the front page, while stories that contained real news were buried or thrown away. Headlines were inaccurate to the point of contradiction, creating lasting false impressions.

It is a tribute to the intelligence of citizens of this country that so many saw through this confusion to the truth of the McCarthy affair, but it is no wonder that so many did not.

3.
The Wire Services, McCarthy's Conduit

REPORTS FROM the three wire services were the source of almost 85 percent of the news published by newspapers about McCarthy in the first month after his Wheeling speech. The 15 percent that did not originate with the wire services came from Washington bureaus of individual papers or groups of papers, from local reporters, or from special agencies such as the *New York Times* service, *Chicago Daily News* service, *New York Herald-Tribune* service, and Newspaper Enterprise Association. The Associated Press was responsible for 75.5 percent of the news furnished by the wire services, the United Press for 16.5 percent, and the International News Service for 5 percent. The other 3 percent was unidentified in the papers that carried it except as "wire dispatches," and usually represented a combination of reports from two or more of these agencies. The newspapers surveyed published 845 AP stories, 184 UP, 57 INS, and 31 from "wire dispatches."*

In 1950 many people, particularly in rural areas, got much of their news from radio. Virtually all radio news came from the wire services. Stories on the radio wire were abbreviated and necessarily distorted, and often sensationalized to make the news catchier. They were inevitably inferior to those furnished to newspapers.

*The circulation of the 129 newspapers in my sample constituted 44 percent of newspaper circulation in the United States at the time they were published. If 100 percent had been surveyed, the wire service share would have risen to more than 90 percent, since most of the papers not included were the smaller ones totally dependent upon the wire services for national news.

Wire service reporters, even those working in Washington, were usually younger than newspaper reporters with similar assignments and were less well paid. For many of them it was a first job, a stepping-stone to a newspaper job. But to get to the Washington bureau of a wire service they had to be bright, aggressive, and ambitious. I was able to interview many of the wire service reporters who covered McCarthy. None of them were proud of their coverage, but it was a difficult story. "It was the most difficult story I ever had to handle," said Marvin Arrowsmith, now chief of the Associated Press Washington bureau. A wire service, he said, does not have the latitude of a newspaper; all of its clients are biased. "No wire service would have lasted five minutes if we hadn't played it right down the middle. ... We were particularly conscious of the necessity for doing it on this story."[1]

John L. Steele, now senior Washington correspondent and assistant to the publisher of *Time* magazine, covered the Senate, which meant McCarthy, for the United Press in 1950. "There was very little opportunity in those days to break out of the role of being a recording device for Joe," Steele said. "I felt trapped. It was the most difficult story I ever had. There is no comparison to anything else. We bear a terrible scar because of that period. That feeling of powerlessness was terrible. We lived it 24 hours a day." Covering McCarthy was such a strain that when Steele left Washington in 1952 for a Nieman fellowship at Harvard he weighed only 132 pounds, down from his normal 150. "If it hadn't been for that Nieman, I don't know what I'd have done," he said.[2]

William Theis, now an official of the American Petroleum Institute, was chief of the International News Service Senate staff in 1940. In his recollection, "all three wire services were so goddamn objective that McCarthy got away with everything, bamboozling the editors and the public. It was a sad period in American journalism." Even newspapers with Washington bureaus did very little interpretation in 1950, he said.

We let Joe get away with murder, reporting it as he said it, not doing the kind of critical analysis we'd do today. The public those days was accustomed to believe damn near anything. It was just a big lark to Joe. He was like a kid in a candy store, trying to grab everything he could. He could say anything, and if only one-third of the people believed it, that was still something.

As a reporter, you did what you could, but things never solidified. He'd talk you blue in the face. Reporters then, and readers, too, didn't have as much sophistication as they have now. The main trouble was the climate of the country; people were ready to believe anything about Communists.

Theis said that the INS was never pressured by the Hearst Corporation, which owned the service, to slant news in McCarthy's favor, although the Hearst newspapers supported McCarthy. The Hearst papers were only a fraction of the INS clientele, and Theis rarely saw a Hearst paper. The problem was that editors and editorial writers refused to believe that McCarthy would make such charges without having the evidence to back them up. "When we tried to tell them something else, we were hitting our heads against a brick wall. Joe saw what a bonanza he had, and he kept riding it. If you jumped on one thing, he'd say another. It was the most difficult story we ever covered, especially emotionally. I'd go home literally sick, seeing what that guy was getting away with."[3]

George Reedy, who later became President Lyndon Johnson's press secretary, also covered McCarthy for the United Press. "We had to take what McCarthy said at face value," he said. "Joe couldn't find a Communist in Red Square—he didn't know Karl Marx from Groucho—but he was a United States Senator. Talking to Joe was like putting your hands in a bowl of mush. It was a shattering experience, and I couldn't stand it. Covering him was a big factor in my decision to quit newspaper work."[4]

Another reporter who covered McCarthy for the INS in the 1950s was Charles Seib, ombudsman for the *Washington Post* when I interviewed him. Seib, too, said that the INS in those days was "a very clean operation," determined to resist pressure. "But the competition was tremendous. We'd fight to get a two-minute beat on a new name, and Joe McCarthy rode this. We were trapped by our techniques. If he said it, we wrote it; the pressures were to deliver. In addition to the time competition, there was pressure to write a lead that would get the play. We were competing with the other services and with our own people, sort of like TV ratings." The editors for whom they were writing were "tilted," and for them, the more sensational the better— "goose it up." "That was true of the whole American press. It was an hysterical time. Practically all of us realized what McCarthy was, but we felt powerless." Seib said that in one respect he and the other wire service reporters, rather than the editors they served, were to blame. The McCarthy controversy was exciting and the reporters didn't really take it seriously. "It was a sort of game for us, as it was for McCarthy. We were so caught up in the game that we didn't worry much about the effects. 'Not my problem,' we said. The thrill was in beating the competition, never mind how. Looking back, though, I see that the devil-may-care journalism we practiced was more dangerous than I realized. That simplistic, gee-whiz reporting, with its phony objectivity, did as much to raise Joe McCarthy from a bumbling unknown to a national menace as the craven behavior of his fellow senators and the White House."[5]

Steele, Reedy, and Seib all believe that the "overnight lead" was the wire service practice that McCarthy exploited most successfully. As Steele described it, "in those days most papers had multiple editions. Editors were always screaming for new leads—a 10 o'clock lead, 12 o'clock lead, all day long. That's where Joe came in. Call him, he'd always have something for a new lead."

In its simplest form, the overnight lead worked like this: President Truman held a press conference at 11 A.M. Washington time. The story went out at once, in plenty of time for most afternoon papers, and the lead—usually the beginning sentence, which had to express the central point of the story—was that Truman had said that he would cooperate with the investigation of McCarthy's charges. The story also said that Truman had declared that only his administration had done anything about ousting Communists from government jobs. That was sufficient for the afternoon papers, but convention demanded that the morning papers get a *new* story. So as soon as the wire service reporter finished his Truman story he had to look for a new angle. In the instance above, what the AP reporter did was to call McCarthy and Senator Bricker (Rep., Ohio), both of whom said that Truman hadn't ousted anyone and that only Congress had nailed Communists—Alger Hiss, for example. The morning papers could then say that Republicans that day had "refuted" President Truman's claim—and in some papers Truman's statement, since it was at the bottom of the story, was lopped off, leaving just the Republican rebuttal.

More often it happened the other way around, because in Washington more news breaks in the afternoon than in the morning, and the morning papers get the first story and the afternoon papers the overnight lead. That played into McCarthy's hands; 36 of the 39 daily newspapers in Wisconsin in 1950 were afternoon papers, with 78 percent of the state's circulation. Wire service reporters, forced to invent new leads every few hours, were often desperate; McCarthy helped them out. Sometimes he was so quick with a quotable comment that he was able to smother the original story, as he 'had in the case of David Demarest Lloyd.

George Reedy said that McCarthy knew all about news cycles, knew everyone's deadlines, and knew just when reporters would have no choice but to print what he said. "His IQ was goddamn high. He could think through to fundamental principles. And, boy, he really had the press figured out." McCarthy's cooperative attitude was described by Dan Hanley, now a *Milwaukee Journal* reporter, who covered McCarthy from Madison for the UP. "I'd call Joe up and say, this was in the *Milwaukee Journal*. 'Is this what you said?' 'Sure,' Joe would say, 'I'll say that for you, or do you want something else? How about this?' And he'd say something new. Or he'd say, 'What do you want me to say? Tell me what you want and I'll say it.' "[6] Murrey Marder, who covered McCarthy for four years for the *Washington Post*, recalls that the initiative usually came from the reporters rather than from McCarthy. "Milt Kelly [AP] or Warren Duffee [UP] would come and say, 'I must have a story,' and McCarthy would go through his files until he found something. McCarthy learned that on Friday the wire service reporters were always in need of stories that could be run on Sunday or Monday, the two dead news days, and he saved up tidbits for them."[7]

Allen Alexander was an AP filing editor in Charlotte, North Carolina, in 1950, responsible for determining which news from incoming trunkline wires would be relayed on the single news wire serving AP clients in North and South Carolina. He described the process at that stage of distribution in this way:

It was quite apparent that many of Senator McCarthy's headline-catching statements were deliberately timed so that they would be bulletined out of Washington around 10 A.M. This assured him of reaching the first editions of the eastern time zone press, including the 25-30 afternoon dailies in the Carolinas.

The 10 A.M. bellringer usually would be followed by a new lead at noon, which would come closer to giving more balance to the original pronouncement. That is, instead of the original unvarnished "Senator Joe McCarthy declared today that John Doe is a lousy, no-good Communist," it would state "John Doe denied today that he is or ever was a lousy, no-good Communist." (This new lead was great for noon newscasters with their in-depth coverage.) By 2 P.M., in time for final afternoon editions, the semblance of a balanced, fair story on the Senator's charges and allegations might be available. All too often, however, this did not take place during the same news cycle.

If this first bulletined story was too blatantly irresponsible, I would on occasion try to delay filing it, knowing that a new, better balanced lead was expectable. But like Canute, I had trouble with an overwhelming tide. AP member newspapers subscribing to competing UP and INS service would message frantically: "Opposition reports that McCarthy said xxx. Where's ours?" What do you tell your superiors when they see a message like that? And when a boss states, "We report the news. Local editors make the judgment as to whether to use it," filing editors are not in a position to discuss philosophy, ethics, or the definition of news. At least they weren't back then.[8]

Alexander said that occasionally he won the battle of suspense by waiting for the more balanced later lead. But usually the member papers thus deprived used the UP or INS story, and his boss would come around to say, "The competition wires got all the play on McCarthy Wednesday. How come? What time did our Washington trunk story come in? What time did you relay it?" The "awful truth"—the time—was on every piece of copy. All of Alexander's experience with stories involving the senator showed that "McCarthy and his inner guard used exquisite timing and that the press was manipulated, perhaps unknowingly in some cases, and in rarer cases willingly."

John Steele, the UP man, said that McCarthy watched the news so closely that a reporter had to go to great lengths to keep his imprint off every story. Once, when Owen Lattimore gave him a statement at 6:30 A.M. on the day Lattimore was to appear before McCarthy's committee, he "got the statement on the wire before Joe could find out about it and dirty it up. Joe was irate."

According to Reedy, McCarthy, by taking advantage of time pressures on the wire services, once forced him (and other reporters) to report a story that was essentially false.

It was a Tydings committee hearing, where McCarthy had said he'd rest his whole case on Owen Lattimore being the main spy. Lattimore was a kind of fuzzy professor who never had any influence in the State Department. The Communist spy business was ridiculous nonsense, and we all knew it. Joe got up and said, "I hold in my hand a letter that Lattimore wrote to the West Coast office of the Office of War Information telling them to fire all the non-Communist Chinese and hire Communist Chinese." We all wanted to see the letter, but he wouldn't give it up.

I had to get an overnight lead for 11 A.M. for the P.M.'s, so I had to go down and write the story. At 11:45 A.M. he let go of the letter. There wasn't a thing in it to back up what he'd said, but there wasn't anything there that disproved what he said, either. In those days you couldn't say that the letter didn't have the remotest bearing on what he'd said. So Joe's story was used.

Most of the wire service reporters who covered him in Washington rather liked McCarthy, at least at first. Several compared him favorably to Nixon, whom they disliked thoroughly. Some, however, said that McCarthy tried to intimidate them.

In an internal *Milwaukee Journal* memorandum, reporter Robert

H. Fleming reported that Friendly of the *Washington Post* and Potter of the *Baltimore Sun* had told him that McCarthy had threatened Steele and Arrowsmith. After Steele pointed out in a story that McCarthy had not kept his pledge to say without immunity those things he was saying on the Senate floor, McCarthy told Steele, "When you write stuff like that, you're helping the Communists. I don't want to have to point that out to your office, so I'm telling you what I think now." "Any kind of criticism," Steele said, "and he'd be all over you, calling you a dupe or worse. Sometimes he'd say, 'I know this won't come out the way I say it, because your bosses are sons of bitches.' He'd say, 'I know that because *I'm* a son of a bitch.' " Fleming said that McCarthy's comment to Arrowsmith, not tied to any specific story, was, "I know you've got six kids, Marv, and I don't want to kick about your work, so I hope there is no reason to do so."[9] (Arrowsmith said he did not remember this and did not recall McCarthy complaining about anything he wrote.)

McCarthy did complain about a story by another AP reporter, John Chadwick, who has covered the Senate since 1952. Theis said that McCarthy tried to get Chadwick fired, working through Riedl, the managing editor of the *Appleton Post-Crescent*, an AP member. The issue was one of interpretation. McCarthy, speaking at a St. Patrick's Day dinner in Chicago on 18 March 1954, stated that he did not give "a tinker's dam" about criticism of his methods as a hunter of Communists "no matter how high or how low" the critics in either political party. W. H. Lawrence wrote in the *New York Times*, "He repeated the phrase 'how high or how low' to leave no doubt with the cheering crowd that one of his targets was President Eisenhower." Chadwick's story said that McCarthy had said he intended to continue uprooting Communists in government despite critcism "from Eisenhower on down." McCarthy told Chadwick he had no right to say that because he had not mentioned Eisenhower by name.

In my interview with Chadwick, he said that he sat next to McCarthy the next morning at a counter at the Milwaukee airport and that McCarthy had refused to speak to him, and that on the way to Oklahoma City, the next stop, McCarthy had made him sit in the tail of the plane. McCarthy began his speech in Oklahoma City by saying that Chadwick had written his story before the speech was given. This was obviously untrue, because the "high or low" phrase wasn't in the text, Chadwick said. After the speech, McCarthy said to him "I hope you don't mind the ribbing" and offered to shake hands. Chadwick refused. "I was burned up," he said. Then McCarthy sat down next to him in the plane, offered him a drink out of the bottle in his briefcase, and talked to him all the way back to Washington. Chadwick considers his lead justified: "McCarthy was always trying to intimidate the reporters."[10]

McCarthy often called Steele from Wisconsin to ask what was going on in Washington, Steele recalls. He would have other people on the line, showing them that he had connections. But he really liked reporters, was interested in everything they did and what they thought, and would often drop in at a reporter's home, carrying a bag of groceries, "shoo the woman out of the kitchen," and cook chicken. Steele said that he was "sort of a loveable clown," until you realized that he had an utter disregard for people.

Steele lived in Georgetown, as did many State Department people, and knew several of McCarthy's victims. They had wives and children, but McCarthy never showed any sympathy for them. "I never heard him say, 'poor bastard,' " Steele said. Most of the State Department people were helpless because they were afraid to talk to reporters, and many of them were overseas when attacked, unable to reply. Steele said that McCarthy had the Senate terrified, too. "McCarthy had no scenario, no game plan," he said. "He did have a certain disarming frankness. He'd say, 'I'm a son of a bitch, but I'm a loveable son of a bitch.' It was all fun and games for a while, but then he began taking it seriously. He became paranoiac." Theis, the INS man, also said that McCarthy was friendly to reporters. "He went out of his way to be palsy-walsy," he said, even if he knew the reporter thought he was a fraud. It made it very difficult for a reporter to build up any personal enmity, he said.

Seib recalled an example of McCarthy's humor. He and Warren Duffee of the United Press went to the senator's office one afternoon. McCarthy was at his desk sipping from a medicine bottle. "If you want to be against McCarthy, boys," McCarthy said, "you've got to be a Communist or a cocksucker," then roared with laughter.

After Reedy was married, McCarthy found an apartment for him in a building in northeast Washington where he himself occupied a bedroom in the apartment of his assistant, Ray Kiermas. McCarthy had arranged for several other reporters to rent apartments there, and he ran the building like a college dormitory, everyone in everyone else's apartment, parties going all the time. "Joe always came in roaring for a drink, but that was a fake," Reedy said. "He'd nurse one drink all evening, or he'd pour it out the window and yell for another. He never really drank much until after the censure." Reedy said that Phil Potter of the *Baltimore Sun* and Murrey Marder of the *Washington Post* did the best job of explaining McCarthy to their readers, "but the readers of those papers were against Joe anyway, so it didn't matter."

The reporter in Wisconsin who knew McCarthy best was Dion Henderson (now the Milwaukee bureau chief for the Associated Press). Henderson traveled with McCarthy throughout the state as an AP reporter, and although he disagreed with him politically, liked him because of his sense of humor. "I hated everything he stood for, and he knew it," Henderson said, "but he was as good a traveling companion as I ever had." McCarthy never did take himself completely seriously, according to Henderson. "His sense of irony was too great. He was full of murky Gaelic premonitions, and he could always look at himself from the outside. He had a sense of the ludicrous."[11]

Henderson said that when McCarthy arrived in Wisconsin from Washington it was customary for him to start the conversation by asking, "What are the right-wing McCarthyites up to this week?" He told the story of covering McCarthy on the day in 1954 when the senator was the keynote speaker at the Republican state convention in Milwaukee.

He'd been out late the night before and he didn't have a speech ready. So on the way to the Milwaukee Auditorium that morning he bought a Time *magazine that had a story about the Army-McCarthy hearings, locked himself in a men's room in a saloon at 12th and State and made some notes. He drank a full glass of Old Fitzgerald while he was writing.*

Then we stopped for another drink at the Mint Bar, near the Auditorium. He was raising the glass to his lips when someone said, "Did you know this was a hangout for queers?" In the same motion, Joe threw the drink over his shoulder and rushed out. A few minutes later he drank another glass of whiskey, neat, in the men's room of the Auditorium, from a bottle he took from his briefcase. [I also observed this incident.]

In his speech, he'd try something out on the audience, and if it didn't get a response he'd try something else. That day he didn't get a response until he said he wasn't going to be a rubber stamp for Eisenhower, and that got a roar from the crowd, so he said it over four or five times. The crowd was so wild that they mobbed him, tearing at his clothes as the cops helped him get out the back door of the Auditorium. His blue suit was soaked black with sweat. He looked at me and grinned and said, "I guess they wanted to touch the hem of the garment."

McCarthy and Henderson worked out a modus operandi when they were on the road. "We'd get to a stopping place at 2 A.M., and I'd ask him for an overnight lead," Henderson said. "He'd go in the bedroom, work for a while, then come out with two or three lines, which he would deliver in an oratorical style. It worked well. He'd have a start on the next day's speeches and I'd have a lead. He always backed up that lead." Nevertheless, he was difficult to cover because he talked in fragments and non sequiturs. "He was impatient with routine, quickly bored. He was quick with lines you couldn't quote, because a reader would misunderstand it. He was too quick sometimes, like the time he told off General Zwicker. That wasn't planned, it just flashed out."

Henderson said that McCarthy never tried to persuade him to slant stories in any way and that he knew what Henderson thought about his politics but never argued with him. Henderson believes that McCarthy was reluctant to argue about politics because Henderson's family had been closely allied to the La Follettes and "McCarthy never did anything to offend La Follette supporters." McCarthy's most positive accomplishment, in Henderson's view, was to demonstrate how easy it would be for "a man on a white horse" to take over in the United States. "He made it impossible for any other demagogue to do that, for at least a generation," he said. "But you couldn't ignore him. He represented a meaningful and significant aberration in American political life, and if anything, we covered him inadequately."

Reporters who covered McCarthy in Washington knew from the beginning that straight reporting—reporting merely what McCarthy said—was playing into his hands. Several of them wrote about this problem, which was referred to as the conflict between "objectivity" and "interpretation," although the idea that this was a conflict of principle was somewhat misleading. Adherence to straight reporting—especially by the wire services—was less a matter of devotion to principle than expediency. All through the McCarthy years, this issue was a subject of bitter debate among editors.

One of the first to make the point about the drawbacks of "objectivity" in covering McCarthy was Richard L. Strout, on 27 May 1950 in the *Christian Science Monitor*.

The business of "straight reporting" never gives the reader much chance to catch up [Strout wrote]. If the reporter had been permitted the freedom of interpretive reporting customarily followed by the great dailies abroad, he could have commented as well as reported. He would have been a historian as well as a photographer with words. But he would have violated one of the dearest rules of American journalism.

Another early analysis was made by Douglass Cater in the *Reporter* of 6 June 1950. During the first three months of McCarthy's charges, Cater said, "the victory of the headlines has been incontestably that of the senator from Wisconsin."

One of the frozen patterns that have hampered press coverage of the McCarthy charges is the distinction between the "straight" reporting of the ordinary reporters and wire-service reporters, and the "interpretive" or "evaluative" reporting of the privileged few. The trouble with "straight" reporting is that it precludes investigation and asking the questions which need to be answered if the reader is to understand what is going on.

Herbert Elliston, editor of the *Washington Post*, had suggested that a second reporter be assigned to important stories to provide interpretation to supplement the "straight" report. Cater pointed out, however, that this would not solve the problem for the small daily wholly at the mercy of the wire services.

Alan Barth, editorial writer for the *Washington Post*, discussed the subject in the *Washington Guild Reporter* of 23 February 1951:

The tradition of objectivity is, of course, one of the great glories of American journalism. It requires a newspaper to keep its editorial opinions out of its news columns. It has produced, on the whole, the fairest and most accurate reporting to be found in any country of the world. It has made a genuine news medium out of what used to be, to a considerable extent, a medium for personal prejudice and political vindictiveness.

But there are always sharpshooters trying to take advantage of press objectivity—trying to peddle as news what is, in fact, propaganda.

Barth said that it was relatively easy to fend off ordinary press agents who tried this, but it was more difficult to cope with elected officials and "the myth that anything said on the record with a straight face by a Senator or a Congressman is news." The House Committee on Un-American Activities was the first to exploit the tradition of objectivity, Barth said, turning irresponsible charges about subversive activity into front-page news.

This technique of punishing by publicity was exploited even more extravagantly by Senator McCarthy, for the deadpan publication of whose nightmare ravings whole forests of pine were felled and ground into woodpulp. The American press must forever carry on its conscience the elevation of Jumping Joe to the status of National High Inquisitor.... I don't know how frauds of this kind ought to be handled by good newspapermen. But I do know the American people are being fooled and that the American press is being used, deliberately, to fool them. Maybe we have a responsibility that goes beyond objectivity.

Better reporting and more interpretation were urged in 1952 by Arthur Hays Sulzberger, publisher of the *New York Times*, before the convention of the Association for Education in Journalism in New York. But Sulzberger did not recommend the abandonment of objectivity as a goal. "Despite everything I have said about the need for interpretation of the news, it does not take the place of the factual news report," Sulzberger said. "It is supplementary and, essential as it is, it is dangerous if not watched and done correctly within rigid limits. The balance between interpretation and opinion is delicate and it must be preserved."[12] (An examination of McCarthy stories in the *New York Times* in 1952 indicates that the editorial staff did adhere to Sulzberger's precepts. News stories were still "straight.")

In his *Newspaper Story: One Hundred Years of the Boston Globe* Louis Lyons wrote that the *Globe* had taken a "neutral bystander's stance" on McCarthy in the early 1950s. "The paper was approaching the end of its dimmest period," he wrote.

But this was a dim period for the press generally; it was particularly vulnerable to exploitation by a demagogue, for its tradition of objectivity had been eroded to a timid neutrality of shallow reporting. What a senator said was news, qualified only by "Senator McCarthy charged that. . . ." The press, largely dependent on the wire services, was deficient in technique to explore the allegations. Very exceptional were the New York Times, Washington Post, Baltimore Sun, Milwaukee Journal and a few more in checking, challenging, and investigating McCarthy's reckless charges.[13]

"Truth has three dimensions," wrote Elmer Davis in *But We Were Born Free*, "but the practice of the American news business—practices adopted in praiseworthy ambition to be objective—too often gives us only one-dimensional news—factually accurate so far as it goes, but very far indeed from the whole truth."[14]

Richard Rovere's description of the objectivity dilemma in his book *Senator Joe McCarthy* is especially pertinent:

In time what appeared to be the susceptibility of the press to McCarthy was held to be the cause of his lamentable successes. Why did the press publish this liar's lies? McCarthy knew the answer: it was not because publishers in general wished to circulate his mendacities or even because he had achieved a glamour that made him irresistible to readers. It was because he had achieved a high elective office, because what he said counted for something (in fact, a great deal, as time went by) in the affairs of this nation, and because there was always the possibility that there was a mystery witness or that he would force Harry Truman to testify. "McCarthy's charges of treason, espionage, corruption, perversion are news which cannot be suppressed or ignored," Walter Lippman once wrote. "They come from a United States Senator and a politician ... in good standing at the headquarters of the Republican Party. When he makes such attacks against the State Department and the Defense Department, it is news which has to be published." It was also, of course, news that a United States Senator was lying and defrauding the people and their government. But—in large part because McCarthy was a true innovator, because he lied with an unprecedented boldness, because he invented new kinds of lies—even those newspapers that were willing to expose him found that they lacked the technical resources.[15]

Robert Griffith, in The Politics of Fear, wrote that McCarthy "turned to his own advantage the structure and functioning of the press itself."

The "straight" news story, for example, played directly into his hands, for while it might not be a fact that Philip Jessup had "an unusual affinity for Communist causes," it was a fact that McCarthy had said so, and thus the story would be printed. Most reporters had neither the time nor the research facilities to evaluate properly the senator's many charges, and wire service tradition of printing the most arresting facts at the head of a story distorted even the most intelligent presentations.[16]

In these and other discussions of objectivity, there has been too little distinction between devotion to a principle and the pragmatic practices of the wire services dictated by competition and the need to avoid offending client newspapers with opposite editorial commitments. Most of the news stories now considered deplorable resulted from such pressures on the wire services. Not that newspapers were blameless; newspapers, too, were much more competitive then than they are today, and local editors, who might have wanted to wait for a more balanced story, as Allen Alexander did, chose to rush to print; and many of them, conscious of the differences of opinion among their readers, undoubtedly welcomed the stories that played it "down the middle." Confusion between these practices and the praiseworthy adherence to objectivity has given that word a bad name; editors today seldom use the term, and it is customary to speak of the newspaper's goal as seeking to be "fair," or to present the truth as best it can be ascertained. This definition permits, or even calls for, something more than "straight" reporting, and it was in this spirit that certain newspapers developed techniques of providing legitimate interpretation of McCarthy's actions as soon as enough was known about his charges to make this possible. One example of this was the practice by the *Milwaukee Journal* of providing bracketed inserts containing the facts about McCarthy's charges; one *Journal* story contained fifteen paragraphs of such corrections. A *Journal* story published 8 May 1950, early in the coverage, read as follows:

McCarthy said that Lattimore has "long been referred to as the architect of the state department's Asiatic policy."

[State department officials and three former secretaries of state have denied that Lattimore played any part in forming policy.]

The Young Republicans guffawed as McCarthy joked about "individuals with peculiar mental aberrations as far as sex is concerned."

[The individual referred to by McCarthy here is no longer in government service.]

Two years later the *Journal* had expanded the practice. In a story of McCarthy's principal campaign speech, on 4 September 1952, inserts of this kind filled 13 inches in a story 52 inches long. Many newspapers adopted similar practices before the McCarthy affair was over, some sooner, some later. Interpretive reports became more usual, sometimes labeled "news analysis" but often without that warning. A reporter of proven competence could be expected to explain as best he could the meaning of the news. Even the wire services did it on occasion: the Associated Press, in its story on the Reno speech, had pointed out that three of the four persons "named" by McCarthy did not work for the State Department.

Only about a dozen newspapers had Washington bureaus large enough to cover McCarthy with their own people. A few more with small bureaus could do an occasional piece of interpretation. Newspapers in Wisconsin could do interpretive reporting when McCarthy appeared in the state, and the few that covered him with their own reporters did. But most papers had no such opportunity.

Telegraph editors, who processed the wire stories, could have performed this function; they could have pulled out the background information and written bracketed inserts for the wire stories. But very few telegraph desks operated that way; it was unusual for a copy editor to use a typewriter.

McCarthy objected even to limited editing by wire service editors. In *McCarthyism, the Fight for America*, McCarthy wrote that in the presence of the wire services he felt "some sense of security"; that traditionally their job was to present the facts without editorializing or distortion, a respect in which they differed from reporters for the *St. Louis Post-Dispatch, New York Post, Milwaukee Journal,* and *Washington Post,* but that later he learned that "the cards were stacked against" these honest reporters:

After several experiences there was impressed upon me the painful truth that the stories written by the competent, honest AP, UP or INS men assigned to cover the Senate or House, might not even be recognized by them when those stories went out on the news tickers to the thousands of newspapers throughout the country. Before being sent out to America's newspapers the stories pass across what is known as a rewrite desk. There certain facts can be played up, others eliminated. For example, so often we found that in the stories about McCarthy, a word like "evidence" was changed to "unfounded charges." [17]

The argument about interpretive reporting by the wire services—particularly by the Associated Press—became an issue that inflamed newspaper editors and publishers over a period of five years. William T. Evjue, the rambunctious editor and publisher of the *Capital Times,* was a persistent critic of the work of the Associated Press on the McCarthy story. Over and over, he charged that the AP was favoring McCarthy in its dispatches. His first blast of high-pitched criticism came on 27 March 1950, stimulated by a biographical feature on McCarthy by Douglas B. Cornell of the AP Washington bureau. Evjue was irritated by Cornell's breezy style of writing about what Evjue considered McCarthy's black crimes—reference to "a bit of income tax trouble." He made his complaint in a talk on his weekly radio program, "Hello Wisconsin," then printed the text on his editorial page:

Last Tuesday the Associated Press sent out a story from Washington that had a lot of significance for an old newspaperman like myself who has been watching the operations of the Associated Press for more than 40 years. It was a long story about Sen. McCarthy that sought to build him up as a sort of Horatio Alger of the United States senate and great crusader against communism. It was palpably a McCarthy build-up and it was, in my judgment, a flagrant violation of the principles of objective journalism. It was a gooey and sticky thing that was a big break for McCarthy in his badly needed rehabilitation. The story even went on to excuse, and obscure, and minimize McCarthy's record in Wisconsin on taxes, quickie divorces and the denunciations of the bar commissioners and the supreme court.

This reminded me, too, that during the 1946 campaign, when the Capital Times *and the* Milwaukee Journal *were exposing McCarthy's tax difficulties, his quickie divorces, the big contributions made to his campaign fund by members of his family who didn't have that kind of dough, and the implications of conducting a political campaign while sitting on the circuit court bench, the Associated Press always seemed timid, evasive and looking for an alibi for not printing this material. We got the impression that the little which the Associated Press did carry over its wires about the McCarthy exposé was done grudgingly and because the AP thought it had to carry something. . . .*

There was no evidence that the Associated Press took Evjue's charges seriously, although some editors and AP managers were glad later that he had made these charges, when the AP was being attacked for "left-wing bias" in its handling of McCarthy news. It gave the managers a chance to say that since they were being attacked from both left and right, they must be playing it down the middle.

John O'Donnell, political columnist for the *New York Daily News,* wrote on 24 April 1950 that McCarthy's speech to members of the American Society of Newspaper Editors in Washington had convinced editors that they were getting distorted news from Washington. O'Donnell said that the press and the Administration had "ganged up" to smear McCarthy as they had smeared the late Senator Robert M. La Follette of Wisconsin: "McCarthy got the same treatment that his Republican predecessor got a generation ago," O'Donnell wrote. "Some of the slanted stories that went out of Washington (and that includes some of the big services) gave the editors and publishers back home a deliberately distorted picture of what was happening." O'Donnell went on to say that the editors were hostile at first, but that after an hour of listening to McCarthy they changed their minds: "Having listened in and noted the reception, we have a hunch there will be some brisk spanking of hitherto important by-line writers by their bosses. It's our further belief that some of the double-domed boys, who, McCarthy told the editors, were egg-sucking so-called liberal columnists, will be missing some syndicate checks."

Following up that appearance, McCarthy sent a letter on 3 August 1950 to the members of the ASNE in which he said that coverage of his activities had improved after his talk but that the improvement had been only temporary. He also charged that the wire services had failed to carry an important story about an affadavit made in Switzerland by a German who had lived in Japan, a document which he said linked Owen Lattimore to a prewar Russian spy ring. The AP said in reply: "The AP has reported in great detail all newsworthy aspects of Sen. McCarthy's charges of Communism-in-government and responses thereto. In this case, it was concluded the Senator's statement lacked news value."

On 8 May 1950 Evjue again attacked the wire services, repeating many of the things he had said in March and blaming the 18 "conservative-minded publishers" who constituted the board of directors of the Associated Press for building up McCarthy because of their hatred for Presidents Roosevelt and Truman.

A charge of left-wing bias became the major issue at the annual meeting of the Associated Press Managing Editors Association in November 1950. The charge came from Charles A. Hazen, managing editor of the *Shreveport Times*, a paper strong in its editorial support for McCarthy. Hazen was backed by Robert Early, managing editor of the *Indianapolis Star*.[18]

Hazen presented a list of 58 instances of what he considered left-wing bias. He accused the AP of being pro-left-wing, pro-Truman, pro-administration, pro-Newspaper Guild, pro-CIO, pro-Acheson, and anti-McCarthy. Some of his charges, he said, were based upon a comparison of AP stories with those in the *New York Times* and with transcripts in the *Congressional Record*; what he received on the AP wire was much shorter than these accounts. Hazen said that he had noticed evidence of bias in AP reports from 1946 on. "I do not believe all is well on objectivity," he said. "We must use stern force."

His accusations were studied and rejected by the APME domestic news committee headed by V. M. Newton, Jr., managing editor of the *Tampa Tribune*. The committee, Newton said, found that the Hazen charges did show evidence of "careless, incomplete and even stupid reporting, an occasional lack of judgment and a general lack of initiative," but did not show evidence of bias. It rejected Hazen's charges, he said, because members were unable to see AP executives as pro-Communists or fellow travelers and because the prevailing view of editors across the nation was that "the AP is too timid, frightened at the very thought of being accused of partiality, and utterly bound by a too rigid adherence to the principle of objectivity."

Early countered that the committee and the APME board of directors were trying to "whitewash" Hazen's charges: "This is more serious than the atom bomb," Early said. "I do not believe that AP management is left-wing or any other kind of wing but there are those down in the line, down in the trenches, who may be influenced. I do think there is a tendency to write biased stories and I do believe AP management can overcome this by closer supervision." He promised to carry the matter further, and said that "the publishers"—meaning the American Newspaper Publishers Association—would take it up.

In support of the committee, Norman Isaacs, managing editor of the *St. Louis Star-Times*, argued that "the files of the AP in New York are as full of Evjue's charges of right-wing bias as they are of Hazen's charges that the AP is left-wing." Ben Reese, managing editor of the *St. Louis Post-Dispatch*, suggested that the *Shreveport Times* did not get complete Washington coverage because it did not subscribe to the AP's full trunk service.

The managing editors supported the committee report and rejected Hazen's charges, and there is no record of further complaints from Shreveport. Evjue persisted, however. On 17 February 1952 the *Capital Times* accused the AP of ignoring a report that a poll of leading political scientists had shown that they believed McCarthy to be the "worst Senator." It also scolded the agency for sending out a picture of McCarthy on the Capitol steps "cleaning Communist influence from government" with a "new broom," and it criticized the wording of the caption because of its "pro-McCarthy assumption" that there was Communist influence in government.

The issue came up again at the 1952 meeting of the APME. Warren Woolard, managing editor of the *Los Angeles Examiner*, introduced a resolution calling upon the APME to provide safeguards against "any abuse of the current trend toward so-called interpretive writing." The resolution was seconded by Richard F. Pourade of the *San Diego Union*. (Both the *Examiner* and the *Union* supported McCarthy editorially.) Norman Isaacs, at this time president of the APME, responded that the adoption of such a resolution "would make every AP man feel he had someone constantly looking over his shoulder." J. F. Weadock of the *Tucson Daily Star*, seconding a motion to table the resolution, said that he, for one, would not work under those conditions. "We are right back again with those who like McCarthy and those who don't," was his comment. The resolution was tabled.[19]

A major debate took place at the 1953 meeting of the APME on whether the AP was doing an "objective, competent and fair job of reporting the activities of Sen. McCarthy." The debaters were Tom Reynolds, managing editor of the *Chicago Sun-Times*, and Pourade of San Diego.[20] According to Pourade, the AP in the beginning had handled McCarthy stories "as though he were pulling political rabbits out of a hat," but over the last two years there had been a gradual change and reporters were taking McCarthy more seriously. "They think maybe, after all, there is something to what he says." In Pourade's opinion, the AP had not reported too much about McCarthy, as some had charged. Vice-President Barkley had spoken one night in San Diego and drawn an audience of only 1,100. McCarthy the next night drew 1,800 to 2,000. This convinced the *San Diego Union* that people were interested in McCarthy, Pourade said.

Reynolds said that the judgment of his telegraph editors was that the AP covered McCarthy "in a quieter manner" than the UP, that it seemed to describe the charges more accurately, and that it tried harder to include replies from those charged. But neither agency did those things well. "McCarthy is still master of the press," he said. "We think McCarthy is a sideshow barker in dealing with the press," said Wallace Lomoe, managing editor of the *Milwaukee Journal*. "First he drops a hint. Then he gives out a name. Third, he gives his version of what the name said or did. And the press carries all three." "I think McCarthy is a cheap demagogue," said Norman Isaacs, at that time managing editor of the *Louisville Times*. He considered the newspapers as much at fault as the wire services in handling McCarthy stories.

In reply to those who said that the AP wrote too much about McCarthy, William Beale, Jr., AP Washington bureau chief, pointed out that McCarthy was chairman of a Senate committee: "He speaks with the full authority of the Senate behind him. You may not like him, but he has the authority of the Senate. We have got to treat McCarthy the same as other committee chairmen. . . . We have no other choice but to report these things as fully and as adequately as it's humanly possible to do."

"The press made McCarthy," said Sam Ragan, managing editor of the *Raleigh News & Observer*, a paper which had criticized McCarthy from the beginning. "We go hog wild whenever he speaks. How much longer are we going to quote irresponsible statements of so-called responsible persons?" Ragan gave the AP credit for doing a good job in obtaining rebuttals from persons named by McCarthy in the last year, but said that it had done this badly at first. In the opinion of J. R. Wiggins, managing editor of the *Washington Post*, the newspapers might be giving too much space to McCarthy charges. "If we circulate . . . day after day, week after week, month after month, the infamous allegation that there's treason in the White House, in the Chiefs of Staff, in the Secretary of State, and in all the other departments of government, we need not be surprised if an hour comes when the American people have confidence in no one."

In 1955, after McCarthy's censure, the managing editors declared that the controversy over how to cover McCarthy was over. As late as 1954, said John Bloomer, managing editor of the *Columbus* (Georgia) *Ledger*, the APME had had long and bitter arguments over "interpretives, background writing, writing in depth as some call it." Now there was "nothing but complete enthusiasm" for interpretive reporting. But at the 1955 meeting of the American Newspaper Publishers Association, William Heath, publisher of the *Haverhill Gazette*, continued to accuse the wire services of "editorial slanting" in reporting the news of McCarthy. He said that many wire service "leads" on McCarthy stories were not supported by the material that followed, and that McCarthy had received "the worst press of any man in recent times."[21]

It is clear that in these years convictions about objectivity were related to opinions of McCarthy. All of the "fundamentalists" on objectivity were from newspapers that supported McCarthy editorially, and all of the editors who defended interpretive reporting were from newspapers that were critical of McCarthy. The *Appleton Post-Crescent*, for example, published an editorial in 1954 praising the wire services for making it clear in 1950 that Senator Tydings bullied McCarthy when he appeared before the investigating committee. "Our great news agencies which we all knew were as fair and unprejudiced as anything could be, simply told the facts from day to day and week to week," the editorial said. "And the public got the pattern." The *Post-Crescent*, of course, supported McCarthy. There is no question but that McCarthy's exploitation of "straight" reporting did cause a gradual but fundamental change in American journalism. It probably took a performance as spectacular as his to move the guardians of objectivity to admit that the *meaning* of an event is as important as the facts of an event. The shift to interpretive reporting was accelerated as television became the principal source of spot news for most people; this made interpretation the meat and potatoes of print journalism. But the beginning was in the McCarthy years, and the first steps were painful. Several of Joe McCarthy's legacies were beneficial, and one of them was the redefinition of the principle of objectivity.

Most of the wire service reporters who covered McCarthy said that they thought the widespread use of interpretive reporting made it unlikely that anyone now could use the press as McCarthy had. Theis, the INS man, said that "even the wire services now make much broader use of interpretation and analysis." "In those days all of that was left to the editorial writers and the columnists, and what they said was watered down because they were usually categorized as 'liberals' and therefore ineffective," Theis said. "I think TV has made the reading public much more sophisticated, too. There's a lot more cynicism around, and readers are less likely to take things for granted."

Seib said that newspapers had "grown" since the 1950s. "I don't know if McCarthy did it or it was just a natural maturing. I think a guy like Lattimore would get a better shake today."

Maybe what would stop it now is the New York-Washington axis. It has a lot more influence now than it did then. We have the New York Times wire and the [Washington] Post-Los Angeles Times wire; the New York Times wire was operating then but not the way it does now. The Times didn't do a very good job on the McCarthy story, not much better than the wire services. That fellow [William S.] White had a flow of words, but he wasn't a very good reporter.

If it wouldn't happen now, it's because the print press realizes its changed role in relation to TV. We're not bringing the news any more—TV does that. We explain it. Television was more important than McCarthy in bringing interpretive reporting. But there could be a time when some demagogue figured out how to "use" TV, and the print press would have to pull it out.

In George Reedy's opinion, the press could handle McCarthy better today because the competition is not as keen and because comment is permitted: "We could report now that the Lattimore letter which McCarthy showed the press did not back up McCarthy's charges," Reedy told me. "Joe's techniques wouldn't work today, but he'd find new techniques. The press didn't *make* Joe; the press is just a form of communication. Whatever the form of communication was, Joe would find a way to use it. Demagogues always find ways to use any communication there is."

Most of the changes in reporting practices came too late to have much of an effect on the McCarthy controversy, however. It was not until April 1954, a month after Edward R. Murrow had broadcast his televised denunciation of the senator and when McCarthy was attacking the Eisenhower administration, that the Associated Press undertook a critical analysis of McCarthy's career. The AP assigned its best-known reporters—Don Whitehead, Saul Pett, Bem Price, Relman Morin, William C. Allen, and Jack Bell—to the job of turning out a series of 18 articles covering everything from McCarthy's childhood to his clash with the Eisenhower administration. It even included a cautious report on some of the early tax problems and questionable judicial rulings that it had failed to carry when they were reported in Wisconsin newspapers four years earlier. While fairly complete, the series did not depart from the AP's tradition of balance and neutrality. It said, for example, that "many observers have spoken of the 'climate of fear' in the nation." This was balanced by a statement that "McCarthy says no one need be afraid except Communists, people who follow the Communist line, or act like Communists."[22]

The series was published in booklet form in May 1954.[23] In a foreword, Alan J. Gould, executive editor, said that there was never any doubt that the AP would publish a comprehensive series on McCarthy but that "the question was when." Gould said that in February 1954 "we decided the time was ripe." The booklet included a collection of comments by editors praising the series, some from papers which had supported McCarthy. One of the editors, Alexander F. Jones of the *Syracuse Herald-Journal and American*, called it "completely objective," and another, John B. Mullaney of the *Cleveland News*, called it "a good down-the-middle job of fact-reporting."

What it proved, more than anything else, was that the Associated Press was still playing the consensus game, that it could move no faster or further than the middle group of newspaper clients, the Republican papers which were slowly edging into criticism of McCarthy as it became apparent to all that he was headed for a showdown with President Eisenhower.

There is no question but that McCarthy used the wire services, deliberately and knowingly, taking advantage of the fierce competition among them and their fear of losing clients. Given the system, the services were unable to prevent this.

4.

The 1952 Election

FEW OF the questions about McCarthy and the press are subject to measurement. We can guess at the effect of an editorial campaign against McCarthy by the trend of letters to the editor, or at the effect of a critical television program by the number and nature of the ensuing telephone calls and telegrams. We can speculate that criticism by the press in Washington, Baltimore, and New York did finally prod President Eisenhower into doing something about McCarthy, or that anti-McCarthy campaigns by newspapers in St. Louis, Denver, or Louisville affected the positions of senators from those areas. We can theorize that live television coverage of the Army-McCarthy hearings in 1954 precipitated a public reaction that made it politic for the Senate to vote censure of McCarthy at the end of that year. But all of this is conjecture.

There was, however, one time and one place where the effect of newspaper support for or opposition to McCarthy could be measured with a high degree of accuracy—the 1952 election in Wisconsin, the only time McCarthy faced the electorate after his commitment to the Communists-in-government issue. McCarthy had achieved enormous publicity during the three years preceding the election, and newspapers had had time to formulate and promulgate their views on McCarthy. In the 1946 election, the issue was absent, and McCarthy was a controversial figure only to the disappointed loyalists of Senator Robert M. La Follette, Jr., who was upset by McCarthy in the primary. This situation is almost ideal for a determination of whether and how the 1952 vote was affected by newspapers. It became apparent in the course of making this determination that a possible mistake in the interpretation of primary returns by political reporters might have been important enough to tip the election to McCarthy. It also became apparent that in the latter days of the 1952 political campaign McCarthy "used" the press more successfully than ever before.

A half-century of political tradition was ending in Wisconsin as Joe McCarthy entered the national political scene in 1946. The Democratic Party had been a negligible force in state politics, and the contests that had counted were in the primaries between the "progressive" faction of the Republican Party and the "stalwart" or conservative faction. From 1934 through 1944, the Progressives had stood as a third party, creating a temporary change in the pattern, but it reverted to the traditional in 1946.

Senator Robert M. La Follette, Jr.—"Young Bob"—was first elected as a Republican in 1925 following the death of his father, Senator Robert M. "Fighting Bob" La Follette. He was reelected on the GOP ticket in 1928 and as a Progressive in 1934 and 1940. In 1946 it was obvious that the Progressive party was on its way out. La Follette's own experience was indicative; as a Republican candidate in 1928 he had won with 89 percent of the vote; as a Progressive in 1934 he drew only 50 percent, the Democratic and Republican candidates splitting the rest evenly. In 1940 he won with 45 percent of the vote, the Republican getting 42 percent and the Democrat 13 percent. In 1944 the Progressive candidate for the Senate got only 6 percent, as Republican Senator Alexander Wiley won with 51 percent.

Progressives in Wisconsin were divided on the question of their political future. The younger members of the party wanted to merge with the Democrats; they were the economic "progressives" in the Progressive party, and for them President Franklin D. Roosevelt had replaced Fighting Bob as a spiritual and political leader. Eventually they did join the Democrats and provided much of the energy and leadership for the rebuilding of the Democratic party in Wisconsin. The other faction was made up by and large of people for whom the principal bond with the La Follettes was foreign policy; they were isolationists. Most of these moved into the Republican party.

La Follette, of course, chose the Republican party. In retrospect, this appears clearly to have been a mistake, and it was also exceptional; other agrarian-reform third parties in the Middle West were merging with the Democratic party at the time. But the old pattern of politics in Wisconsin was so fixed in La Follette's mind that the Democratic alternative was unthinkable. It is likely that he was so immersed in his work in Washington that he lost touch with political changes taking place in his home state.

McCarthy, endorsed by the regular Republican organization, won the 1946 primary by 5,378 votes, in a total Republican vote of 440,097.

La Follette carried the largest number of counties, chiefly in the western and northwestern parts of Wisconsin, but the only county in which he piled up any appreciable margin was Dane (Madison), where his candidacy was supported by William T. Evjue and the *Capital Times.* He won Dane County by about 6,000 votes. McCarthy amassed his winning margin in the industrial counties of eastern Wisconsin—1,000 in Racine, 2,000 in Outagamie, 3,000 in Waukesha, and 10,000 in Milwaukee. According to Robert Griffith in his book *The Politics of Fear,* La Follette lost in the heavily populated industrial areas of Racine, Kenosha, and Milwaukee "not so much because workers supported McCarthy, but because they entered the Democratic primary in support of Howard McMurray."[1] McMurray, however, was unopposed for the nomination, and the incentive for such a move seems unclear.

A number of writers have ascribed McCarthy's strong showing in Milwaukee to the Communist party, noting that the *CIO News,* in the hands of a pro-Communist faction of the CIO, had urged its readers to vote for McCarthy as a means of defeating La Follette, who had repeatedly warned against the expansionist ambitions of Russia in eastern Europe. In the opinion of Paul Ringler of the *Milwaukee Journal,* there was no question but that Harold Christoffel, a Milwaukee union official, tried to influence his followers in the United Auto Workers union to vote against La Follette. But "the idea that this was the decisive factor in electing McCarthy over La Follette was a Bill Evjue [*Capital Times*] doctrine," Ringler said. "It may well have been one of the factors, but we were never able to figure it as *the* factor in our intensive study of the Milwaukee county election returns."[2]

Another factor was the part played by the national Democratic party, although I am unable to confirm any of the versions of what this tactic was. My own recollection is that the Democratic national committee sent in $10,000, funneled by the Wisconsin national committeeman, the late federal judge Robert E. Tehan, to Richard S. Davis, the *Milwaukee Journal's* drama critic. Davis took a leave of absence to run an underground political unit aimed at persuading Democrats to cross over to vote for McCarthy as the easier man to beat in the general election.[3] Ringler does not remember this, but does recall that some state Democrats were advocating such a crossover.[4]

Philip Potter, political reporter for the *Baltimore Sun* in the fifties, remembers being told by Thomas Corcoran, a Washington lawyer and White House insider, that President Truman had tried through Robert Hannegan, the Democratic national chairman, to persuade La Follette to run as a Democrat in 1946. Angered by La Follette's refusal, he had induced Howard McMurray to run, and had encouraged Democrats and Progressives who had supported La Follette in the past to vote in the Democratic primary so as to enable McCarthy to defeat La Follette.[5] This version was challenged by (among others) George Reedy, on the grounds that Truman despised politicians who switched parties. According to Ringler, Reedy could not believe that Truman would have asked La Follette to switch, or that he would have worked to punish him because he didn't.

More important than either of these factors, however, was the failure of the *Milwaukee Journal* to endorse La Follette. Ringler remembers that La Follette telephoned him to ask him to set up a meeting with *Journal* executives and editorial writers. "This was considered earth-shaking, since the *Journal* had feuded violently with the La Follettes since the senior Bob opposed [entering] World War I. No La Follette had entered the *Journal* building, at least since 1924." Ringler said that La Follette met with him, J. D. Ferguson, the editor, and Will C. Conrad, the chief editorial writer, in Ferguson's office.

La Follette said that he must have the Journal's *endorsement to win the primary. He said that he no longer had any organized support in the state; that the Progressive backers of years past were mostly inactive. He had been too busy with the reorganization plan before Congress to do any serious campaigning. He said that perhaps he had erred badly in taking the party into the GOP, but that had seemed to him its proper and historic home.*

He said he believed, and hoped, that the Journal, *which had strongly supported his reorganization plan, and had editorialized favorably about him on other issues, would overcome its past prejudices against the family and support him now.[6]*

Ringler argued in favor of endorsement but was told that the *Journal* did not endorse in primaries. (It did, however, endorse McCarthy's opponent in the 1952 Republican primary.) It was Ringler's feeling that Conrad, an "intense La Follette hater," convinced Ferguson. The *Journal* did not endorse. According to Ringler, the *Journal* was very influential in state and local elections in those days, and its endorsement might have made La Follette the winner.[7] My estimate is that a *Journal* endorsement was worth at least 20,000 votes in Milwaukee in those days, much more than enough to reverse the outcome.

In Wisconsin's open primary, voters are not registered by parties; in the rural areas they are not required to register at all. Voters are given ballots for each party offering candidates in a primary; they mark one and throw the others away. Most Democrats in Wisconsin until recent years behaved like independents; they voted first in the

Republican primary, usually in the hope of defeating the organization-backed Republican, and knowing that they would get another chance to defeat him in November if the first try failed. This often worked; Democrats and independent voters crossed over to defeat right-wing Republican challengers twice, as Wiley, a moderate, won four terms in the Senate.*

Most of McCarthy's opponents in 1952, both Republicans and Democrats, thought in the old way: fight him in the Republican primary. All through 1951 there were efforts to persuade one or another major Republican to run. La Follette was approached by both Republicans and Democrats; he considered the Democratic offer, tendered by Averell Harriman in March 1952, but decided against it, reportedly because he thought it was still politically unrealistic to run as a Democrat in Wisconsin.[8] There were flurries of speculation about former Governor Oscar Rennebohm and Supreme Court Justice Henry Hughes, but these fizzled out. Most McCarthy opponents hoped that Governor Walter J. Kohler, a moderate Republican who was privately contemptuous of McCarthy, would run; labor offered its support. Kohler considered running, but the regular Republicans were dead set against it; he finally announced that he would seek reelection as governor. The *St. Louis Post-Dispatch* said of this, on 5 July 1952, "When threats and pressures were brought against his senatorial candidacy, Gov. Kohler folded up. . . . He chose expediency and now he blesses the evil growth he should have helped the American people cut out of the body politic."

Next came a boom for Jim Dan Hill, president of Wisconsin State College, Superior, and commanding general of the 32nd Infantry Division of the Wisconsin National Guard, an undeniable patriot who disagreed with McCarthy. For a year, Leonard F. Schmitt, of Merrill, Wisconsin, had been saying that if no one else ran against McCarthy in the primary, he would. Schmitt was a Republican and had been elected district attorney in a northern county on that ticket. He had been a delegate to the Republican national convention in 1936 and had a good military record, but he was not widely known. He urged Hill to run and said he would support him if he did, but Hill was unable to make up his mind, and on 24 June 1952 Schmitt became a candidate.

*Many who crossed over to vote for Wiley developed a kind of loyalty to him, however, and voted for him again against his Democratic opponent. Only in 1962, when Wiley was finally nominated without a Republican primary fight, did he lose, to Governor Gaylord Nelson. In 1978 the old pattern reasserted itself. Lee S. Dreyfus, a maverick Republican, was able, with the support of many Democrats, to defeat the candidate endorsed by the Republican organization and to go on to upset the incumbent Democratic governor.

He made a vigorous campaign. He had the support of the Wisconsin State Federation of Labor and he was endorsed by the *Milwaukee Journal*, the *Capital Times*, and a few smaller papers. He got money from some Eisenhower Republicans, in and out of Wisconsin, who saw McCarthy as Eisenhower's biggest political problem in the election. Schmitt tried to make himself known by conducting four "talkathons," marathon radio and television talks in which he answered questions from listeners.

McCarthy campaigned very little. He underwent surgery that summer for a ruptured diaphragm and spent the rest of the time convalescing at a resort in northern Wisconsin. He had money, though, as a result of his endorsement by the Republican organization, and his supporters hammered hard, in newspaper advertisements, on the theme that Schmitt was less than a "real" Republican. The advertisements quoted stories from the 25 October 1950 editions of the *Milwaukee Journal* and the *Capital Times*, reporting that Schmitt had advocated voting for the Democratic candidates for governor, senator, and attorney general after losing the primary race that year for the Republican nomination for governor. There were indications that the attack was effective; some Republicans seemed angrier about Schmitt's "fraudulent" claim to Republicanism than about his attacks on McCarthy. Typical of their attitude toward Schmitt was this excerpt from the editorial in which the *Portage Daily Register* endorsed McCarthy. The *Register* said that the right man might have taken the nomination away from McCarthy because many conservative Republicans were not satisfied with him. "But Len Schmitt is not the man to win that nomination. His close alliance with the Progressive-Democrats and his contemptuous slur at the regular Republican organization are not the measures needed to win the thousands of moderate Republicans whose votes are needed to defeat the state's junior senator."

The Democrats had a primary contest, too, between two respected candidates, Henry S. Reuss and Thomas E. Fairchild. Most Democrats regarded both candidates with equal esteem, and the race generated little excitement. Newspapers ignored it for the most part, caught up in the old game of the Republican primary.

On 14 September 1951, the administrative committee of the Democratic state organization declared that McCarthy could not be defeated in the Republican primary and urged Democrats to stick to their own ballot. The statement adopted by the group said, "The independent voter and the active liberal will have their only real opportunity to return him [McCarthy] to private life at the general election when a Democratic candidate offers them a positive alternative to McCarthyism. . . ."[9] Not all Democrats adhered to this strategy, however. On 26 August 1952, William Proxmire, the unopposed Democratic candidate for governor, urged supporters of General Eisenhower to vote for Schmitt, saying that Eisenhower's criticism of McCarthy's attack on General Marshall constituted "a ringing endorsement" of Leonard Schmitt. "If Eisenhower could vote in Wisconsin, he would vote for Schmitt," Proxmire said.[10]

McCarthy's one major speech in the 1952 primary campaign was delivered in Shorewood, a Republican suburb of Milwaukee, in the high school auditorium, on September 3. The crowd was large and enthusiastic, and the speech was broadcast over 31 Wisconsin radio stations. It was chiefly an attack on Adlai E. Stevenson, the Democratic nominee for president, in which McCarthy attempted, through half-truths and innuendo, to link Stevenson with Alger Hiss and others who had been fired from government jobs. The McCarthy-Schmitt primary was a big story nationally, and reporters were there from newspapers all over the country. Among them was Joseph Alsop, the columnist. At one point in the Shorewood speech McCarthy quoted what he said were conversations between himself and James Forrestal, the late secretary of defense, whom he called "one of the greatest friends I ever had." This infuriated Alsop, who really had been a close friend of Forrestal. Alsop stood up in the orchestra pit where the press tables were, shook his fist at McCarthy, and yelled, "That's a lie! You never even knew him!" McCarthy ignored Alsop, talked over him just as he had talked over Democratic senators on the Tydings subcommittee, and few in the crowd noticed the disturbance. No one but Alsop was much excited by the speech until McCarthy made a passing reference to "the press." The crowd erupted. "Tell the *Journal*, Joe!" people yelled. "Show the *Journal*!" The shouting continued. As it died down, McCarthy chuckled into the microphone and said, "Yeah, I'll give it to the *Milwaukee Daily Worker*." This set them off again.[11] As that rally ended, about 50 women, shouting and waving umbrellas, converged on the orchestra pit where the reporters were trapped. "Get the *Journal* reporter!" they yelled. "Where's the *Journal* reporter?" I was the *Journal* reporter, but I didn't say so. Miles McMillin of the *Capital Times* stepped in front of the crowd and said: "Ladies! Are you going to vote for Eisenhower?" Some said they were. "At my paper," said McMillin, "we think he's a Communist." They stopped. "What paper?" one asked. "The *Chicago Tribune*," McMillin said, and in the confusion that followed I slipped past them and out a side door. McCarthy's comments about the press had been very restrained that night, but it didn't take much to get his supporters worked up.

McCarthy swamped Schmitt in the September 9 primary, 515,481 to 213,701. His vote was larger than the combined vote for all other candidates on the ballot—five Republicans and two Democrats—which totaled only 435,492. For the Democratic nomination, Fairchild nosed out Reuss by less than 3,000 votes; the total Democratic vote was less than Schmitt's losing vote. Four out of five voters had chosen the Republican ballot.

The *Milwaukee Journal's* analysis the next day was headed "Democrats Helped Pick McCarthy, Votes Show; Received More Support in Some Democratic Areas Than He Did in Solid GOP Districts." The story said, "It is the inescapable conclusion that many Wisconsin Democrats crossed party lines not to defeat McCarthy but to nominate him." It cited examples of Democratic wards, suburbs, and cities where large numbers of votes were cast for McCarthy, while few were cast in the Democratic contest. It noted that McCarthy had barely won over Schmitt in normally Republican suburbs, and concluded, "The two big political questions before the primary were whether the Democrats would cross over and whether the people of Wisconsin had been impressed with McCarthy's campaign against alleged "Communists" in government. The answer to both questions was in the affirmative." The *Wisconsin State Journal* interpreted the primary vote similarly in its September 11 comment, and quoted McCarthy as saying that he couldn't tell whether Democrats had crossed over, "but if they did, they gave us a pretty good break." The *State Journal's* political columnist, Sanford Goltz, wrote that precinct figures showed "without question" that many who ordinarily voted Democratic "came over and voted for what has been called McCarthyism."

The Associated Press story by Don Whitehead was cautious on this point. "McCarthy's spectacular victory indicated that perhaps he had some support from switch-voting Democrats who crossed the line to give him help. But this was only speculation and there was no way to check it.[12] Richard J. H. Johnston, reporting from Milwaukee for the *New York Times* September 10, essayed an explanation: "More than 536,000 voters, including Democrats who crossed to the Republican lists, voted for the Senator yesterday. However, analysts admitted their bafflement at the fact that, having crossed over, Democrats in large numbers voted for, not against, the Senator. . . . They may have been voting as midwesterners and not as Democrats."

The *Milwaukee Journal's* interpretation of the primary vote went by special correspondence to the *Washington Post, St. Louis Post-Dispatch, Kansas City Star, Nashville Tennessean, Boston Globe, Louisville Courier-Journal,* and *Time* magazine, so that this discouraging story was widely disseminated.[13] Other newspapers arrived at similar conclusions independently. "Senator McCarthy," said the *Washington Post* in a September 11 editorial, "had the support of the regular Republican organization in Wisconsin—a rather well-organized machine. But since a number of Democrats undoubtedly crossed over to vote against him in the Republican primary, and since the size of his plurality was extremely impressive, it is impossible to write off his victory as machine-made."

The *Baltimore Sun* on September 15 wrote that the McCarthy landslide in Wisconsin "is explainable only on the premise that many Democrats crossed party lines (as is permitted in the Wisconsin primary) *to vote for McCarthy*. The main reason could only have been that McCarthy is an outspoken, if an unscrupulous, critic of Administration policy." "The Wisconsin primary," said the *Appleton Post-Crescent* on September 15, "not only demonstrated that the rank and file of the Republican voters were overwhelmingly in favor of McCarthy but were matched by the rank and file of Democratic voters." The *New York Times* said editorially on September 11, "The only explanation for the astonishing drop in the Democratic total Tuesday is that a great many Democrats must have crossed over to the Republican side (as under Wisconsin law they have the right to do) and voted not against McCarthy, but for him. Even in Democratic strongholds Mr. McCarthy ran ahead of his opponent."

The *Chicago Tribune* was exultant. In its September 11 editorial, titled "McCarthy's Triumph," it wrote, "When the votes were counted, it was found that McCarthy had wiped the floor with his opposition. The people of Wisconsin knew their senator and knew that the charges against him were false and malicious. The Democrats who moved into the Republican party for the day did so, for the most part, to indorse McCarthy."

The size of the McCarthy win impressed many newspapers. "On the basis of the primary figures," said the *Philadelphia Bulletin* on September 11, "—with McCarthy's total vote a good 100,000 greater than those of all other Republican and Democratic candidates—there would seem to be little hope for an upset in November." The *Columbus Dispatch* commented on September 11, "His renomination by a landslide has vindicated and supported his issue. It is the best single bit of news the Republicans have had during the campaign."

Post-primary editorials made three other points about the McCarthy win. One was that opposition to the Korean War had had a good deal to do with the big McCarthy vote. Arthur Krock of the *New York Times* and columnist David Lawrence both made that point, as did the *St. Louis Post-Dispatch*, which said, on September 17: "People who are unhappy about the Korean War (as who is not?) can find an outlet for their feelings in McCarthy. He does not tell them how to solve the Korean crisis, but he tells them that softness toward Communism and treason in high places created it. This is a lie, but people who are stirred by emotion more than by rational analysis can vote against the Korean War by voting for McCarthy."

There is no question that dissatisfaction with the war was a major factor in McCarthy's victory. Many of the voters who were interviewed coming from the polling booths mentioned the Korean War. The more recent bitterness over the Vietnam War has dimmed the memory of that other bitter war in Asia. It was the main reason that Democrats fared so badly in congressional races in Wisconsin in 1950, and it was a major factor in Eisenhower's victory over Adlai Stevenson. Another thing that many editorial writers speculated about was whether the opposition of "outsiders"—apparently meaning the press outside Wisconsin—had worked to favor McCarthy. They also wondered whether the intensity of the criticism from certain newspapers in Wisconsin had made voters feel that McCarthy was being "picked on." The *Wausau Record-Herald* on September 10 wrote that McCarthy won "in the face of concerted efforts not only by those who opposed him within the state but also by forces throughout the land which made a national issue of McCarthy and the manner of his fight with Communism in government." "McCarthy had the advantage," said the *Philadelphia Inquirer* on September 11, "not only of united Organization support, but of the resentment felt by many Wisconsin Republicans at the outpouring of unsolicited advice from outsiders bidding them how and how not to cast their votes." And this was the point of the September 11 editorial of the *Chicago Tribune*:

Against McCarthy were arrayed the state's leading newspaper and some lesser ones, the leading newspapers of neighboring Minnesota and Iowa, some supposedly influential Republicans, and all the influential Democrats. Most of the popular radio commentators sought to destroy him and in this endeavor were supported by many of the most widely read magazines.

Sen. McCarthy had been the object of a smear campaign that had continued, day in and day out for years. . . . No man in public life in our day has been so persistently and so plentifully smeared.

The other idea that grew out of McCarthy's big primary victory was that other Republican candidates, and particularly General Eisenhower, would now have to depend on the senator to pull them through in November; they would be "riding McCarthy's coattails." Again, the *Tribune*: "It is now clear that Sen. McCarthy doesn't have to ride on anyone's coattails and it is also clear that if Gen. Eisenhower is to win in Wisconsin, he will have to ride the McCarthy coattails. . . ."

This belief was not confined to those who favored McCarthy. On 28 October 1952, the Associated Press questioned editors meeting in Milwaukee on prospects in the coming election. One of the editors was Harry Maier of the *Sheboygan Press*, a paper that opposed McCarthy and supported Stevenson. In Maier's opinion Eisenhower would carry Sheboygan County with 54 percent of the vote. (Eisenhower got 59 percent.) "The Democratic campaign lacks force as a result of the jolt taken from McCarthy's large primary vote," he said. (McCarthy ended up with 47 percent of the Sheboygan County vote.) Another editor whose paper opposed McCarthy and supported Stevenson was John D. Rice of the weekly *Monroe County Democrat*. Rice predicted that Eisenhower would get 54 percent of the vote in Monroe County. (Eisenhower got 70 percent.) "In my opinion," Rice said, "McCarthy is considerably stronger in this territory than the general." (McCarthy got 68 percent in Monroe County.) Another weekly editor who had taken a stand against McCarthy was George Hough of the *Vernon County Censor*. He told the AP that McCarthy's strong support of the GOP national ticket would carry a lot of votes and that McCarthy's political activity was "steaming up a lot of enthusiasm." (Eisenhower got 65 percent of the vote in Vernon County, McCarthy 63 percent.) Artemas Bonner, editor of the *Antigo Daily Journal* (strongly pro-McCarthy), said that McCarthy's support of Eisenhower would be "enough to take Langlade County out of a 'safe Democratic' category," leaving it divided equally. (Langlade County gave Eisenhower 64 percent of the vote, McCarthy, 63 percent.) Another McCarthy supporter, John B. Chapple, editor of the *Ashland Press*, said that Eisenhower was gaining in Ashland County, "helped by the Joe McCarthy landslide." (Eisenhower got 54 percent in Ashland County, McCarthy 52 percent.)

These comments indicate the devastating effect of the McCarthy primary victory on the thinking of editors in Wisconsin, friend and foe of McCarthy alike. In every case they overestimated McCarthy's strength and underestimated Eisenhower's appeal. Not one, obviously, thought that Tom Fairchild, the Democratic nominee, had the slightest chance of winning in November. We can only guess at the primary's effect on editors who might have been flirting with the idea of a Fairchild endorsement, or who might have summoned up enough courage to withstand the pressures of local McCarthyites if the outcome of the election could have been affected by their actions. But if it's hopeless, they must have thought, why ask for trouble?

Newspapers already in the field against McCarthy did not relent. The *St. Louis Post-Dispatch* spoke for many in an editorial which appeared on September 17: "Now that Senator McCarthy has been renominated by Wisconsin Republicans, those who opposed him are being widely advised to throw in the towel and accept 'the people's verdict.' We do not intend to take that advice ourselves, and we hope that the valiant army of McCarthy's opponents in Wisconsin will pay no more heed." McCarthy's opponents in Wisconsin were not silenced. On September 10, the day after the primary, the *Milwaukee Journal* published, under the heading "The Man They Nominated," a list of McCarthy's misdeeds and a bitter denunciation of those who, knowing these things, nevertheless voted for McCarthy. This editorial, written by Paul Ringler, was more widely reprinted than any other *Journal* editorial. It said, in part:

This is not only appalling—it is frightening.

It betrays a dulled moral sense, a dimmed instinct for truth, for honor, decency and fairness.

It rewards falsehood, chicanery, deception, ruthlessness, the tactics of smear and fear, and contempt for the constitutional principles that safeguard American human and legal rights.

It will cause misgivings for the future across the land, for it evidences the dangers which confront our fundamental freedom.

One paper that reprinted that editorial, not surprisingly, was the *Capital Times*, and in his Sunday evening radio talk, printed on Monday, September 15, Evjue assured his listeners that he was not giving up. "Our chin is still up," he said. "We will continue this fight until Wisconsin is rid of the ugly cult of mccarthyism." He said that the outlook for November was "not as bad as the Republican newspapers would have you believe," and found comfort in the fact that McCarthy had received "only" about 100,000 votes more than the anti-McCarthy candidates—Schmitt, Reuss, and Fairchild.

Democrats were saying this, too. On September 13, James E. Doyle, state party chairman, said that Fairchild would start with about 40 percent of the vote cast in the primary and that in the past the Democratic vote had doubled, tripled, or quadrupled between the primary and the election. Doyle predicted (incorrectly) that Adlai Stevenson would carry the state, helping Fairchild, and (correctly) that McCarthy would trail the rest of the GOP ticket.

Several political analysts have contended that McCarthy won in November because political writers overemphasized the importance and nature of his primary victory and especially because the vote was interpreted as a Democratic crossover to McCarthy. This view was put forth in an article in *The Reporter* on 28 October 1952 by James G. March, "McCarthy Can Still Be Beaten." March argued that Democrats who crossed over to the Republican primary voted for Schmitt and that almost no Republicans voted for Schmitt. He doesn't say it, but his argument also would have to include the point that Republicans turned out to vote for McCarthy in very large numbers—large enough to pile up big margins for McCarthy over Schmitt in Democratic territory—49,000 in Milwaukee County, for example. March's argument was that McCarthy did "most poorly"—that is, got his smallest percentages of the combined Schmitt-McCarthy vote—in counties where Democrats were traditionally strongest, and that he won by the largest proportions in traditional Republican strongholds.

If it was true that there was a significant Democratic vote for McCarthy, McCarthy should have done better where the Democrats were strong and where they voted in the Republican primary than he did where the Democrats were weak or stayed in their own primary. ... On the other hand, the eleven counties in which McCarthy did best, running five to one over Schmitt, should have been those counties in which there were Democratic votes for him.

In an analysis of the vote in the 10 most Democratic counties in Wisconsin, March concluded that a Democratic crossover to McCarthy took place only in two small rural counties, Portage and Florence, and that a highly significant crossover to Schmitt took place in Dane, Douglas, and Milwaukee counties.

March said that his analysis eliminated the most important basis for the feelings of futility that overcame the anti-McCarthy forces after the primary. He then made an argument similar to Doyle's—that a presidential election brings out normally apathetic voters (presumably Democrats) and that some Republicans would split their tickets to vote against McCarthy. He concluded that Fairchild's candidacy was not hopeless.

The biggest blow to his chances has been the interpretation thus far placed on the primary results. ... The impact of this interpretation cannot be underestimated. Every study of political and social attitudes indicates that the man on the fence, the person who is undecided, is extraordinarily sensitive to the subtle need for emotional support from relatives, neighbors, friends, and even the press.

It is among these many undecided voters, whose importance to the Fairchild candidacy is indisputable, that the popular pronouncement that the vast majority of Wisconsin citizens, Democrats and Republicans alike, appear to be solidly behind McCarthy, has had and will have a devastating effect.

It seems unlikely that there were many undecided voters in Wisconsin in that emotional campaign, but it was true that the prevailing interpretation of the primary vote did have a dire effect on Fairchild's campaign. People who concluded that a McCarthy victory in November was inevitable were not inclined to contribute to a seemingly hopeless campaign. Neither Fairchild nor the Wisconsin Democratic party had money for advertising; in most newspapers Republicans bought several pages of advertising during the last week of the campaign, the Democrats almost none. McCarthy ads were placed both by his own campaign committee and by the state GOP organization, whose advertisements sometimes boosted McCarthy alone and sometimes as the leader of the Republican slate of candidates. Equally important, a candidate perceived as a loser becomes less auspicious as a maker of news; his press releases can be safely ignored. Fairchild's campaign statements and appearances were given relatively little space in Wisconsin papers. Whether it was correct or not, the reports of the Democratic crossover vote had the kind of effect that March deplored.

Any study of voting in a Wisconsin primary is highly speculative. We speak of a "crossover" as though all voters had firm loyalties to political parties, but in Wisconsin the number who considered themselves party members was undoubtedly small; my guess is that a majority of Wisconsin voters in those days considered themselves independents. It is an axiom of politics that those with strong party ties are more likely to vote in primaries, but the size of the primary vote in 1952 indicates that many who did not ordinarily do so voted in the primary that year; the turnout was more like that of a general election. The 1946 primary in which McCarthy defeated La Follette was a hotly contested vote by comparison to most, but the vote in that primary was only half the size of the vote in the general election. The vote in the 1952 primary was about 60 percent of the vote in the 1952 general election, notwithstanding the fact that a president was elected in November. And the vote was almost as large as the vote in the 1946 general election. This would seem to indicate that many independents voted in the primary, which makes the analysis of crossover voting more difficult. That astounding primary vote might have been defined more sharply through a post-primary poll or by assigning reporters to interview voters as they left the polls. A number of newspapers began doing this in 1976, and reporter/pollster teams did it in almost every presidential primary in 1980.

Whatever damage a possibly incorrect interpretation of the primary vote did to the campaign against McCarthy was probably less important than the mere numbers of votes cast for him—more than for all other candidates combined. It was probably less important, too, than what occurred in the media as the bitter campaign worked toward its climax in November. In its editorial of 15 September 1952, the *Appleton Post-Crescent* made a prediction: "Three men probably will get their names on newsprint during the next seven weeks more than anyone else: Dwight D. Eisenhower, Adlai Stevenson and Joe McCarthy. The man who was a little-known circuit judge in Appleton six years ago may get more ink than either of the other two." This turned out to be true, especially in Wisconsin, where McCarthy's votes were. It did not happen at once, because McCarthy did little campaigning for a while after his primary victory, but he "got the ink" in the last week of the campaign by using the press more skillfully and successfully than ever before. He did it by running against Adlai Stevenson, ignoring the race for the Senate, and campaigning as a political leader with a national following that gave him a right to intervene in the race for the presidency. He did this not as a Republican—he never did say anything good about General Eisenhower—but as the ultimate authority on Communism and the only one tough enough to do a dirty job like trying to make a Communist out of Adlai Stevenson.

No one knows how successful he was in tarring Stevenson, but one result of the effort was plain: he dominated the news in Wisconsin newspapers the last week, burying the unfortunate Fairchild under an avalanche of headlines in newspapers that favored him and those that fought him alike. All the news wasn't good for McCarthy that week, but all the news was *about* McCarthy.

Fairchild stumped the state for two months, making 10 or 12 speeches a day from a sound truck. His appearances were rarely noted even by local newspapers. McCarthy traveled across the country, conferring the title of "Communist fighter" upon allies like Senator Harry Cain of Washington and that of "Communist sympathizer" upon Senate enemies like William Benton of Connecticut. John Wyngaard, the state political columnist, wrote on October 30 that McCarthy "had hardly campaigned at all in Wisconsin" because he had "the best instinctive understanding of voter behavior of any politician of his time" and he knew that he was safe in the Wisconsin election. McCarthy's only concern was a Republican majority in the Senate, Wyngaard said.[14]

McCarthy's out-of-state forays were not all triumphs; his appearance in the state of Washington was a fiasco in which he aborted two speeches and ended up squabbling with the Washington State Press Club and with KING-TV, Seattle's largest television station. On October 22 his plane was unable to reach Everett, Washington, because of fog, and he spoke at a rally for Cain by telephone from Vancouver. He got to Seattle in mid-afternoon, and skipped dinner to write the two "major speeches" he intended to deliver that night.

The first of these speeches was given at the Gridiron Dinner of the local press club, and McCarthy grew restless as he sat through a mock political convention. "I didn't travel 2,300 miles to be a funnyman," he grumbled. "I want to make a speech about some serious things the American people should know." The reporters told him he could make any kind of speech he wanted, but when he did speak, he found that the club's tradition called for heckling the speakers. McCarthy didn't like it. "Make your speech later," he yelled at one heckler in the gallery. "I've only got a few minutes." He started his usual speech about the tactics necessary in fighting Communists. "You can't fight skunks with kid gloves and lace cuffs," he said. Heckling and booing grew louder as he repeated his attack on General Marshall, and after 15 minutes he stopped, saying that he had to leave for the television station. There he was confronted with a demand that he delete from his prepared speech a charge that two employes of Drew Pearson had Communist affiliations, a charge that the station manager said might be libelous. McCarthy refused to make the deletions and stormed out, threatening to complain to the FCC.[15]

McCarthy's few speeches in Wisconsin consisted of innuendoes about Stevenson's Communist connections and threats of further revelations. On September 21 at Reedsburg, McCarthy said that Stevenson spent a great deal of his time talking about McCarthy. "That's because he knows we're checking his record from the time he went into the Agriculture Department at the time when Mother Bloor established a Communist cell," McCarthy said. "When we get through with Adlai we'll give him to the American people and then if anyone wants Adlai they can have him but I don't think they will."[16]

McCarthy drew an audience of 700 at the Reedsburg Lions Club dairy festival, and he was interrupted by applause 15 times. The crowd reacted most enthusiastically to his charge that the war in Korea was the work of Communists in Washington rather than an attempt to halt Communist aggression. On the day before, at the same event, Fairchild had drawn a crowd of only 400. There was no reaction whatever to his appeal for common sense and fair play, and only a few people came up afterward to shake hands.

It was during this period that McCarthy made the often-quoted remark that encouraged those who saw him as a potential fascist. He was speaking to the Wisconsin Buttermakers' and Managers' Association convention at Chippewa Falls. "If you'll give me a slippery elm club and put me aboard Adlai Stevenson's campaign train," he said, "I could use it on some of his advisers and I might be able to make a good American out of him."[17]

The speech McCarthy made on October 27 in Chicago, the major event of his campaign and one of the major events in the presidential campaign, was an equivalent of the "slippery elm club" speech. The *Chicago Tribune* reported that 6,000 people had contributed to pay for the broadcast of the speech over 55 television stations and 550 radio stations. McCarthy spoke before an audience of 1,700, of whom 1,286 had paid $50 a plate for dinner. The *New York Times* reported that $78,000 was collected in all.

McCarthy's speech charged that Stevenson and five "advisers"— Arthur M. Schlesinger, Jr., Bernard DeVoto, James Wechsler, Archibald MacLeish, and Wilson Wyatt—were sympathetic to Communism and had aided the Communist cause. He said that all of his charges were supported by public documents, and the occasion was advertised as McCarthy's "documentation" speech. The television audience certainly got the impression that documents backed up his charges; many in the audience probably also got an impression that McCarthy was actually calling these people Communists. Later studies proved that although the charges were related to the public documents McCarthy cited, in most cases the documents did not prove, and often disproved, the charges. In Wisconsin the story of the speech was a banner headline in almost every daily paper. It enabled McCarthy to dominate the news right up to the day of the election, as he amplified his charges, as others attacked him, and as he replied to his attackers. Fairchild was forgotten.

In the last week of the campaign, 832 news stories about McCarthy, Fairchild, or both appeared in Wisconsin's 39 daily newspapers and the three out-of-state papers with large circulations in Wisconsin. McCarthy's name appeared in the headlines above 665 of these stories—80 percent of them. Fairchild's name appeared in only 112 headlines—13.6 percent.

Students of the press have long been in agreement that the headline is the most important element of a news story, serving both as an index for the reader who is "shopping" the paper and as an ultimate, concentrated digest of the news story.[18] Surveys have shown that many readers advance no further than the headline and the first few lines of the lead; for them, this is the story. That is why it was so important when the writers of headlines played into McCarthy's hands in the early days of his anti-Communist adventure. By the end of 1952 the editors knew more about McCarthy and were not making that kind of mistake; the striking thing about headlines in 1952 was simply that the word *McCarthy* was in so many of them and *Fairchild* in so few.

This difference was multiplied by the placement of stories. Headlines containing McCarthy's name appeared on front pages 209 times. Every daily paper in the state had at least one page-one story with *McCarthy* in a headline during the last week before the election.

Headlines bearing Fairchild's name appeared on only 30 front pages and in only 14 of the 42 newspapers. In 12 papers, Fairchild's name appeared in no headline at all during the last week of the campaign. McCarthy's name appeared in headlines 35 times in each of three papers, the *Capital Times*, the *Wisconsin State Journal*, and the *Milwaukee Journal*. It appeared 20 or more times in nine other papers.

Patterns of partisanship were apparent in the use of headlines. In the *Appleton Post-Crescent*, for example, McCarthy's name appeared in 25 headlines, Fairchild's in two. In Green Bay it was 15 and two; in Beloit 11 and one; in Ashland 12 and one; and in Antigo 14 and none. The *Chicago Tribune* had 15 McCarthy headlines, none naming Fairchild. The *Milwaukee Sentinel's* score was 14 McCarthy, Fairchild none. The ratio was almost the same in papers that were officially neutral. In the *Marshfield News-Herald* it was 20 and two; in the *Wausau Record-Herald* 20 and three; the *La Crosse Tribune* 12 and two. And even the five papers that endorsed Fairchild gave McCarthy from three to six times as many headlines as they did Fairchild. (See table 2, p. 229, for details.)

There were so many McCarthy news stories, pro and con, available during this week that a news editor could pick and choose to suit his newspaper's politics, as shown by the list on page 233. An evaluation of the use of news stories favorable to or critical of each candidate shows clearly that Wisconsin papers extended editorial positions to the news pages through the process of news selection.

The *Capital Times*, opposing McCarthy, published 21 stories critical of McCarthy and only one that might be called favorable. It also published eight stories favorable to Fairchild. The *Milwaukee Journal* published 22 critical of McCarthy, nine favorable. For the *Sheboygan Press* it was 20 critical, five favorable. On the other side, the *Appleton Post-Crescent* printed 17 stories favorable to McCarthy, five unfavorable. The *Milwaukee Sentinel* printed nine favorable, two critical. In the *Green Bay Press-Gazette* it was 9-4; in the *Beloit Daily News*, 6-3; the *Ashland Press*, 11-1; the *Oshkosh Northwestern*, 20-5; and the *Antigo Journal*, 12-0.

The only exceptions were the *Wisconsin State Journal*, a pro-McCarthy paper which published 18 stories critical of McCarthy to 14 favorable, as well as four favoring Fairchild, and the *Twin Cities News-Record* in Neenah, also pro-McCarthy, in which the critical stories outnumbered the favorable 6-3. (See table 3, p. 230, for details.)

Every paper in Wisconsin carried a big story on the Chicago speech, and several ran the text. Then came statements from the people attacked, denying Communist leanings. Americans for Democratic Action (ADA), of which McCarthy had accused Stevenson of being a

founder (he wasn't even a member), restated its anti-Communist position. The Democratic national committee produced an analysis of
McCarthy's charges and a rebuttal to each charge. This story, distributed by the AP, ran several columns in the *Milwaukee Journal* and
the *New York Times*, two of the papers that used it. There were
statements praising McCarthy's speech by Governor Kohler, Senator
Taft, Senator Nixon (the Republican nominee for vice-president),
Thomas E. Coleman, Wisconsin GOP chairman, and Senator Dirksen.
There were denunciations of the speech by President Truman, Senator
Sparkman (the Democratic nominee for vice-president), Senator Benton, and George Haberman, Wisconsin AFL-CIO president. Almost
every columnist expressed an opinion, and almost every newspaper
delivered an editorial judgment on the speech.

Once again, by the delivery of outrageous charges, McCarthy had
maneuvered the media into utter concentration on him and the issues
he raised. Even those newspapers fighting him most doggedly fell into
the trap. The immediate effect was a blackout of news about Fairchild,
but the headlines that questioned Stevenson's loyalty may have had
an effect on the outcome of the presidential election, too, for example:
"Senator Hits Governor For 'Aid to Red Cause'; Calls Nominee Part
of Hiss-Lattimore-Acheson Group; Fits Together 'Jig Saw Puzzle' of
Candidate" (*Chicago Tribune*); "Stevenson Has Aided Red Cause,
McCarthy Charges" (*Minneapolis Star*); or "McCarthy Paints Adlai
as 'Soft' Toward Reds" (*Chicago Sun-Times*).

The attack on Stevenson provides one of the best examples of the
problem faced by reporters who tried to sort truth from falsehood in
a McCarthy speech, or who tried to make sense out of the jumble of
half-truths, out-of-context insinuations, and innuendoes—the problem
that caused the Washington wire service reporters to describe covering
McCarthy as "the most difficult story." This had been a problem for
reporters of the speech at Reno, Nevada, in February 1950, and of the
speech in the Senate—"the 81 cases"—later that month.

News stories reporting the Chicago speech show that editors and
reporters were attempting to answer McCarthy's charges at the same
time the charges were made. The *New York Times*, for instance,
wrote:

*McCarthy did not always make it clear just when Stevenson was
a member of such groups as the Institute for Pacific Relations. But in
listing Stevenson as a prominent member of the World Citizens Association, he said he had evidence that the Democratic nominee was
a member as late as 1948, although he said Stevenson's staff maintains
he was a member only in 1941.*[19]

The story distributed by the Associated Press for afternoon newspapers on October 28 included some reactions to the speech and the refutation of one of McCarthy's charges. McCarthy had said that his investigators had found 200,000 "astounding documents" in a Massachusetts barn, documents which showed that Communists in the Institute of Pacific Relations were shaping the policies of the State Department. One document, he said, showed that "Alger Hiss and Frank Coe recommended Adlai Stevenson as a delegate to a conference which was to determine our postwar policy in Asia," and that Hiss was a convicted traitor and Coe had been named under oath seven times as a member of the Communist party. "I repeat that I did not state that Stevenson was a Communist or pro-Communist, but I must believe that something was wrong somewhere," McCarthy said. The AP followed that with a parenthetical insert:

(McCarthy made some important omissions. The document, written in 1952, shows Hiss was so unacquainted with Stevenson that he referred to him as Stevens. He did correctly identify him by his position of assistant secretary of the navy. McCarthy failed to say the same document also suggested as speakers Admiral Thomas C. Hart, the former Republican senator from Connecticut, and Gardner Cowles, the publisher of the Des Moines, Ia., Register. McCarthy further failed to mention that there is no evidence that Stevenson was invited to speak or even attented the meeting.)[20]

None of the stories mentioned the remark that epitomized McCarthy's speech. This was the pretense of mis-speaking—"Alger . . . I mean Adlai"—a device McCarthy liked so much that he repeated it, with a giggle, admiring his own cleverness. It was not in the text.

In its editorial of October 29, the *Chicago Tribune* issued a challenge: "It was not a flamboyant speech. It was a careful collection and appraisal of evidence. The only answer to it is presentation of proof that Mr. McCarthy's evidence is faulty. It remains to be seen if Gov. Stevenson and his friends can make such an answer." Stevenson's friends did make an answer, a point-by-point refutation of 18 of McCarthy's charges issued by the Democratic National Committee on Saturday, November 1. The analysis was distributed that day by the Associated Press from Washington and was published in Sunday newspapers.*

---

*The principal writer of the analysis was Anthony Lewis, a researcher for the National Committee, later a reporter and columnist for the *Washington Daily News* and the *New York Times*. (Lewis interview, 25 January 1976.)

What follows is an excerpt from the speech in which McCarthy sought to plant the idea that Stevenson had been endorsed by the Communist party, and the Democratic reply, as both were reported in the *New York Times* of 2 November 1952:

McCarthy Said:

"I hold in my hand a photostat of the Daily Worker of Oct. 19, 1952. That is only eight days old. They damn [Gen. Dwight D.] Eisenhower and Eisenhowerism. They refer, and I quote, 'to our hatred for Eisenhower' and then go on to say that they do not like Stevenson too well. They slap him on the wrist and say if Communists want to vote for Stevenson—go ahead and do it but don't vote straight down the line. Vote for Communist-controlled Progressive party candidates and pile up a big vote for those Communist candidates on the ticket."

The Facts:

Nowhere in the Daily Worker for Oct. 19, 1952, nor for any other date, does there appear any such statement. What the editorial for the date cited by Senator McCarthy does say (in part) is:

"(Some) who are deeply troubled by the war in Korea and who have begun to see that the Democratic party today is, in fact, a war party, are even grasping at the 'peace' demagogy of Eisenhower.

"For our part, we believe only a vote for the Progressive party will register a positive vote for peace. We believe that those who will vote Progressive, constitute the most alert and most militant section of the population and that the American people, as they become more conscious of the truth, will turn to them for leadership.

"The best way to register the true will of the people is, of course, through getting the biggest possible vote for Vincent Hallinan and Mrs. Charlotta Bass, and through the best possible results in local Progressive, coalition and Communist campaigns."

[McCarthy's charge, however, impressed the editors of at least two small Wisconsin newspapers, whose headlines on October 28 read: "McCarthy Says Reds Support Stevenson; Quotes from Article in Daily Worker" (*Baraboo News-Republic*); and "McCarthy Says Reds Endorse Adlai" (*Jefferson County Union*).]

Whether or not Stevenson introduced Alger Hiss at a Northwestern University lecture proved be fairly easy to check. Again, from the November 2 Times:

McCarthy Said:

"Whether or not Stevenson introduced Hiss [at a Northwestern University lecture Nov. 12, 1946] is relatively unimportant [but] I am

curious, so I made some check as to his veracity [in saying he was not in Chicago Nov. 12 and so could not have introduced Hiss]. In the news of Nov. 11, 1946, it was reported that Stevenson would make a speech at 4 P.M. the following day at the University of Chicago. Stevenson, we have found, was paid the sum of $250 for appearing to make that speech that day."

The Facts:

Governor Stevenson's University of Chicago lecture, "Civil-Military Relations in the U.N.," for which he was paid $250, was originally scheduled for Nov. 12, 1946, but postponed to Nov. 21.

Prof. Jerome Kirwin, a political science professor at the University of Chicago, made a study of the university's official calendar and found that Stevenson had delivered his lecture on Nov. 21. The calendar carried this note: "Postponed from Nov. 12." The $250 check presented to Stevenson also carried the Nov. 21 date.

Governor Stevenson was not in Chicago Nov. 12 and never introduced Hiss in any lecture.

A number of McCarthy's charges were directed at Schlesinger; Schlesinger had written much on the issue of Communism. McCarthy's technique was to extract one sentence, or part of a sentence, removing it from context. The example the Times gave was typical:

McCarthy Said:

"Perhaps the most revealing article written by Stevenson's speech writer appeared in The New York Times on Dec. 11, 1949, on page 3, and listen to this, if you will. I quote: he says: 'I happen to believe— I happen to believe that the Communist party should be granted the freedom of political action and that Communists should be allowed to teach in universities.'

"Nothing secret, nothing's secret about it, it's in The New York Times Dec. 11, 1949, Stevenson's speech writer saying I think that Communists should be allowed to teach your children, my good friends."

The Facts:

The New York Times article referred to is found on Page 3, Book Review Section, Dec. 11, 1949. It is a review by Schlesinger of "Primer of Intellectual Freedom," edited by Howard Mumford Jones. McCarthy quoted part of one sentence from the review. The prepared text of McCarthy's speech quoted the complete sentence, but it can be doubted that McCarthy ever intended to read it. The full sentence from the review follows:

"I happen to believe that the Communist party should be granted freedom of political action and that Communists should be allowed to teach in universities so long as they do not disqualify themselves by intellectual distortions in the classroom."

The body of the Schlesinger book review was a sharp criticism of Professor Jones for underestimating the threat of communism in "Primer of Intellectual Freedom." These are some excerpts from the review which McCarthy did not read:

"Fascism first disclosed sinister possibilities in the total manipulation of thought and belief; the U.S.S.R. has now extended the same possibilities into an appalling campaign to rewrite history, to expurgate philosophy and to enslave science. . . . Nowhere does [Jones] suggest that communism is a totalitarian faith with grave implications for the freedom of inquiry. . . . To write in 1949 as if communism was in no sense a threat to liberty is vastly to misrepresent the whole problem of preserving liberty. Professor Jones' solicitude about intellectual freedom would be more impressive if there were any evidence that it extended to those suffering under Soviet totalitarianism."

Again, in attacking James Wechsler, editor of the New York Post, McCarthy told only part of the story, as the Times showed, and the omissions made the statement an actual lie:

McCarthy Said:

"The next—one of the men selected by Stevenson as one of his ghost writers—is a man Jim—James Wechsler. Wechsler and his wife both admit—both admit having been members of the Young Communist League. . . . Some light is shed on the importance of this man in the Stevenson camp by the list of long-distance phone calls between the Governor's office in Springfield and this man who says 'I belonged to the Young Communist League'—Wechsler. Here's a list of the phone calls between Wechsler and the Governor's Mansion.

The Facts:

Wechsler and his wife have openly stated they were members of the Young Communist League during college days. They renounced communism in 1937, long before Whittaker Chambers, Elizabeth Bentley or Louis Budenz, and for the past fifteen years have been among the most active anti-Communist crusaders in the United States. Alicia Patterson, a niece of Col. Robert R. McCormick and a director of The Chicago Tribune, wrote in her newspaper Newsday:

"Wechsler has admitted, openly and whenever asked, that he was a member of the Young Communist League while he was in college; he has asserted, and the assertion has not been gainsaid, that he quit the Commies in 1937 and has fought them ever since. His record in the last fifteen years bears that out.

"I do not happen to agree with many of Wechsler's views, but never-theless he has been engaged in a steady and effective attack on Stalin and his cohorts."

Governor Stevenson's Springfield headquarters, as is customary with all political campaign headquarters, has been in frequent tele-phone communication with major metropolitan newspapers. This in-cludes papers which support Eisenhower—The New York Times and The Chicago Tribune.

McCarthy's attack on Bernard DeVoto, the historian and magazine columnist, again told only part of the story. McCarthy chose to make it appear suspicious by quoting the *Daily Worker* on the facts; the story had also appeared in the *New York Times* and other papers.

McCarthy Said:

"The Communist Daily Worker on Feb. 13, 1947, reports that Ste-venson's man (Bernard) DeVoto headed a group seeking a permit for a meeting for the wife of Gerhardt Eisler the Communist who had disappeared behind the Iron Curtain and who as of tonight is heading up the anti-Communist (sic) group in East Berlin."

The Facts:

Mr. DeVoto led a delegation from the anti-Communist American Civil Liberties Union in February, 1947, protesting attempts to ban a speech by Eisler's wife. Neither Mr. DeVoto nor the Civil Liberties Union had anything to do with arranging the speech, but they upheld anyone's right to talk. Acting Mayor John B. Kelley of Boston con-curred in their view, and refused to revoke the license.

Mr. DeVoto said, Oct. 28, 1952: "I did nothing then I would not do for Joe McCarthy. I think the United States will survive both McCarthy and the Communists."

An even more detailed analysis of the October 27 speech and an-other that McCarthy made on the night of November 3 in Appleton was made by a Northwestern University law professor, Willard H. Pedrick, in 1953. Professor Pedrick concluded that the speeches were libelous but that it was probably not worth suing McCarthy. He wrote:

On the basis of the analysis set out at considerable length above, it seems clear that under the law of many states, if not all, the two McCarthy speeches under consideration were libelous. The charge of sympathy for and aid to Communism is defamatory and cannot be defended as true on the facts claimed by the Senator. Nor should the charges be privileged as fair comment. . . .

All things considered it would not be at all sensible for the indi-

viduals concerned to sue on the basis of the two McCarthy speeches. The law of libel like the "munificent bequest of a pauper's will is a promise to the ear to be broken to the heart." The sad fact is that notwithstanding all the pious doctrine, virtually any sort of baseless charge can be made in this country against a candidate and his supporters.[21]

If McCarthy's statements were libelous, so were most of the headlines with which newspapers reported the story. Among the 42 daily newspapers in and around Wisconsin, 22 reported in headlines that McCarthy had accused Stevenson of giving help (or aid) to Communist (or Red) causes. Another 19 said that Stevenson was "surrounded by" or "linked to" "leftists" or "left-wingers." Others said Stevenson was charged with being a member of "the Acheson-Hiss-Lattimore group" or that he was advocating "Kremlin-shaped policies."

Papers supporting General Eisenhower pointed out that no one in the Eisenhower camp had approved McCarthy's attack. "The speech was really made on behalf of extreme right-wingers of the McCarthy stripe who are seeking re-election," said the *New York Times.* The *Washington Post,* however, called upon Eisenhower to repudiate McCarthy's allegations.

In the opinion of the *Washington Post* of 29 October, it was impossible to assess the effect of McCarthy's speech. Some people, it said, might be impelled to switch to Stevenson out of sheer revulsion, and others might go the other way because of McCarthy's assertion that the success or failure of international communism was at stake.

Most of the newspapers opposing McCarthy took the position that the speech would not affect the voting. "Senator McCarthy's widely advertised 'exposure' of Governor Adlai Stevenson fell flat in the mud," wrote the *Pittsburgh Post-Gazette* on October 30. "The American people had a look at Senator Joseph R. McCarthy in action Monday evening," said the *Cleveland Plain Dealer* on October 28, "and a majority of them, we are convinced, did not like what they saw. . . . Besides being intemperate, McCarthy's speech was unconvincing and ineffective and we do not believe it aided the cause of Gen. Eisenhower." "The 'Stevenson Story' written by that well-known author, Senator Joseph R. McCarthy, is not likely to hit any best-seller list," said the *Washington Star* on October 28. "For it is composed of the same old frothy material, high in coloration but short in substance, that went into the production of the Senator's earlier Communist 'exposes.' " The *Baltimore Sun* wrote on October 29, "After listening to the $76,000 McCarthy harangue and checking with a bipartisan segment of local observers, it is our conclusion that the 'great exposure' changed not a single vote. The voters who were for Stevenson are still for him and those who were for Eisenhower still incline that way."

But not all newspapers were sure that McCarthy had been unconvincing. The *Christian Science Monitor* expressed the opinion, on October 29, that "it is quite possible that honorable men, including a candidate for the nation's highest office, have been damaged. . . . Too many Americans are ready to find fellow citizens guilty without waiting for courts or even to hear what the accused has to say." "By inference, insinuation, and innuendo," wrote the *Sheboygan Press* on October 31, "McCarthy creates the impression that anyone who likes Adlai is a, well, maybe not a Communist, but certainly 'soft to communism.' . . . The claim that Stevenson is 'soft to communism' is fantastic. Yet this is precisely the impression McCarthy deliberately creates and brazenly wants you to accept without any foundation in fact."

My assessment is that the speech did hurt Stevenson. In those days, the mere accusation of being "soft on Communism" made people suspicious of the targeted person. The Eisenhower people played this cleverly; their advance statement of dissociation freed Eisenhower of direct responsibility, and he could accept the benefits of the attack without onus. He did not, as the *Washington Post* and other papers demanded, repudiate the speech. The page-one banner in the *New York Times* on Sunday, October 26, the day before the McCarthy speech, was "Eisenhower Tells Harlem He'll Fight Bias; Says Rival Favors Appeasing Communism." The news story said that Eisenhower had issued a statement saying that Stevenson had laid down a "soothing and appeasing formula" for combatting Communism and had taken "not one single exception to the course of action and policy" pursued in Asia by the Truman administration.

Some people were impressed by McCarthy's "documentation" and reacted as did the *Green Bay Press-Gazette* in an editorial on November 1: "Before Senator McCarthy made his nationwide broadcast last Monday the reply of Little Steve [the *Press-Gazette*'s fanciful name for Stevenson] had been outlined. It consisted of Smear! Smear! Smear! It continued in that way without regard for the meaty propositions that McCarthy established from written texts."

Many people said in 1952 that the newspapers fighting McCarthy were actually helping him, that the stream of critical editorials, the large number of stories and columns out of Washington, and the exposure of his personal and financial derelictions had made a martyr of him and had created a wave of sympathy that would be translated into votes on November 4. Those who said this most often were McCarthy sympathizers—there were a few of these even in the *Mil-*

waukee Journal's editorial offices—but some people believed it. McCarthy tried to play for the "sympathy vote" in the campaign; in almost every speech, he said that he was being smeared by those vicious left-wing newspapers, the *Milwaukee Journal* and the *Capital Times*.

The obvious way to determine whether and how newspaper opposition to McCarthy did affect the vote is to compare the vote in the 1946 Senate race with that of 1952 in the newspapers' circulation areas. The same test can be applied to areas in which newspapers supported McCarthy in 1952.

One of the first to speculate about this question was Louis H. Bean, the political analyst who had achieved fame by correctly predicting President Truman's reelection in 1948. Bean examined the characteristics of voters in counties that gave McCarthy a higher percentage of the vote in 1952 than in 1946 and in counties that swung most drastically away from McCarthy in 1952.[22] He found that McCarthy had improved his standing among farmers, in low-income areas, and among the less-well-educated. To him, the most significant point in his analysis was that metropolitan and urban centers had turned sharply against McCarthy in 1952. "The press is undoubtedly partly responsible for his [McCarthy's] loss in political strength in the Milwaukee and Madison areas and his failure to make headway except in rural areas where knowledge of his character and his methods is not widespread," Bean concluded.

Of the 42 daily newspapers circulating in Wisconsin in 1952, including three out-of-state papers with significant circulation in the state, 16 endorsed McCarthy; five endorsed Fairchild. The rest made no endorsement in the Senate race.

Newspapers that endorsed Fairchild were these:

The *Milwaukee Journal*, which ran three pro-Fairchild and four anti-McCarthy editorials in the last week of the campaign, and 22 news stories unfavorable to McCarthy as against nine that might be considered favorable. Four stories favored Fairchild.

The *Capital Times*, which carried one pro-Fairchild and six anti-McCarthy editorials, as well as 21 stories critical of McCarthy and eight favorable to Fairchild.

The *Sheboygan Press*, which carried one editorial endorsing Fairchild and five criticizing McCarthy, 20 stories critical of McCarthy and five favorable, and eight stories favorable to Fairchild.

The *Eau Claire Leader*, with one editorial endorsing Fairchild and six news stories favorable to and six critical of McCarthy.

The *Eau Claire Telegram* (same ownership), with one pro-Fairchild editorial, six news stories favorable to and 10 critical of McCarthy, and two stories favorable to Fairchild.*

The *Chicago Sun-Times* ran four editorials criticizing McCarthy and 12 critical news stories against two favorable. The *Minneapolis Star* ran one editorial criticizing McCarthy, and critical news stories outnumbered the favorable eight to two. Neither of these papers made an endorsement.

On McCarthy's side were these:

The *Appleton Post-Crescent*, which published three editorials supporting McCarthy that week, and 17 news stories favorable to against five critical of him.

The *Green Bay Press-Gazette* (same ownership), which ran three pro-McCarthy editorials, nine favorable news stories, and four critical ones.

The *Milwaukee Sentinel*, three pro-McCarthy editorials, and nine stories favorable to him against two unfavorable.

The *Oshkosh Northwestern*, five pro-McCarthy editorials, 10 stories favorable and five unfavorable to McCarthy, and three stories favorable to Fairchild.

The *Chicago Tribune*, four pro-McCarthy editorials, including an endorsement, nine stories favorable to him and five unfavorable.

The *Janesville Gazette*, two pro-McCarthy editorials, and four favorable stories to two unfavorable. Coverage was relatively light.

The *Antigo Journal*, whose pro-McCarthy passion matched the emotional level of the anti-McCarthy *Capital Times*, endorsed Eisenhower and McCarthy in an editorial which also blasted the *Milwaukee Journal*, Senator Wayne Morse of Oregon, who had campaigned in the state against McCarthy, and Leonard Schmitt, with whom they were still angry. The *Antigo Journal* also denounced the "rabid literature" of a farm committee supporting Fairchild. The *Journal* ran 12 news stories favorable to McCarthy and none critical.

The *Wisconsin State Journal*, with three editorials backing McCarthy, was an exception to the general rule in that its news stories critical of McCarthy outnumbered its favorable stories 18 to 14, and it carried four favorable to Fairchild.

Seven other papers carried one editorial each endorsing McCarthy, and all carried about twice as many favorable news stories as unfa-

*The Eau Claire papers were like two editions of the same paper. The morning paper's circulation was almost entirely outside the city and the evening paper's within it.

vorable. They were the *Beloit Daily News, Marinette Eagle-Star, Waukesha Freeman, Jefferson County Union, Monroe Evening Times, Two Rivers Reporter,* and *Manitowoc Herald-Times.* The *Twin Cities Record,* in Neenah, also endorsed McCarthy but carried more critical news stories than favorable. (See table 3, p. 230, for a detailed tabulation.)

In mid-October, Fairchild issued a statement saying that Wisconsin editors had been intimidated by McCarthy: "I have talked to editors who have stated they are on my side but do not feel they can say so in their newspapers. The right of the press to take and express a stand on any subject is basic to American democracy. If it fails, then all the freedoms we cherish are in similar danger."[23] Fairchild, now Chief Judge, U.S. Court of Appeals for the Seventh Circuit (Chicago), has written me that he no longer remembers which editors he was talking about but that he does remember "frustration about news coverage. ... It seemed also that when we got a story, the headline was more likely to be 'Foe Hits McCarthy' than to reflect my name." Fairchild wrote that "in fairness," he thought that his press coverage might have suffered because of his decision to run an affirmative campaign stressing economic and other traditionally Democratic issues rather than attacking McCarthy. He and his campaign strategists decided on this course in the hope of retaining the support of normally Democratic voters who might have been swayed by McCarthy's anti-Communist image. He said, further, that he had been thoroughly discouraged until about the middle of October. He had entered the primary late, in July, and was still in debt from his 1950 run for the Senate against Wiley. He was not really prepared for the campaign and was fearful of making "off-the-cuff" attacks on McCarthy lest they be shown up as lacking documentation. The out-of-state anti-McCarthy money had gone to Schmitt, and it took a long time to convince people and newspapers that a Democratic candidate against McCarthy had a chance. Ultimately the money came, but much of it came too late. "I remember a trip through the central part of the state visiting editors of weeklies, making the traditional street speeches and the like, and wondering why on earth I was doing it," Fairchild wrote. Late in October, though, there was a change, and support started coming from people he had no reason to feel were on his side. "My own explanation of the change in attitude is the speech Joe made in mid-October to the effect that he would like to climb on the Stevenson train with a slippery elm club and make good Americans out of the Stevenson campaign workers. Up to that point, the idea that McCarthy and Hitler might have something in common got no reception. After that speech, people started to make the point for themselves."[24]

One paper whose editor would have liked to endorse Fairchild but didn't was the *Racine Journal-Times*, edited by the brother of Howard McMurray, the Democratic nominee whom McCarthy had defeated in 1946. James O'Brien, the *Journal-Times* editorial writer, says that the editor, Donald McMurray, was trying to shift the paper's editorial position away from the 100 percent Republicanism of the previous publisher, Frank Starbuck, McMurray's father-in-law. The first gradual step in this direction was the decision not to endorse either candidate in the Senate race; O'Brien and McMurray thought that this was as far as they could go at that time without offending their readers. In Racine, no endorsement was interpreted as an anti-McCarthy position, and it helped Fairchild in Racine County.[25] Another paper which followed the same pattern was the *Wausau Record-Herald*, which had criticized McCarthy editorially but made no endorsement. The *Watertown Times* made no endorsement but carried 10 news stories critical of McCarthy and only two favorable during the last week of the campaign.

The *Milwaukee Journal's* influence in its primary circulation zones was dramatically evident. In the "city zone," where *Journal* circulation reached saturation, McCarthy's share of the vote was 17 percent less in 1952 than it had been in 1946. Further afield, in the 10 counties in the *Journal's* "retail trading zone," McCarthy's vote dropped 8.5 percent, despite the fact that several smaller newspapers in this zone—the southeast quarter of the state—supported McCarthy. In all but three of the 11 counties in these two zones (and those three were on the outer fringes of the retail trading zone), McCarthy ran far behind the eight-year average Republican vote for the county, while Eisenhower and Kohler ran well ahead of the GOP average in every county (see table 4, p. 231).[26]

The effect of vigorous newspaper opposition to McCarthy was equally clear in Dane, Sheboygan, and Eau Claire counties. In Dane County (Madison), home of the *Capital Times*, the McCarthy vote had been relatively low in 1946 (48 percent); it fell off another 10 percent in 1952. In Sheboygan County, where *Milwaukee Journal* influence reinforced the campaign of the *Sheboygan Press* against McCarthy, the McCarthy vote fell off by 10 percent. In the city of Sheboygan, the drop was 14.3 percent. In Eau Claire County, where the two local papers endorsed Fairchild, the McCarthy vote fell off 10 percent, too. The nearby Minneapolis newspapers, which had also criticized McCarthy, probably augmented the local influence. In Dane, Sheboygan, and Eau Claire counties and in Milwaukee and its two nearest suburban counties, McCarthy ran—in this landslide year for the Republicans—more than 9 percent behind the eight-year Republican average. He lagged behind Governor Kohler by an average of 16 percent, indicating that large numbers of normally Republican voters were splitting tickets to vote for Fairchild.

The effect of vigorous newspaper support of McCarthy was also clear. In Brown County, where the *Green Bay Press-Gazette* backed McCarthy faithfully, the McCarthy vote rose from 65 percent in 1946 to 67 percent, reversing the statewide trend. In the city of Green Bay, where the influence of the paper would be expected to be greatest, the McCarthy vote rose even more—by 4 percent. In Outagamie County, where the *Appleton Post-Crescent* supported McCarthy, the McCarthy share of the vote declined only slightly, from 71 percent to 70, and his vote in the city of Appleton rose almost 1 percent, from 71.5 to 72.3. In neighboring Neenah-Menasha, where the *Twin Cities Record* had endorsed McCarthy, the senator's 1952 share of the vote rose by one-half of 1 percent. The *Post-Crescent* also circulated in these cities. In Janesville, McCarthy's share rose by 3 percent, as it did in Antigo, where the local paper had backed him so fiercely.

Statewide, McCarthy's vote declined by 7 percent from his vote in 1946, so that a decline of less than 7 percent constituted a shift from the state norm in McCarthy's favor. This could be interpreted as meaning that declines of 4 percent in Marinette, 5 percent in Beloit, and 6 percent in Oshkosh were actually evidence of pro-McCarthy influence. Applying this standard, McCarthy's share of the 1952 vote exceeded the state norm in every area where a local daily newspaper supported him, outside of the *Milwaukee Journal-Capital Times* zones of influence. (See table 5, p. 231, for details of vote shifts.)

In the Milwaukee area, the *Sentinel's* endorsement of McCarthy, and that of the suburban *Waukesha Freeman*, had no visible effect. In Waukesha, McCarthy's vote fell off 23 percent from 1946; this decline, however, undoubtedly stems primarily from the fact that Waukesha County was Milwaukee's most rapidly growing suburb in those six years, and many who voted there in 1952 were city people who had brought their political allegiances with them when they moved out. In the Madison area, the McCarthy vote declined sharply despite the support of the *Wisconsin State Journal*, whose daily circulation was only a little less than that of the *Capital Times*, and which published the only Sunday paper, with a circulation of 68,748.

This pattern seems to indicate that full information about McCarthy was more important than editorial campaigns, as Bean had hinted. Readers in Milwaukee and Madison had access to a great deal of information about McCarthy that was not available in remoter parts of the state.

There were nearly 300 weekly newspapers in Wisconsin in 1952, and since most readers of weekly newspapers are likely to be subjected to the influence of some daily newspaper, the effect of the weeklies on their readers' opinions is more difficult to ascertain. About 10 percent of them opposed McCarthy in their editorial columns, and about 20 percent supported him. Most weeklies endorsed one or more—or all—Republicans, often without naming them. But when weekly editors did take a strong position on one side or the other of the McCarthy issue, they seemed to have an effect on the McCarthy vote in the city or the village in which the weekly was published (see table 6, p. 232). The influence of small newspapers was not unimportant. As Ben H. Bagdikian, a shrewd observer of newspaper practice, wrote in *The Effete Conspiracy*, "Because rural papers have a disproportionate political impact and because they happen to be the major carriers of canned opinion, we are confronted with a perverse rule: The smaller the newspaper, the greater its relative influence in national politics."[27]

In most places, it took courage on the part of a weekly editor to take a stand against McCarthy. The angry readers who telephoned or wrote to the reporters or editors of a metropolitan paper were either politicans or strangers, but in a small town the people who were angry were neighbors, fellow church members, merchants, advertisers—the people the editors saw every day. Life for these editors was a series of angry confrontations.

To oppose McCarthy in a small town could also be dangerous commercially. McCarthy's attempts to institute advertising boycotts of *Time* magazine and the *Milwaukee Journal* never had any perceptible effect, and a few lost ads would not have hurt either publication. But the loss of a major advertising account could be a serious thing for a weekly paper, and at least one weekly, the *Delavan Enterprise*, suffered such a loss after Robert F. Rogan, editor and publisher, criticized McCarthy for his attack on General Marshall. "It wasn't a very vicious editorial," Rogan said. "I took a crack at the Senator for putting Eisenhower on the defensive by having to defend his friend and super-patriot, General Marshall. I pointed out that as far as Americanism is concerned, I'll take the Marshall brand in preference to McCarthy's." Rogan didn't blame McCarthy for the lost account but said that the action represented a "trend" in the community. "All the people who care about politics in Delavan are for McCarthy," he said, "and it's like a religion with them."[28]

Political opinion on McCarthy varied more in the weeklies than in the daily newspapers. Views expressed were more personal, often emotional and less inhibited. News coverage was spotty, sometimes concentrated on one party, sometimes punctiliously fair.

At least two of the anti-McCarthy weeklies—the *Rice Lake Chron-*

otype and the *Grant County Independent*—handled the campaign
with flair and professionalism. The quality of writing in the editorial
columns was good, and news stories were informative. The *Chronotype*, with a circulation of 4,781 (1950), was one of the largest weeklies
in the state. Its editor and publisher was Warren D. Leary. Rice Lake
is in Barron County, in the northwestern quarter of the state, the
largest city in the 150 miles between Chippewa Falls, in the center,
and Superior, at the northern corner. Most of the statewide candidates
stopped there to campaign. For a weekly, the *Chronotype* carried an
uncommonly large amount of political news. In the last month before
the election, its coverage seemed balanced, with news of candidates
of both parties, including McCarthy and Fairchild. Editorially, however, it said that McCarthy lacked integrity and that he constituted
"a dire threat to our basic liberties." In the final week, the paper
endorsed Fairchild and Stevenson. That last issue also carried two
full pages of Republican advertisements and one small Fairchild ad
headed "Smash Communism in the Courtroom," intended to demonstrate that Fairchild, too, was against Communists. Was the paper
influential? In Barron County, McCarthy's share of the 1952 vote fell
off 2 percent from 1946, and in Rice Lake itself, the McCarthy vote
fell 7 percent.

The *Grant County Independent*, in Lancaster, was owned and edited by Norman Clapp, a former aide to Senator La Follette who later
became chairman of the Wisconsin Public Service Commission. The
paper (circulation 1,481) regularly won prizes for excellence in state
newspaper judgings. Its hometown was in the southwestern corner
of the state, the corn-belt country where the Republican vote averaged
about 80 percent. Clapp's aggressive journalism and his political views
were resented in Lancaster, and he was bitter when he sold out in
1960. His comment in 1976 was that he was sure he had influenced
no one on the McCarthy issue. He said that the *Independent* could
be influential on local matters but that when it came to state or national
affairs "we couldn't reach them."[29]

On October 3, 1952, Clapp criticized Republicans for being cynical
by being happy because a military general had said that there were
Communists in the CIA. On October 10 he wrote that McCarthy's
record on farm legislation showed that he was not interested in ag-
ricultural issues. He reprinted an editorial from a nearby weekly
which contrasted Fairchild's calm approach to the Communist problem with that of a McCarthy spokesman who bluntly advocated guilt
by association. On October 24 the paper endorsed Stevenson, saying
that Eisenhower had lost its respect by failing to stand up to McCarthy.
On October 31, in an editorial headed "There's a Moral Issue in

Tuesday's Election," the *Independent* said, "The real issue in Mc-Carthy's re-election is decency, honesty and the respect for the individual American's right to think and speak without fear. Tom Fairchild, the Democratic candidate, is a man of the highest character and integrity, as well as a man of proven ability."

Despite Clapp's pessimism, the *Grant County Independent* did have an effect. The voters of Lancaster cast 4 percent fewer votes for McCarthy than did the voters in Grant County as a whole. They were a little less in favor of McCarthy in 1952 than they had been in 1946, while in the county the McCarthy vote rose 3.5 percent over 1946. The numbers were small, but the direction was clear.

No editor fought McCarthy more exuberantly than Abe Van Meter of the *New Richmond News*, in west-central Wisconsin. Van Meter disliked both McCarthy and Nixon but urged votes for Eisenhower "even if it means voting for Poor Richard, too." His name for McCarthy was "Polecat Joe." He had his own cartoonist, unusual for a weekly, and on October 9 a cartoon showed a weary Eisenhower, weighed down by millstones labeled "Tearful Nix," "Polecat Joe," and "Wisconsin Old Guard." In his column "Honest Abe" on October 16, Van Meter suggested that Fairchild had a good chance of winning. The headline on a story about Fairchild's speech in New Richmond said that the candidate made a "fine impression." On October 23 a cartoon in the *News* caricatured McCarthy grinning as he prepared to beat Stevenson with a slippery elm club. On October 30 "Honest Abe" warned that McCarthy would say you were a Communist if you voted for Democrats. His final editorial, endorsing Fairchild, seemed to show a weakening of his support for Eisenhower. "We could get a worse deal than we got with the Democrats, especially if the Republicans are going to let Polecat Joe run loose. . . . We'll rue the day we let the polecat get the upper hand." The McCarthy vote in 1952 declined 4 percent from 1946 in New Richmond, but Van Meter's campaign could not be considered successful on the basis of a comparison with the vote in the county. The McCarthy vote in St. Croix County declined even more—by 7 percent. On another basis of comparison—McCarthy's vote versus Governor Kohler's—the *News* ranked as highly influential, however. In New Richmond, McCarthy ran 13 percent behind Kohler.

Some of the papers on McCarthy's side were equally vigorous. (See table 7, p. 232, for vote shifts favoring McCarthy.) In the *Peshtigo Times*, in northeastern Wisconsin, every story, column, and editorial in the last month of the campaign was a variation of the charge that Democrats were Communists. On October 9 in an editorial headed "Let's Face Facts on Senator Joe," the *Times* contended that McCarthy had exposed Alger Hiss, that he was right in attacking General Marshall, that his charges had resulted in 2,004 "loyalty dismissals," and that he had been "vilified in the public press." On October 16 the paper published a column by Senator Wiley (who had been frightened by McCarthy's primary victory) which said that "the fight against atheistic Communism does count" and that Democratic tactics were "cover up, shut up, and smear up." A week later, the paper endorsed Eisenhower, Kohler, and McCarthy in a front-page editor's column which declared that there was "no 'delicate' way of driving Communists out of their holes." It also said that there had been Communists in government as far back as 1917 and that the Democrats had done nothing about it. On October 30 the *Times* urged its readers to vote for "Ike and Joe and the rest of the Republican candidates." In Peshtigo, the McCarthy vote in 1952 declined by 5 percent, while the McCarthy vote in surrounding Marinette County went down 8 percent from 1946. McCarthy even ran ahead of Kohler in Peshtigo, making it, by this standard, the most effective of the pro-McCarthy weeklies.

The *Chilton Times-Journal*, in east-central Wisconsin, on 28 August 1952 attacked General Eisenhower for being "wishy-washy" in his support for McCarthy and said that the general had blessed the New Deal, approved the war in Korea, and failed to attack Stevenson for giving a character deposition for Alger Hiss. There was nothing left to campaign on, it lamented. On 12 July 1951 the paper had written, "The American people know there have been Communists in government from the records of convictions and confessions. They know there are in it 'liberals' who do the work of Communists. They admire McCarthy for braving the criticism and scorn to do a job that he—and they—believe should be done." The McCarthy vote in Chilton rose 8 percent over 1946, while the vote in Calumet County, of which Chilton is a part, rose only 4 percent.

The *New London Press-Republican*, in northeastern Wisconsin, supported all Republicans. In his "Chatter Box" column, the editor told his readers that he had lived in Alabama and knew that Senator Sparkman, Stevenson's running mate, was bigoted. He said that he liked Taft best but could "make do" with Eisenhower and Nixon. On October 16 he ridiculed Fairchild for saying that some Wisconsin editors were abstaining from supporting him out of "fear." Fairchild might have been ignored by the press because they didn't know he was in town, he said. Fairchild came to New London without any "public warning," and he himself had heard about it only later. The next week the paper did cover a Fairchild speech in detail, with a picture. The rest of the stories were about Republicans. The paper urged a straight Republican vote. McCarthy's share of the vote in New

London rose 2.5 percent over his vote in 1946, while his vote in surrounding Outagamie County declined by 1 percent.

The *Vilas County News-Review*, in Eagle River, supported McCarthy fiercely. "Yep, we're 100% for Sen. Joe McCarthy, and we know why," the editor wrote in a column on 28 February 1952. "We know that if the rotten smears and foul blows he is being dealt finally bring him, battered and bloody, to defeat, it will mean the end of representative government, government by the people, and the beginning of government by 'smear gangs.' " The "parlor pinks" and the "pseudo-intellectuals" were using "every dirty, foul, gouging, groin-punching, rabbit-punching trick in the books," the editor said, but McCarthy was fighting "like a freight conductor leaping from ice-covered car to ice-covered car, when a false step means death." The McCarthy vote in Eagle River, where McCarthy often vacationed, rose by 3 percent over 1946. So did the McCarthy vote in Vilas County.

On the basis of comparing the local vote with the vote in the surrounding county, the campaigns of eight of the 15 anti-McCarthy weeklies could be considered effective. The others of the eight, besides those mentioned, were the *Darlington Republican-Journal*, the *Delavan Enterprise*, the *Glenwood City Tribune*, the *Mauston Star*, the *Montello Tribune*, and the *Monroe County Democrat*. Six of the eleven pro-McCarthy papers could be considered effective: those discussed, as well as the two pro-McCarthy papers in Richland Center.

A comparison of McCarthy's vote with Kohler's brings slightly different results. Among the anti-McCarthy weeklies, the *Mellen Record* would be seen as the most influential; McCarthy ran 15.4 percent behind Kohler in Mellen. By this standard, other effective anti-McCarthy papers, besides those mentioned, were the ones in Sparta (-10 percent) and in Montello and Delavan (-9 percent). The other effective pro-McCarthy papers were in Eagle River (even), Marion (-.5 percent), Richland Center (-1.4 percent), and Mosinee (-2.5 percent).

Although it is not as clearly defined as in the case of the dailies, evidence supports the view that where a weekly newspaper outside the sphere of influence of a strong daily took a stand on McCarthy, it did influence the voting in the local community.

There is no way in which newspapers could have avoided giving McCarthy the massive, disproportionate coverage he got during the last week of the campaign. The Chicago speech attacking Stevenson was news, as were the rebuttals and counter-charges that filled the newspapers during the last week. Other things, however, might have been done differently.

If editors had not been so impressed with the size of McCarthy's vote in the primary, and if that vote had been interpreted as something other than a Democratic crossover to McCarthy, Fairchild's campaign might not have been so universally viewed as hopeless. Money might have been more forthcoming and the campaign regarded as newsworthy.

Newspaper opposition, no matter how unrelenting, did not help McCarthy; it hurt him. Those opposing McCarthy need not have doubted. If more editors had realized how vulnerable McCarthy was, if more editors had not underestimated their own power to influence their readers, and if more editors had been willing to stand up to the vociferous McCarthy supporters in their own communities, the result on 4 November 1952 might have been different.

5.

The "Camp-Following, Mocking-Bird, Bleeding-Heart, Left-Wing" Press

OUTAGAMIE COUNTY Judge Urban Van Susteren says that he and one other man, the late Otis Gomillion, knew McCarthy better than anyone else. Whenever McCarthy returned to Appleton from Washington, he and Van Susteren would hole up for a long talk. What did they talk about? The press, always the press, Van Susteren says. McCarthy would analyze the work of each reporter and explain exactly why he wrote the way he did. Van Susteren believes that McCarthy really understood the press.[1]

McCarthy talked about the press, too, in almost every speech he made outside the Senate and in everything that was published under his name. Nearly one-fifth of his principal publication, *McCarthyism: The Fight for America*, is devoted to accusations against the "left-wing press" and against individual reporters.

In 1953 and 1954 McCarthy customarily began his speeches by introducing reporters to the audience in this way: "There's Miles McMillin of the *Madison Daily Worker*. There's Bill Bechtel of the *Milwaukee Daily Worker*. There's Dick Johnston of the *New York Daily Worker*. Stand up, Dick, and show them what a reporter for a Communist newspaper looks like." Then he would add, "I'm not saying Dick's a Communist; it's just the two percent at the top of his paper that are Communists." After the speech, McCarthy would usually throw his arm over the reporter's shoulders and say something like, "That was just good fun." Reporters tried to avoid these introductions as well as McCarthy's show of friendliness.

"He embarrassed me one night at the South Side Armory," said Paul Ringler, the *Milwaukee Journal* editorial writer. "It was a rally in 1952, and I wanted to see firsthand what was going on. Frieda [Mrs. Ringler] and I sat up in the balcony, and I didn't think he could see me, but in the middle of his speech he said, 'Isn't that right, Paul? That's Paul Ringler of the *Milwaukee Journal* up there in the balcony.' "[2]

John Hunter, a political reporter for the *Capital Times*, had a similar experience. "I got tired of being pointed out, so I would sit way in the back instead of the press row," Hunter said. "I did this once at Reedsburg, and McCarthy said, 'Where are you hiding, John Hunter? Come out from behind that post.' Then afterwards he came around and nudged me and said, 'How'd I do today?' "[3]

I can neither find nor recall any instance of this raillery being reported in newspapers. Not many of his seriously expressed accusations against newspapers found their way into print, either; there was a convention among reporters in those days that it was somehow immodest to report comments about your newspaper, pro or con, and it was unseemly to build up your competitors, either, by mentioning attacks on other newspapers. Many stories in the *Milwaukee Journal* carried a line to the effect that McCarthy's audience reached a peak of enthusiasm when he attacked the *Journal*. The only stories about his attacks on the *Journal* that were carried at any length were those in which the attack was new and specific and those in which he proposed a boycott of the paper by advertisers or subscribers. But the impression that one gets from reading and recalling McCarthy's statements about the press is that his interest in the subject was so great as to be almost an obsession.

The most pervasive mistake made by those who have written about McCarthy and the news media is that of referring to "the press" in general, as if all newspapers and other media had reacted and performed in exactly the same way to McCarthy and his accusations. We have seen, in the examination of newspaper performance in the month after the Wheeling speech, how differently newspapers handled news about McCarthy and how varied were the editorial reactions that followed the news; some papers supported McCarthy, some opposed him, and some—the vast majority—equivocated. McCarthy did not consider the press a monolith. He concentrated his attacks upon those newspapers he knew were opposing him; his "left-wing press" list did not include a number of other press critics such as the *Raleigh News & Observer* or the *Tampa Tribune* or even the *Chicago Sun-Times*, which he apparently did not read or hear about. There is evidence that his reading of newspapers, like the operation of his office and his research methods, was haphazard and casual. He did not even read Wisconsin papers systematically; stories which first appeared in the *Milwaukee Journal* went unremarked, as a rule, until the same story appeared in the *Washington Post*. When he sued the *Syracuse Post-Standard* for libel in 1951, it was on the basis of a clipping of an editorial that someone had sent him, and it is likely that some newspapers got onto his list in that way.

In May 1952, Edward L. Bernays, a public relations man in New York, polled editors and civic leaders to determine, in their judgment, the 10 best newspapers in the country. Eight of the 10 were on McCarthy's "left-wing" list—the *New York Times, Christian Science Monitor, Washington Post, Milwaukee Journal, Louisville Courier-Journal, St. Louis Post-Dispatch, New York Herald Tribune,* and *Baltimore Sun.* Others on the "left-wing" list were the *Capital Times, New York Post, Denver Post,* and *Portland Oregonian,* as well as *Time* magazine.

McCarthy did not often mention the *Sheboygan Press*, the only other Wisconsin daily that consistently criticized him, but on 20 May 1951, speaking to a group of Young Republicans in Sheboygan, he said that the *Press* was "allowing itself to be used as a tool by the Communist party." He said the paper was "of the same stripe" as the *"Daily Workers"* in Madison and Milwaukee. The *Press* noted that this was the first time the paper had been attacked by McCarthy.[4]

His remarks showed particular concern for the opposition of the widely respected papers. On 12 September 1950, speaking to the Wauwatosa Republican Club, he said:

The heads of every one of our intelligence agencies say that, except for Communist utilization of the so-called respectable newspapers and radio stations they could destroy the entire movement. Papers that regularly follow the Communist line, like the Washington Post, *the* St. Louis Post-Dispatch *and the* Capital Times *don't do much damage. But so-called respectable papers like the* Milwaukee Journal. . . .[5]*

His view was not unlike that of another Washington anti-Communist described by Daniel Bell in a 1955 essay:

A few years ago I encountered Robert Morris, the counsel then for the Jenner Committee on internal subversion. He complained of the "terrible press" his committee was receiving. What press, he was asked; after all, the great Hearst and Scripps-Howard and Gannett chains, as well as an overwhelming number of newspaper dailies, had enthusiastically supported the work of the Committee. I wasn't thinking of them, he replied. I was thinking of the New York Times, *the* Washington Post, *the* St. Louis Post-Dispatch.[6]

McCarthy's attacks upon the most respected and influential newspapers is consistent with his attacks upon other respected institutions and individuals, the State Department, Harvard, the "young men born with silver spoons in their mouths," and, eventually, President Eisenhower. He seized almost every opportunity to attack what is now known as The Establishment. If he had not chosen the "Communists in government" theme, he might well have been a successful populist agitator. The intellectual conservatives who supported him recognized this streak in him, and it kept them from total identification with his pursuit of their cause.

McCarthy's feud with the *Capital Times* pre-dated his emergence as an anti-Communist. The *Capital Times* was not an "establishment" paper; its philosophy was fiercely populist, and it employed a sledge-hammer editorial style. The paper had been devoted for several decades to the support of the La Follette political dynasty, and it provided the only significant newspaper support in the state for Senator Robert M. La Follette in the 1946 Republican primary. McCarthy's defeat of that hero solidified its enmity, and the paper was constantly critical of McCarthy's performance as a senator in the years that followed.

McCarthy struck back on 9 November 1949 when he released a copy of a letter he had sent to 400 daily and weekly newspaper editors in Wisconsin "wondering" whether the *Capital Times* was "the Red mouthpiece for the Communist party in Wisconsin." The statement ended with the suggestion that a boycott of the *Capital Times* was a proper response to his charges: "It is for the people of Madison and vicinity to decide whether they will continue by advertisements and subscriptions to support this paper in view of the above facts—especially in view of the fact that the man who is editor publicly proclaimed that the man hired as city editor was an active and leading member of the Communist party."[7] The city editor to whom he referred was Cedric Parker, who promptly denied that he was a Communist and said that McCarthy had attacked him because he had investigated his income tax returns.[8] The editor, William T. Evjue, said that the Communists "hate the *Capital Times* more than any other newspaper in Wisconsin."[9] McCarthy repeated his charges two days later in a speech in Madison and displayed a photostat of an "open letter" from Evjue, published 14 March 1941, in which Evjue said that Parker was "the Communist leader in Madison."[10]

The *Milwaukee Journal* ridiculed the implication that Evjue was a Communist, in an editorial that was reprinted by many Wisconsin newspapers. It said, in part:

The best test perhaps, of Mr. Evjue's position is the Senator's own. "If a fowl," he quotes, "looks like a duck, walks like a duck, swims like a duck and quacks like a duck, then we can safely assume that it is a duck." Mr. Evjue looks like a capitalist, walks like a capitalist, and quacks in a voice entirely his own, sometimes like a capitalist, sometimes like the Delphic oracle, sometimes like the Mad Hatter— and always entertaining.[11]

McCarthy, nevertheless, thought he had scored a point against Evjue. He repeated his charges about Parker frequently in 1950 and 1951 and periodically challenged the editor to a debate on the subject. (Perhaps the most significant aspect of the incident is that it shows that McCarthy's awareness of the political value of the "Communist" charge preceded the crusade that began at Wheeling, a development that is commonly ascribed to a lunch at Washington's Colony restaurant in January 1950.)

In his book *McCarthyism* the senator repeated his charges about Evjue and Parker four times, in almost identical language, as he accused the *Capital Times* of being the principal source of the "smear attack" against him. In a speech to the Wisconsin Young Republican convention on 7 May 1950, McCarthy said that the *Capital Times* "does a more effective job of spewing forth Communist line sewage than any paper other than the *New Masses* and the *Daily Worker*." That was the general theme of his attacks against the paper for the next four years; repetition, not originality, was the essence of his style.

The *Capital Times* fought McCarthy with all its resources. Evjue and Miles McMillin, the editorial writer and columnist, spoke and debated about McCarthy throughout the state and elsewhere; McMillin, Parker, Hunter, and Aldric Revell, another columnist and political reporter, made investigative reports about McCarthy's failure to pay income taxes on wartime stock market profits and his questionable actions as a judge; McMillin, a lawyer, filed a suit seeking to disbar McCarthy for violating the Wisconsin constitution by running for the Senate while holding a judgeship. Evjue criticized McCarthy almost every Sunday in his "Hello Wisconsin" talks on radio station WIBA, and reprinted the talks in the paper's special Monday edition. *Capital Times* reporters organized groups to sign petitions or buy advertisements opposing McCarthy; they wrote letters to the editor under various names, attacking McCarthy; no day went by without some attack. McMillin made frequent trips to Washington to gather fresh material with which to attack McCarthy. Unlike most reporters, McMillin liked to confront McCarthy personally at political meetings.

On one occasion, McCarthy had McMillin ejected from a hotel in La Crosse where McCarthy was speaking to a meeting of local service clubs. Outside the hotel, State Senator Gaylord Nelson and Assemblyman William Proxmire (both to become U.S. senators) were talking from a sound truck, and each time McCarthy paused, they heckled him. This was getting on McCarthy's nerves, McMillin said, and "when I got up to ask a question, Joe blew up. 'Get him out!' he yelled. 'That's a representative of a Communist newspaper.' Those Rotarians and Kiwanians surrounded me and shoved me out the door."[12]

Another confrontation took place that year at the Republican state convention in Madison, where McCarthy began a press conference by talking about Communists at the *Milwaukee Journal*. "You've charged there are Communists at the *Milwaukee Journal*," McMillin said. "Name one." McCarthy didn't reply. "I insist on an answer," McMillin said. McCarthy sat there, silent. Art Bystrom, the AP reporter, was impatient. "Come on," he said to McMillin, "let's get on with it." Robert H. Fleming of the *Journal* was furious. "Shut up," he said to Bystrom, and Bystrom did. "I'm not going to answer that if we sit here all day," said McCarthy. So they sat there for 15 minutes in silence, and then McCarthy got up and left.

According to McMillin, the wire services never ran stories that were adverse to McCarthy, and Wisconsin editors and the Associated Press "went easy" on McCarthy out of "fear, gutlessness, and concern about their social status."

But there were doubts and internal differences about the handling of McCarthy news within the *Capital Times*, too. Most of the paper's desk men thought that the paper was "overplaying" McCarthy, and even Evjue was afraid of McCarthy. "He was afraid of the Catholics," McMillin told me. "He considered them a monolithic force. He'd take things out of McCarthy stories all the time. He'd say, 'Everything I have is tied up in this paper.'" In 1947, McMillin had dug up the story about McCarthy's failure to pay taxes on stock income during World War II, but Evjue wouldn't run it immediately. "We've got to be careful," he said. "We're charging him with a felony." Then he called J. D. Ferguson, editor of the *Milwaukee Journal*, and told him what they had, and Ferguson sent over Frank Sinclair, the *Journal's* tax specialist, who called the state tax commissioner and got confirmation on a confidential basis. "So the *Cap Times* and the *Journal* had page-one stories the same day," McMillin said. "Evjue was afraid to do it alone."

Evjue's apprehension was reflected in the play given each story of McCarthy's attacks on other papers; he desperately wanted company as a McCarthy target. When, on 25 May 1950, speaking in Rochester, New York, McCarthy included the *Washington Post*, the *New York Post*, and the *St. Louis Post-Dispatch* along with the *Capital Times* as newspapers that followed that "*Daily Worker* line," Evjue was exultant. A long story on this development was followed by an editorial, a radio talk, and the reprint of that talk in the *Capital Times*. In these, Evjue suggested that the *Milwaukee Journal* should be added to McCarthy's list, and he quoted critical editorials from other newspapers to show that he was not alone in his opposition to McCarthy.

Evjue's fear was understandable. His was the smallest paper attacked consistently by McCarthy and the only one that might have been vulnerable to a boycott; no one knew at that point what McCarthy's supporters were capable of doing. Under the circumstances, Evjue's continued opposition to McCarthy was an act of courage, even if he was too cautious for such a firebrand as McMillin.

Although the paper had been denouncing him regularly in its editorial columns for five months, McCarthy did not add the *Milwaukee Journal* to his list until the first week of July 1950, when he described the *Journal* as "the Milwaukee version of the *Washington Daily Worker* or the *Washington Post*." Perhaps he waited this long because the *Journal* had said good things about him in the past and he still hoped to get back in the paper's graces. Paul Ringler described the earlier attitude of the *Journal* toward McCarthy in an unpublished editorial written 2 January 1951:

The Journal *was friendly to Joe McCarthy at first. We did not oppose him in the primaries of 1944 or 1946, or in the general election of 1946. We did not endorse him, but we helped him indirectly by editorials critical of his opponents. We had a friendly editorial in the midst of the 1944 campaign. After his nomination in 1946, we spoke kindly of him. After his election, we said he had the abilities to make a good senator. Members of our staff were on the best of terms with McCarthy; it was long his practice to have lunch with them whenever he came to the city.*[13]

Perhaps McCarthy's thinking was influenced by the *Journal*'s historical opposition to the Socialist party and its candidates in Milwaukee and by its postwar crusade against Communists in the Milwaukee labor movement, based on material leaked by the Milwaukee office of the FBI. Labor leaders in the city regularly castigated the *Journal* up until 1950 as a "red-baiting" newspaper. And in 1948 the *Journal* had endorsed Thomas E. Dewey, the Republican nominee for president.

My guess is that McCarthy was genuinely surprised at the reaction of the *Journal* and other basically conservative papers to his Communists-in-government charges. He and others in his camp never did understand why anti-Communist newspapers regarded his brand of anti-Communism as a threat to civil liberties rather than a threat to Communists. Even the *New York Post*, on McCarthy's list of the "most communistic" papers, was running a series by Murray Kempton on Communist infiltration of New York City labor unions when McCarthy opened his campaign in Wheeling.

Once started on the *Journal*, however, McCarthy kept up a regular barrage, probably influenced by his audiences. His supporters could not easily follow his confusing arguments as to why some obscure federal bureaucrat was a Communist influence, but they could understand a vitriolic attack on the state's largest newspaper, and they liked it. They cheered on 30 July 1950, in Fond du Lac, when McCarthy called the *Capital Times* and the *Journal* "the poisoned water holes in this state," and said that one of the Communist movement's chief objectives was to "get men placed on the so-called responsible papers so that when the chips are down they can bank on them."[14]

In September, speaking to the Wauwatosa Republican club, McCarthy began the exposition of a theme he pursued for the next year—that a New York lawyer controlled the editorial policy of the *Journal*: "I'm going to tell later," he said, "about Louis Weiss, an attorney for the now-defunct fellow-traveling newspaper *PM*, who happens to be not only the good friend and adviser but also the brother-in-law of the chief of the *Journal*'s editorial staff, Lindsay Hoben. He controls the editorial policy of that paper."[15] Louis S. Weiss was a member of the New York law firm of Paul, Weiss, Rifkind & Garrison. He was an attorney for Marshall Field III, the department store magnate, in many enterprises, *PM* among them. His wife was a younger sister of Mrs. Hoben.

On 11 April 1951, speaking to the Wisconsin Retail Furniture Association in Milwaukee, McCarthy tried to tie the *Journal* to Alger Hiss through Weiss:

> . . . *I think it is important to explore the reasons why a paper upon which I would say about 95, 96, 97 percent of the employes are just as loyal as the people in this room and I know a sizeable number working on the paper are not communistic. You wonder why a paper of that kind follows communistic issues at all times when the chips*

are down. . . . I have a list of all those who contributed to the Hiss defense fund in both his first and second trials. One of the men who collected the money for the defense of Alger Hiss was the New York lawyer for PM called Louis Weiss. His brother-in-law is chief of the editorial writers for the Milwaukee Journal, *Lindsay Hoben. . . .*[16]

He then said that two *Journal* editorial writers had contributed to the defense of Alger Hiss. "So it is not too surprising," he said, "when you find that paper editorially coming to the defense of the top unexposed Communist men. And if this isn't true, I suggest the *Journal* deny it and we will give them the names of the editorial writers."

The *Journal* did promptly deny the charge and challenged McCarthy to name the editorial writers. On April 7, McCarthy told an AP reporter that he was going to name them in a speech that night at Fort Atkinson, Wisconsin. Robert H. Fleming of the *Journal* asked him about this before the speech. "I don't know that I'll name them tonight," McCarthy said, "but I have the names all right." Fleming asked who they were. "They're two of the editorial writers, so you can guess," McCarthy answered. "I don't want to give out the names yet, because we want to be sure we have the complete list. What we've got is an auditor's list, and we've checked all the names on it. Every one of them stands up." Fleming said he didn't believe him. "Why, you know who they are," McCarthy said. ". . . But I'm not giving out the names tonight."[17] He did not give out the names, but he did say that Weiss, who was dead, was "a Communist if there ever was one."

Later in April, Fleming went to Cambridge, Massachusetts, to talk to Richard Field, a Harvard law professor who was treasurer of the Hiss fund. Field told him that he had the only existing list of contributors, that there were no *Journal* editorial writers on it, and that there never had been an "auditor's list." He could not let Fleming examine the list, but if Fleming gave him names he would check the list to see if any appeared. Fleming typed out 11 names—eight editorial writers and three *Journal* editors—and Field gave him a letter saying that those names did not appear.[18] McCarthy never did name anyone, and eventually he stopped making the charge about the editorial writers.

Fleming did the largest share of the *Journal's* investigation of McCarthy, discovering, among other things, that McCarthy's claims about his war record—that he was wounded in action and that his leg was burned and broken in an airplane accident—were false.[19] Fleming obtained navy records showing that McCarthy's only injury was suffered in a shipboard celebration of the crossing of the equator.

My own investigation revealed the extensive financial contributions and lavish entertainment of McCarthy by Texas oilmen. The story

noted that McCarthy had voted in favor of oil interests and against
the seeming interests of his constituents on three key issues in the
Senate between 1950 and 1953, but quoted the oilmen as saying their
contributions resulted not from these votes but from their appreciation
of McCarthy's fight against "Communists."[20] This story was reprinted
and widely distributed by the political action committee of the CIO
in Washington.

Some comparisons between press coverage of McCarthy and of the
Nixon Watergate affair have suggested that if the press had been as
diligent in investigating McCarthy as it was in investigating Nixon
and Watergate, McCarthy might have been toppled earlier. The suggestion is not valid; between the *Journal* and the *Capital Times*, almost
every aspect of McCarthy's record was investigated and his derelictions exposed, over and over. No one cared, though, because it was
not McCarthy's character, morals, or deportment that concerned people; the only issue that mattered was the Communist issue.

Fleming went to Washington often to confer with members of Senator Benton's staff who were investigating McCarthy, and with other
reporters and editors from papers opposing McCarthy. He talked with
Philip Graham, publisher of the *Washington Post*, and with Irving
Dilliard, chief editorial writer of the *St. Louis Post-Dispatch*, about
the possibility of pooling efforts and money to hire professional investigators to check rumors about McCarthy, but nothing came of
this.[21]

The *Journal* several times was offered affidavits by persons who
said that they had had homosexual relations with McCarthy, but the
editors never seriously considered publishing them. (They were published later by Hank Greenspun in his *Las Vegas Sun*.) One person
at the *Journal* who did advocate publication was Murray Reed, a
former city editor who had been retired but who so loved the newspaper and his life there that he had been permitted to stay on in the
city room as "executive city editor." Reed was a throwback to an
earlier, saltier period of journalism—the "Front Page" era—and he
was fiercely loyal to the paper. He proposed that a political reporter
call every person known to be closely associated with McCarthy and
ask whether the senator was a homosexual. If all of them said he was
not, Reed said, the paper could run a story beginning, "Thirty-five of
McCarthy's closest friends deny that he is a homosexual," or, if some
of them refused to answer, the story could say, "Twenty-eight out of
35 of McCarthy's closest friends deny. . . ." Reed's suggestion was
rejected.

One of Fleming's letters to C. Stanley Allen, Senator Benton's administrative assistant, was intercepted by someone friendly to Mc-
Carthy and turned over to the senator, who leaked it to George Dixon,

a Hearst columnist, much to the *Journal's* embarrassment. The letter was written in a grandiose, conspiratorial style, speaking of "The Project"—meaning the effort to expel McCarthy from the Senate—and suggesting that the message be destroyed upon reading. Dixon devoted two columns to lampooning Fleming and the *Journal*, which was easy to do with such material.[22] Ferguson, the *Journal's* editor, was irritated. "Don't write any more letters," he told Fleming. "Use the telephone, and if you think that's tapped, take a plane. But don't write letters."

On 12 September 1950, in a speech to the Wauwatosa Republican Club, McCarthy called for a boycott of businesses that advertised in the *Journal*. "Now if every housewife advises the advertisers in that paper that she will not buy a cent's worth of goods advertised in papers that are smearing good, loyal Americans, that will have an effect."[23] He repeated this call on several occasions in the Milwaukee area, but the campaign had no perceptible effect on *Journal* advertising, and no advertiser reported any pressure of this kind from customers. The senator told Fleming he had not expected the boycott to work. "I don't have any idea I can break the *Journal*. Off the record, I don't know that I can cut its profits at all. . . . But if you can show a paper as unfriendly and having a reason for being antagonistic, you take the sting out of what it says about you. I think I can convince a lot of people that they can't believe what they read in the *Journal*."[24]

McCarthy's attacks on the *Journal* were fewer in 1953 and 1954; he was moving toward a confrontation with President Eisenhower and was preoccupied with Washington affairs. His only new tactic was to exclude *Journal* reporters from press conferences, a practice which had the effect of turning other members of the press against him. On 8 May 1954 he refused to allow Harry Pease, a *Journal* reporter, to participate in a press conference in Wausau. There was no point in talking to a *Journal* reporter because, he said, "I do not believe it is a newspaper, only a propaganda sheet."[25] Later that year he forced me to leave a house in Fort Atkinson, Wisconsin, before he would begin a press conference. Bob Howard, a *Chicago Tribune* reporter, said to me in a loud voice, "Don't worry. I'll fill you in on everything the son of a bitch says."

The *Journal* never wavered in its opposition to McCarthy. Ringler, who with the late John Reddin wrote most of the McCarthy editorials, said that the paper's editorial position was fully supported by Harry Grant, chairman of the board, a conservative.[26] Altogether, from the date of the Wheeling speech to McCarthy's death seven years later, the *Journal* published 201 editorials criticizing McCarthy.

Although McCarthy listed the *New York Times* as one of his "Daily Workers," he never criticized the *Times* with the same vigor he expended on the two Wisconsin papers and the *Washington Post*. Roy Cohn, his aide, did criticize the *Times* for some specific stories, but McCarthy never did more than taunt its reporters.[27]

The *Times*'s news stories were not the kind that would irritate McCarthy, written as they were in the classic grey prose that its editors preferred, in long sentences and with a puritanical adherence to the principle of objectivity. *Times* accounts of McCarthy's activities in the Senate ran longer than those in any other newspaper, but they did not tell readers what an event meant or why it was happening, nor was it described. Notable exceptions to this prosaic coverage were occasional columns by James B. Reston, and later on, reports from Wisconsin and other parts of the country by William H. Lawrence, another political reporter, John Oakes, an editorial writer, and Reston.

As it did for other news organizations, the five-year McCarthy period produced changes in news practices at the *Times*. Departure from strict objectivity came slowly, however, and as late as August 1952 Arthur Hays Sulzberger was not ready to make the leap to interpretive reporting, as noted earlier. But by March 1954 policies had changed, and Lester Markel, Sunday editor, speaking to the Women's National Press Club in Washington, could say, "If we are responsible for inflating McCarthy, we should take on the job of deflating him, not in the editorials but in an interpretive way." If McCarthy's charges were on page one, stories that prove the allegations unfounded should be on page one, not on the editorial page.[28] The newspaper reflected this view. By 1954 there was a good deal of interpretation in *Times* stories, and Reston's columns had more bite than they had had in 1950.

Most of the *Times*'s reporting of McCarthy in the Midwest was done by Richard J. H. Johnston of the paper's Chicago bureau. Johnston recently recalled experiences with McCarthy and said that when people ask him what it was like to cover McCarthy, his answer is that "it wasn't easy."

But there was some fascination for all of us in covering Joe, because while his kind has appeared frequently on the stage of politics, he was the top banana for his kind of act in his time, and while it was a burden and a trial for some of us, it was a joyous thing for Joe at all times. I finally came to the conclusion that in the strictest sense of the word he didn't understand a goddamn thing he was doing except that it was getting him a lot of notoriety and this he loved.[29]

In 1957 Johnston's editors in New York wanted him to do a story on who would inherit McCarthy's organization and carry on his crusade. They wouldn't believe him, he said, when he told them that there wasn't any organization, that when McCarthy left the scene "it would all fall down like a house of cards in a little breeze."

Johnston said that McCarthy had set him up as the enemy in Fargo, North Dakota, by introducing him to the crowd in this way: "I've got a man traveling with me all the way from New York, from the *New York Times*, that's the other branch of the *Daily Worker* in New York. This fellow is a pro-Communist, too, but he's a nice fellow who just does what he's told. They pay him, and when they say 'jump,' he jumps."

Then [Johnston continued], when Joe started to speak and I stopped taking notes—there wasn't any press section and I was in the front row of seats—the guy on one side of me said, "go ahead and write." I said, "He said all that before." The guy said, "When Joe talks, put it down. What are you, some kind of Communist?" Then later when I did take notes, a guy on the other side said, "Boy, they don't miss a thing, do they? They're going to hang Joe with this one."

Like other reporters who covered McCarthy, Johnston puzzled over the senator's motivation and goals. Once, in Duluth, Minnesota, he asked McCarthy what he would do, whom he would attack when the last Communist went to prison and all his enemies were defeated. "You'll have to have somebody to attack," he said, "you can't just sit there." According to Johnston, McCarthy said, "Maybe I can attack the Catholic church." Johnston said, "That's a good one." Then McCarthy said, "I didn't mean that, don't put it in the paper." But Johnston is not sure that he didn't mean it, that keeping up the momentum was not McCarthy's greatest concern.

Vice-President Nixon held a press conference in Chicago shortly before McCarthy was censured in 1954, Johnston said, and afterward, in a lounge outside the bar in the Sheraton Hotel, Johnston mentioned that McCarthy had been there the day before. "What's the matter with him?" Nixon asked. "Is he crazy, do you think?" Johnston said he didn't know, he wasn't a psychiatrist. It seems ironic to Johnston now (after the Watergate scandals) to think of Nixon asking whether Joe was crazy. "It's too bad Joe didn't live to see Nixon *in extremis*," he said.*

The *New York Times*'s one experience as a target of McCarthyism

---

*People tend to think that since Nixon and McCarthy both achieved fame as baiters of "Communists" in government, the two must have been allies, even friends. Another indication to the contrary came from Judge Van Susteren, McCarthy's close friend, who said that McCarthy disliked Nixon so much that "you could almost say he hated him." "Yes," he said, "he did hate Nixon." (Van Susteren interview, 5 May 1976.)

was at the hands of the Senate internal security subcommittee, headed by Senator James Eastland, Democrat of Mississippi, which held closed hearings during the latter months of 1955 as part of an investigation into the alleged influence of Communists on American newspapers. The investigation was directed by J. G. Sourwine, a protégé of the late Senator Pat McCarran of Nevada. Of the 38 witnesses who were asked about present or past affiliations with Communist organizations, 25 were *Times* employes and five others had formerly worked there. Sourwine tried to convey the impression that the accused employes were in positions in which they could influence *Times* policy along Communist lines. In an editorial published 5 January 1956, the *Times* said that it had been singled out for attack because of its opposition to things for which Eastland and the subcommittee stood—segregation in southern schools, McCarthyism, and the abusive methods of some congressional committees. Many other newspapers published editorials along the same lines. The hearings ended on January 7, with Eastland saying that new hearings would be held later but that no more *Times* employes would be called. No more hearings were held, and two weeks later Sourwine resigned as counsel.

In its editorial of January 5, the *Times* had said that it would not knowingly employ a Communist in the news or editorial departments because a Communist could not be trusted to report the news objectively or comment honestly. But the question for the *Times* was what to do about those who were no longer members of the Communist party but who had pleaded the Fifth Amendment before the subcommittee, or had admitted their own past associations but refused to testify about others who might have been party members. General Julius Ochs Adler, the general manager, wanted to fire all the former Communists. Turner Catledge, the editor, took the position that the *Times* should not fire people for taking the Fifth Amendment—exercising their constitutional rights—and Sulzberger, whose decision it was, gradually came around to that view.[30]

Irving Dilliard, editor of the *St. Louis Post-Dispatch* editorial page, told the American Society of Newspaper Editors in New York on 19 April 1956 that the Eastland subcommittee's investigation of the *New York Times* had been an invasion of freedom of the press that might have intimidated other newspapers. He pointed out that 112 of the 193 newspapers in the nation's 100 largest cities had taken no position on the Eastland inquiry. Only 35 of these papers were critical of the subcommittee and 33 supported the investigation. "Did Senator Eastland's boldness in concentrating on the *New York Times* so impress the press that many editors found it desirable to avoid commenting?" Dilliard asked.[31] The reluctance of most newspapers to take a position on a controversial issue of vital importance to the press was much like their reluctance to challenge McCarthy during the first month of his rampage.

Dilliard's paper was one of those which criticized McCarthy early and harshly, and its editorials were backed by the powerful cartoons of Daniel Fitzpatrick—"Fitz"—who was second only to Herblock in his ability to portray McCarthyism as an evil. This stand was not maintained without difficulty, however. Dilliard, directing the editorial page, and news executives such as Ben Reese, Raymond Crowley, and Donald Grant, were under almost constant pressure from the publisher, Joseph Pulitzer, to be cautious in the campaign against McCarthy.[32]

One of these cautionary messages was sent to Dilliard on 13 March 1950, only a month after McCarthy's Wheeling speech. Pulitzer wrote that he recognized that there was "plenty of politics" in McCarthy's charges against the State Department and that the Republicans were trying to smear the Democrats as pro-Communists, but that he thought that the paper should call on Tydings to "go slow in his role of prosecutor and his efforts to throw a smokescreen over the whole thing." "After all," he wrote, "the charges have been made and an investigation is on," a statement that indicated that he thought there might be something to McCarthy's charges after all. This was not at all the line Dilliard was taking on the editorial page.

Pulitzer's memoranda to Dilliard over the next four years were a succession of notes that pleaded, wheedled, or demanded that the editor be kinder to McCarthy and the Republicans. The *Post-Dispatch* was officially an "independent Democratic" paper, but Pulitzer was determined that President Truman should not be reelected. His memoranda indicate that he intended to support General Eisenhower against Truman if that contest occurred, and that he might have considered supporting Senator Robert Taft of Ohio, the arch-Republican and isolationist, against Truman.*

In a memorandum to Dilliard dated 10 November 1951, Pulitzer urged that the paper avoid seeming to "pick on" Taft. "I cannot imagine how we could support Taft next year," he wrote. "On the other hand, I cannot at the moment see how we could support Truman. It is barely conceivable that between now and then the unpredictable

---

*It was widely believed during this period that President Truman would seek reelection, a possibility that served to muffle criticism of McCarthy and Taft in many newspapers. Truman did in fact run, to the extent of permitting his name to be entered in the New Hampshire primary, where he was defeated by Tennessee senator Estes Kefauver, who won all the delegates. A few weeks later, Kefauver won all of Wisconsin's delegates over a stand-in for Truman, after which Truman withdrew as a candidate. In both states, the official Democratic organizations had supported Truman.

Taft, thanks to Eisenhower's influence, might swing into line on foreign policy, McCarthy and other issues. If that should happen we
might be embarassed by our record of hyper-criticism."

Pulitzer also persisted in his view that McCarthy might really be
concerned about Communists in government. On 18 March 1951 he
wrote Dilliard, "Henceforth in denouncing McCarthyism we should
not seem to overlook or excuse the fact that the Democrats might have
and should have shown a greater willingness to recognize the existence of Communist dangers here at home. Where there was so much
smoke there must have been some fire, and the Democrats should
have been quick to recognize it. McCarthy was wrong; so was Truman."

On 28 January 1953, Pulitzer wrote managing editor Crowley to say
that a question had been plaguing him since the *Post-Dispatch* had
reprinted a *Milwaukee Journal* story debunking McCarthy's war record. If the story was accurate, he asked, how could the Marine Corps
subsequently award McCarthy a number of medals for his wartime
service? He could not believe that the Marine Corps would have done
this purely as a result of political pressure by McCarthy, he wrote.

On 14 May 1953, in a memorandum to Crowley, Pulitzer proposed
a McCarthy story divided into two parts, one dealing with his "successes or partial successes (as in the case of John Carter Vincent) in
rooting out subversives and disloyalty" and the other with instances
of the unfair means he used—"guilt by association, irresponsible accusation, etc."

*In other words [he wrote], it is my impression without having looked
up the record that this scalawag regardless of his evil methods has
accomplished some good. If this impression stacks up I believe the
P-D in the interest of realism should be open-minded enough to print
the record. Doing so, I believe, would strengthen our editorial opposition to his methods.*

Writing again to Crowley on 7 July 1953, Pulitzer said that the night
before he had been challenged about McCarthy:

*I was asked the familiar question—granting that McCarthy has been
loose in his charges and may well have smeared some innocent people,
in short, that his methods have been bad, have not the results on the
whole been good? Is not his objective a worthy one and if he had not
uncovered so many Communists and so many who take refuge in the
Fifth Amendment and refuse to answer questions who would have
done so?*

*I should seriously like to see an article which might well quote the
foregoing question and might undertake, with the utmost fairness and*

generosity to McCarthy, to give the answers. I shall want to see the
copy before it is released.

This story was written, and its publication resulted in a disagree-
ment between Pulitzer and his son, Joseph Pulitzer, Jr., functioning
as associate editor, over the paper's handling of McCarthy. In a memorandum to Crowley on the story of the "good" and the "bad" about
McCarthy, Pulitzer, Jr., said he doubted that the article had contained
enough about McCarthy's "notorious early history" in Wisconsin:

In other words, should the Post-Dispatch *be content to recount the*
"good" and the "bad" . . . or should we undertake a major exposé
along the lines of "The McCarthy Record," which was compiled by
a distinguished Wisconsin citizens' committee? The full record, I be-
lieve, would reveal the man beyond a shadow of a doubt as a scoun-
drel, a demagogue, and a dangerous public enemy.

The elder Pulitzer was still worrying about McCarthy's war record
on 4 September 1953 when he wrote Dilliard to ask whether McCarthy
had been a tail gunner or not. He noted that a citation issued by
Admiral Nimitz's office referred to him as a "rear gunner." If there
was any doubt about this aspect of McCarthy's career, the editorial
writers should "drop it once and for all."

The rest of Pulitzer's memoranda on McCarthy asserted a decline
in public interest in McCarthy and admonished Dilliard to play him
down. On 27 April 1954 Pulitzer said that the Hooper ratings for the
Army-McCarthy hearings, measuring television viewing, were slip-
ping and that the paper should be on guard against boring its readers
with "too much of anything." Two days later he wrote Dilliard to say
that after the editorial page had carried a whole column of letters
about McCarthy they might "go slow" in printing more McCarthy
letters; he had watched the hearings on television two nights in a row
and did not plan to watch any more. On April 30 he was more specific,
writing Dilliard, "Please, please, please lay off the McCarthy hearings.
To me—and I believe to the great majority—they are the most terrific
bore. Offhand, I would say that one editorial, one letter and one cartoon a week would be about right." On May 4 he praised an editorial
on McCarthy but said, "Can't we be satisfied with it and turn our
minds and the minds of our readers to subjects of equal or greater
importance?" The final word to Dilliard on McCarthy, on December
6, was a command: "I must ask that the words 'McCarthy' or 'Mc-
Carthyism' or any oblique reference to either shall not appear on the
editorial page without my specific approval in the issues of December
7, 8, 9, 10, 11 and 12."

The banishment of McCarthy from the pages of the *Post-Dispatch* was virtually eternal, for this was the week following the senator's censure. Nor did any but Wisconsin newspapers carry much news of McCarthy from that time until his death two and a half years later.

The *New York Post*, a fiercely liberal but strongly anti-Communist afternoon tabloid, got into the fight slowly; it carried only one small story on McCarthy during the first two weeks of the campaign that began at Wheeling. Its first editorial was on 22 February 1950. But from 8 March on, with the start of hearings in Washington, it provided steady coverage and a barrage of critical columns, cartoons, and editorials. It was one of the first half-dozen papers to make the senator's "left-wing press" list.

On 4 September 1951 it began a 17-part series by Oliver Pilat and William V. Shannon titled "The One-Man Mob of Joe McCarthy," which covered the senator's career as a judge, his war record, his alleged support by Communists in the 1946 primary, his income tax troubles, his support by the "real estate lobby," the Lustron booklet, the Malmedy hearings, the Wheeling speech, the attack on Dorothy Kenyon, his relations with homosexuals, his links to the "China lobby," his part in the Tydings campaign, his "fascist" supporters, and his attempts to "gag" the press.

In the article on his relations with the press, Pilat and Shannon wrote that McCarthy had "followed a consistent policy of trying to coerce not only correspondents and commentators but also the great news services like Associated Press and United Press into giving him favorable treatment. He goes over the heads of the reporters to the publishers, small-town editors, radio sponsors, advertising agencies and local pressure groups in order to whiplash his critics into line or else destroy them. He attacks not their competence but their patriotism."[33]

The series was a highly emotional but remarkably thorough compilation of everything unsavory that had been dug up about McCarthy's past. Most of it was familiar to readers of the *Milwaukee Journal*, the *Capital Times*, and the *Progressive* magazine, but this was the first time that much of this material had been published outside Wisconsin.

On 24 April 1953, when McCarthy called James A. Wechsler, editor of the *Post*, before his Senate investigating subcommittee, he insisted that the summons did not result from the series of 17 critical articles.[34] He said that Wechsler was called because some of the books he had written had been purchased by the State Department for use in overseas libraries. Wechsler said, however, that McCarthy's questions were directed at the *Post's* editorial policies, not his books. Wechsler had joined the Young Communist League at Columbia University in

1934. He quit the party in 1937, making a public announcement of this and the fact that he had cooperated with the FBI. He opposed the Communists from then on, in his work and his writing, and he helped defeat a Communist effort to take over the American Newspaper Guild. He appeared twice before McCarthy's subcommittee in closed sessions. On 7 May 1953 McCarthy acceded to Wechsler's demand that a transcript of the hearings be made public, and the transcript was published the next day in the *New York Times*.

The transcript showed that McCarthy had questioned the editor repeatedly on the editorial position of the *Post*. He asked whether the *Post* had attacked J. Edgar Hoover, head of the FBI, and whether the *Post* had ever praised the FBI. He asked whether Wechsler had consistently criticized the chairmen of the House Un-American Activities Committee, and whether he had opposed Senator William E. Jenner, the Indiana Republican who headed the Senate internal security subcommittee, and about his position on Greek-Turkish (anti-Communist) aid. Then McCarthy began the argument he pursued throughout the hearing: "If you or I were a member of the Communist party, and we wanted to advance the Communist list, perhaps the most effective way of doing that would be to claim we deserted the party, and if we got into control of the paper, use that paper to attack and smear anybody who actually was fighting communism. Now, without saying whether you have done it, you would agree that that was a good tactic, would you not?"

Wechsler said that he knew of no case of such a thing happening. He pointed out that McCarthy had an ex-Communist on his staff, referring to Howard A. Rushmore, a former Communist who sat at McCarthy's side during the hearings. McCarthy answered that there was a big difference between "the ex-Communist on our committee and your ex-communism, real or alleged," saying that Rushmore had given all his information about Communists to the FBI and that "he does not spend his time, you see, trying to smear and tear down the people who are really fighting communism."

"Senator, let's face it," said Wechsler. "You are saying that an ex-Communist who is for McCarthy is a good one and an ex-Communist who is against McCarthy is suspect." "I feel you have not broken with your Communist ideal," McCarthy said. "I feel you are serving them very, very actively. Whether you are doing it knowingly or not, that is in your own mind. I have no knowledge as to whether you have a card in the party."

Before the second hearing, Wechsler presented a list of persons he had known to be Communists. He asked that the list not be made public. He also said that McCarthy had raised questions of freedom of the press that warranted an investigation by the American Society of Newspaper Editors. McCarthy said that if that happened, he hoped that the ASNE would also investigate "the lack of ethics and the lack of truth in the newspaper you edit."

McCarthy demanded that Wechsler produce evidence that the *Post* had really opposed Communists. Wechsler cited his support of Whittaker Chambers in the Hiss case and the exposure of Communist control of the Henry Wallace campaign for president in 1948. McCarthy did not comment on the allusion to Chambers, but dismissed the exposure of the Wallace movement as unimportant because Wallace had never had a chance of being elected, and suggested that what Wechsler really was trying to do was to protect "the old Acheson crowd that has been so thoroughly infiltrated by Communists." "I may say that your purported reformation does not convince me at all," he said. "He [Wechsler] has been the chief ring leader in smearing the head of every Un-American Activities Committee," McCarthy concluded. "There has been no change in his writings since he admits he was active in the Communist movement as far as I can see." Wechsler's last word was that McCarthy's basic test of patriotism was an editor's attitude toward him and his committee, and "I believe I am here because of our editorial policy."

The *New York Times*, in an editorial on 9 May 1953, agreed with Wechsler. It said that it had concluded that McCarthy "was using his undoubted right of investigation as a cover for an attempt to harass and intimidate an editor who has bitterly and uncompromisingly opposed Mr. McCarthy." It said that McCarthy's repeated references to the editorial policy of the *Post* had shown clearly what was in McCarthy's mind, and that it was "close to an infringement on one of America's basic freedoms" if he used his power as chairman of an investigating committee to accuse an editor of continued subservience to "the Communist ideal" because the editor's writings were not to his liking.

On 10 May 1953, Basil L. (Stuffy) Walters, executive editor of the *Chicago Daily News* and president of the American Society of Newspaper Editors, directed the group's freedom of information committee to study the transcript of the Wechsler hearings and report its conclusions to the ASNE board of directors. J. Russell Wiggins, managing editor of the *Washington Post*, chaired the committee.

While the committee studied, the issue was debated by radio panels, on university campuses, and in editorial columns. Arthur Krock, the *New York Times*'s senior pundit, argued on 22 May 1953 that while McCarthy may have tried to intimidate the press, he had not actually invaded the area protected by the constitutional provision that "Congress shall make no law ... abridging the freedom of the press." Further, Krock said, the press should not raise the issue unless there was a "plain" invasion of the freedom of the press to print and to withhold. This produced a flood of letters to the *Times*.

The Wiggins committee was unable to reach a unanimous decision. Four members of the committee, including Wiggins, issued a separate report saying that McCarthy's actions constituted "a peril to American freedom." It said that "freedom of the press in the United States ... could not long survive the repeated exercise by Congress of unlimited inquiry into the conduct of newspapers." No member of the committee defended McCarthy's actions, but its report said that members were undecided whether the incident constituted a clear and present danger to freedom of the press justifying a specific challenge, a position much like Krock's.

The *Denver Post*, on the "left-wing" list, did not immediately join the fight against McCarthy. Edward J. Dooley, its managing editor all through the McCarthy period, recalls that Colorado was solidly isolationist and fiercely anti-Communist in those days and that the paper's editorial policy was militantly anti-Communist.[35] This was reflected in the *Post's* first McCarthy editorial, on 21 February 1950, which warned readers that "there are many traitors among us" and that "we must root them out lest they destroy us."

According to Dooley, Palmer (Ep) Hoyt, editor and publisher, had thought at first that there must be something to McCarthy's charges because they were made by a United States senator. But he grew suspicious as McCarthy's numbers (of Communists) kept changing, and came to the conclusion that the senator was "shooting from the hip." Then he decided that what McCarthy was doing was "outrageous" and jumped into the fight with both feet. "We really got a hell of a lot of heat," Dooley said.

The strong reaction of its readers was apparently one reason for the *Post's* lasting reputation as a courageous critic of McCarthy. The paper also carried the strongly critical syndicated columns of the Alsop brothers and Drew Pearson, which reinforced its editorial position. But what the *Post* is known best for, particularly in the newspaper fraternity, is a memorandum of February 1953 from Hoyt to Dooley on how the paper could avoid being "used" by McCarthy; it was circulated in virtually ever newspaper office in the country, debated at meetings of newspaper editors, and attacked by the American Civil Liberties Union. It stands as one of the milestones in the evolution from purely "straight" reporting to interpretive reporting.[36]

In the memorandum, Hoyt wrote that "in view of the mounting tide of McCarthyism," he wanted to suggest precautions against "loose charges, irresponsible utterances and attempts at character assassination." The memorandum instructed the news staff to evaluate the sources of charges, to weigh each story to see what they would do with it if official immunity were lacking, and to consider whether the story could not be held until an answer could be received from the person or group accused. These things were not controversial; most responsible newspapers by this time were doing something of the sort. The argument arose over two further points.

One was a suggestion that when members of the news staff knew of their own knowledge that a charge was false, they should "apply any reasonable doubt they [might] have to the treatment of the story." This advice granted a reporter unheard-of latitude; it would permit, conceivably, the inclusion of a flat statement that an accuser was lying.

The second suggestion was that stories could be played down or put into sharper perspective by headlines and placement. "It seems obvious that many charges made by reckless or impulsive public officials cannot and should not be ignored," Hoyt wrote, "but it seems to me that news stories and headlines can be presented in such a manner that the reading public will be able to measure the real worth or value and the true meaning of the stories." In the case of "wild accusations" by McCarthy, the memorandum continued, reporters should remind the public that McCarthy's name was synonymous with "poor documentation and irresponsible conduct." When a story could not be ignored, it might be placed in the middle or lower part of page one, or inside the paper under a small headline. Hoyt wrote that he would like to see a "kicker line" saying "Today's McCarthyism" or "McCarthy Charges Today" over each story.

The staff was instructed that no news story would be complete unless each person attacked by McCarthy had a chance at rebuttal, and it was urged to put pressure on the wire services to furnish speedier rebuttals from McCarthy victims. If rebuttals were not available, editors should insert a "precede" or a "drop-in" saying that similar charges had proved untrue or that those accused had not had a chance to answer.

The American Civil Liberties Union, in a letter to newspaper publishers from Patrick Murphy Malin, executive director, said that the ACLU's free speech committee was concerned that the last two suggestions by Hoyt could result in slanting the news, and that use of the "kicker" would suggest to readers that everything Senator McCarthy said was false, "which is a broad assumption."[37]

Dooley does not recall that the *Post* went as far as Hoyt's memorandum suggested, but the memorandum did result in changes in the handling of McCarthy stories there and probably at a number of other newspapers.

Hoyt made a number of impassioned speeches in which he enjoined other editors to realize the menace of McCarthyism. One of these was on 21 November 1954 at Tucson, Arizona, in which he called Mc-Carthy "a grave threat to all our basic liberties":

During the years in which the dark shadow of Joe McCarthy has spread over the landscape, by no means have all newspapers shown him up for what he is—a grave threat to all our basic liberties by his contemptuous flouting of the rights of individuals. . . . Thus it is necessary for newspapers to function more sharply, more adequately than ever before. And, believe me, there is nothing wrong with this country that repeated strong dosages of the facts will not correct. Even McCarthyism will melt away before this treatment.[38]

In his book *McCarthyism*, McCarthy (or whoever it was who wrote under his name) cast his first chapter in the form of a flashback to 8 March 1950 as he sat in the Senate caucus room waiting to testify before the Tydings subcommittee. As he looked around, he wrote, he saw Richard L. Strout of the *Christian Science Monitor* shaking hands with Rob Hall, a reporter for the Communist *Daily Worker*. He had always thought of the *Monitor* as it had been 20 years before, a respected paper noted for its coverage of foreign news. But as he saw that handshake, the story of Gunther Stein, "the *Christian Science Monitor*'s correspondent in China," flashed across his mind. General MacArthur's intelligence headquarters had exposed the fact that Stein was a Communist and a member of a spy ring, he wrote, after which Stein had disappeared until the spring of 1950, when he was arrested by French police as a Communist spy.*

McCarthy had assumed at first that the *Monitor* had been deceived by Stein when they hired him as a correspondent, but "began to wonder" when he watched Strout and Hall "cheek by jowl" all through the hearing and when he read "the venomous distorted parallel stories which they both wrote."

Knowing that many fine, trusting deeply religious people would get their picture of the evidence of Communists in government from the

---

*According to Anderson and May in their book *McCarthy: The Man, the Senator, the "Ism"* (p. 284), Erwin D. Canham, editor of the *Monitor*, said in 1952 that Stein had never been on the staff of the *Monitor* but that in 1937 on the advice of William Henry Chamberlain, an anti-Communist writer, the paper had accepted special correspondence from Stein. This relationship ended long before publication of spy charges against Stein, Canham said.

pen of Strout, I was disturbed. However, I was doubly disturbed with the thought that if a columnist for a paper like the Christian Science Monitor *could so closely follow the Communist line, no publication and no institution in the entire country could be secure from Communist infiltration.*[39]

Strout's report of that March 8 hearing was a piece of lively description and detached interpretation which could not have resembled anything that appeared in the *Daily Worker*. It told how the committee, "in a mood of angry partisanship," had tried in vain to get "yes or no" answers from McCarthy and how Democrats had constantly interrupted the Republican senator as he delivered his charges about Dorothy Kenyon. Strout's stories and the columns by Joseph C. Harsch during the hearings gave readers of the *Monitor* an accurate picture of what was happening in those hearings and told why it was happening. The *Monitor* carried no editorial on McCarthy during this period.

Strout said (in 1976) that the *Monitor* never did adopt a strong editorial position against McCarthy. The senator or his supporters put a lot of pressure on the paper's board, a group of conservative, religious people, and they were cowed. They were afraid about some correspondent in Asia (Stein, obviously). "Everybody had some Achilles' heel they were hiding in those days," Strout said.[40]

The *Washington Post* was one of the first newspapers to be critical of Senator McCarthy's campaign against "Communists in government," and it was the second newspaper—after the *Capital Times*—to be attacked by McCarthy. In a Senate speech on 6 July 1950, McCarthy warned that some people were saying that "anyone who places the finger upon dupes and traitors in Washington" is found guilty of spreading disunity in the Korean War effort. "Already," he said, "this cry has reached fantastic pinnacles of moronic thinking. Take, for example, the local *Daily Worker*—that is, the *Washington Post*."

The *Post's* coverage of McCarthy was probably the best in the nation. Its editorials, most of them written by Alan Barth, were calm and reasoned, but forceful and unremitting. Herblock's cartoons were devastating. But equally important was the daily reporting of McCarthy's doings, first by Alfred Friendly and then, for four years, by Murrey Marder. The *Post* also, through its correspondents, regularly carried many stories on McCarthy's activities in Wisconsin and other parts of the country. Especially demanding of space was the detail of the defense of persons accused by McCarthy; McCarthy's charges sounded simple, but an accurate and adequate explanation of the facts behind the charges took many columns of type. Friendly, writing in 1977, explained the decision to provide this kind of coverage. "The paper was in dire financial straits," he wrote. "Its space for news was a fraction of what it now provides and every inch was valued in ounces of gold. Yet, seeing what had to be done, the paper vouchsafed those who covered the story a good two columns a day, a grotesquely disproportionate allocation in the light of its meager news space. There was no other way to provide coverage of a sort that let the reader decide the truth for himself."[41]

As early as 9 March 1950, the *Post* devoted more than four columns a day to the McCarthy story, as hearings got underway before the Tydings subcommittee. Four years later, on 11 March 1954, it carried nine stories, an editorial, a column, and a picture, a total of 234 inches, almost 10 columns of McCarthy news.

Murrey Marder had covered the Hiss trial in 1949, then gone to Harvard for an academic year on a Nieman Fellowship. He started covering McCarthy in January 1951. Friendly, who had covered the early McCarthy speeches and the Tydings committee, became assistant managing editor and picked Marder as his replacement. This assignment was not unexpected, and Marder had given a lot of thought, while at Harvard, to the best way of reporting the McCarthy story. "I started with the premise that the existing method of coverage was not satisfactory," he explained in an interview. "We were caught in an illusory concept of objectivity, a narrow definition of journalism— don't intrude on the story—that served as a vehicle for McCarthy's multiplying accusations."[42]

The *Post* had been carrying two kinds of stories about McCarthy; one was brief and totally factual, and the other all interpretation, a synopsis. The latter was what Friendly had been writing, and the paper was "getting a lot of flak about it," Marder said. "The bobtailed stories were not telling enough. The synopsis was controversial because it did not record enough specifics. Was there a third track? I decided it was in-depth daily reporting, avoiding any obvious interpretation, but relating it to what had happened the week before and the month before."

"In-depth daily reporting," which Marder did for the next four years, produced a number of internal problems for the *Post*. It took a lot of space, and some of the editors argued that they were expanding and exaggerating McCarthy's importance by devoting two columns a day to his doings. For Marder, it was a time problem. To do what he wanted to do, to give the McCarthy story some perspective, demanded research—research that had to be done on deadline. "So many names were spewed out at those hearings that before I could start I had to index my notes," Marder said. "Phil Potter [*Baltimore*

Sun], Don Irwin [*New York Herald Tribune*], and I would sit there for a long time trying to sort out the charges. Some days there were 100 names." Then Marder would return to the newspaper office, digging into his files to relate McCarthy's new charges with older ones or to find the original source of the charges. "I'd be there until 11 or 12 o'clock every night," Marder said. "I'd write part of the story for the first edition and the rest for the 11:30 deadline, then I'd be fiddling with it until past midnight."

Marder's stories over the four years were detailed and precise and events were all in context. They contained no interpretation, much less opinion, and while there was information enough to satisfy an interested reader, there was little that would make even a McCarthy partisan angry. Barth's editorials and Herblock's cartoons excited the readers; Marder kept them informed. Marder said that he did not recollect McCarthy ever complaining seriously about his stories. "Sometimes he'd tease me. He'd say, 'That was a fairly accurate story you wrote this morning. You'll be in trouble at the *Post*. I think I'll call Phil Graham and tell him I like your coverage. That'll bring the roof down on you.'"

In Marder's view, McCarthy was fundamentally "a mischievous child." "He didn't give a damn about Communism or anything else," Marder said. "It was all a game with Joe. He'd browbeat a witness and then he'd go up and grin at him and expect him to be friendly. That mischievous quality of his was the hardest thing to put into print, especially with the journalistic standards of the day." When McCarthy made a charge against someone, Marder said, his voice would rise to a high-pitched tremolo; then as he finished, he'd go back to his speaking voice, in a much lower register. It was as if he were two different persons.*

Some historians have contended that McCarthy was serious rather than cynical about his charges. "It's probably true that a point came where he started to believe his own stuff," Marder said, "but I don't know if he was serious about Communism in 1953 or just worried about people closing in on him." McCarthy was worried when people in the political center began to challenge him after his attacks on the Army, according to Marder.

The *Washington Post* strongly supported Eisenhower for president in 1952, and Phil Graham, the editor, was certain that the election of a Republican president would remove McCarthy from the public eye.

---

*Sometime in 1951 McCarthy offered me a job on his staff in Washington; he said he'd pay me twice whatever the *Journal* was paying me. I was astounded. "How could you think I'd work for you after what I've written about you?" I asked. "Oh, that doesn't matter," he said, "If you worked for me you'd write it different." That seemed to me to demonstrate his cynicism, or at least his lack of seriousness.

On election night he said to Marder, "This is the end of the McCarthy period. We'll have to find something else for you to do." "You're wrong," Marder said. "You're going to have to put two men on McCarthy now." And that, of course, was the way it turned out. In Marder's judgment, some people never did understand McCarthy. One day a book publisher called him and asked him to write a book about McCarthy's "secret plan to become president of the United States." Marder laughed, and the publisher was offended. "Don't you know about it?" he asked. "I'm told you're the leading authority on McCarthy and you don't know about the plan?" "You'd better find someone else," Marder said. "Joe doesn't have a plan about who he's going to have lunch with tomorrow. He never has any plans."

Marder said that no responsible newspaper could ignore McCarthy before his censure by the Senate. "He was hitting on the most sensitive issue of our times, the East-West issue. You had to take him seriously. It was a period of national turmoil, at least as serious as the reaction to the Vietnam war. Careers and families were destroyed, people committed suicide. Fear was in the atmosphere; you always had to know who you were talking to. It threw into jeopardy all the great American attributes—freedom of speech, thought, and association. Anybody who had been in public life was vulnerable, and you had to think back through all your associations. It was the closest we ever came to a real totalitarian atmosphere."

Before it happened, some of the reporters argued over whether censure of McCarthy would have an effect. Marder said he had thought it would destroy McCarthy's credibility. "And it did," he said. "It stripped him of respectability. We no longer had to consider his daily pronouncements as carrying the weight of a respectable senator. If he hadn't been censured, it would have gone on as it did before."

The *Post* was not always the fat, profitable paper it is today. In 1950 there were four newspapers in Washington, and the *Post* was third in circulation with 184,000, back of the *Star* with 216,000 and the *Times-Herald* with 276,000. On 17 March 1954, Eugene Meyer, the *Post*'s publisher, bought the *Times-Herald* from Col. Robert R. McCormick of the *Chicago Tribune*, eliminating from the capital the only newspaper supporting McCarthy, while elevating the anti-McCarthy *Post* to first in circulation among Washington papers, a position it has never relinquished. It made the *Post* the only morning newspaper in Washington. The morning paper in a capital city is almost a part of government; it helps set the agenda for Congress and the Executive; its news values are absorbed by everyone in government, and its judgments make some issues urgent and others less important. "The sale of the *Times-Herald* to the *Post* was a real blow to Joe," said Willard Edwards, who specialized in anti-Communist reporting and covered McCarthy for the *Chicago Tribune*'s Washington bureau, which was also the *Times-Herald* bureau. "It meant that there was no local morning paper on his side, and the local morning paper is everything in Washington. It was a great blow to all the McCarthy people."[43]

Colonel McCormick had purchased the *Times-Herald* in 1949 for $4,500,000 from seven "faithful employes" to whom it had been left in 1948 by Mrs. Eleanor M. Patterson, a cousin of the colonel and a member of the family which controlled the *Tribune* and the *New York Daily News.* Colonel McCormick discussed the purchase in a speech to his advertising department on 16 November 1950. "When we purchased the *Times-Herald* in Washington last year," he said, "it was not for political reasons, but it gave us an opportunity to take Americanism into the national capital. Before that, the *Times-Herald* had not been a political force. Now the Republican victory in Maryland [over Tydings] was preponderantly the work of the *Times-Herald.* . . ."[44]

Colonel McCormick had been listed as publisher of the *Times-Herald* since the acquisition, and his niece, Mrs. Ruth M. (Bazy) Miller, as editor. But on 6 April 1951 the colonel took over as both editor and publisher. He was 70. He said that he had looked all over for an editor who could make the paper a success. "They told me I was the only one who could handle the job."[45] But Colonel McCormick was sick—he died the following year—and the *Times-Herald* was losing money, advertising, and circulation. The only buyer willing to pay the Colonel's price was Meyer, and the sale at $8,500,000 was considered a good business deal. Nevertheless it must have been a bitter decision for McCormick, whose *Chicago Tribune* had for 10 years denounced and ridiculed the *Post* in its editorial columns.

The *Chicago Tribune* did not follow the general practice of ignoring the existence of other newspapers with differing editorial positions. In his exercise of personal journalism, Colonel McCormick regarded other newspapers as competitors in the political arena, and he hailed each victory of a *Tribune*-endorsed candidate as a personal victory over another paper. The papers he disliked were much the same as those on McCarthy's "left-wing press" list, and his name-calling was even more imaginative than McCarthy's.

On 6 January 1943 a *Tribune* editorial accused Meyer and the *Post* of being part of the "Pantywaist Press," whose policies were the result of social aspirations. Others he put in this group were the *New York Herald-Tribune*, Time, Inc., the Marshall Field papers, the *San Francisco Chronicle*, and the *New York Post.*

On 21 February 1944, a policy story by Frank Hughes, a member of the paper's Washington bureau, was headed "Smear Brigade Sets Stage to Keep F.D.R. In." The *Tribune* lumped the "smear newspapers" into two groups. One was made up of the "independent Republican" papers, "a wing of the international press ... that has sold out its readers to Mr. Roosevelt" by backing Wendell Willkie, "the man Mr. Roosevelt can always beat," for the Republican nomination. These papers were the *New York Herald-Tribune*, the *Milwaukee Journal*, the Cowles newspapers in Des Moines and Minneapolis, the Lee Newspaper syndicate, and Time, Inc. The other group was described as those whose policies were the result of the social aspirations of their publishers. It included the *New York Post, Philadelphia Record, Cleveland Press, Cleveland Plain Dealer, Cleveland News, St. Louis Globe-Democrat, St. Louis Post-Dispatch, Louisville Courier-Journal*, Marshall Field papers, and *Washington Post*. In a subsequent story on 23 March 1944, Hughes wrote that Henry Luce, "the fuehrer of the *Time-Life-Fortune* magazine axis," had been the first "to exploit the tactic of the smear." This tactic was later perfected by Meyer's *Washington Post*, Hughes said. In an editorial of 7 April 1944 headed "The Wood Pussy Press," the *Tribune* said that "a few newspapers have been trying to attract attention to themselves by attacking *The Tribune*." These, it said, were the *Daily Worker, New York Post, Herald-Tribune, PM, Louisville Courier-Journal, Milwaukee Journal, St. Louis Post-Dispatch, New Masses, American Mercury, Time* and *Liberty* magazines, and *Washington Post*. "The *Daily Worker* and the *New Masses* are more honest than the rest of them because they admit their treasonable intent," the editorial said, exactly the argument that McCarthy made so often in later years.

On 12 April 1945 the *Tribune* applied to the War Production Board for newsprint to start a morning newspaper in Milwaukee. The paper's announcement said that the issue on the Republican side of the recent Wisconsin presidential primary had been "Wendell Willkie versus the *Tribune*" and that Willkie's loss in the primary showed that a newspaper like the *Tribune* would fill a "long-felt need" in Wisconsin. (The *Tribune* periodically threatened to start a newspaper in Milwaukee, but Colonel McCormick was, at the bottom, a businessman, and the losses predicted by his accountants kept him from making the move. *Tribune* circulation in Wisconsin declined steadily in postwar years.)

On 29 May 1950 the *Tribune* responded to a *Washington Post* editorial which had charged McCarthy with "witch hunting" by saying that the *Post* had led a witch hunt against critics of President Roosevelt. The *Post*, it said, "[is] so deeply involved with communism that it has borrowed a spare red herring from Mr. Truman and is dragging it across the trail." On 10 July 1950 the *Tribune* wrote that editorials in the *Washington Post*, the *New York Post*, and *Life* magazine had "followed a central thought so faithfully as to suggest that they were the product of some single directive." Six days later, in an editorial headed "Is It Feminism?" the *Tribune* said that the *New York Herald-Tribune* and the *New York Post* followed similar editorial policies because both were headed by women "who seem to prefer the over-bearing arrogance of Englishmen to the deferential courtesy of Americans." The *Washington Post*, it said, belongs to Eugene Meyer but is dominated by Mrs. Meyer and "is on the Red side of purple." *Time* magazine, it said, has the same approach because "Henry Luce has borrowed Dorothy Thompson's panties and is unable to fill them out completely." On 1 September 1950, the *Tribune* listed a group of papers, this time including the *Capital Times*, as the "Insect Press," with "pitiful circulations . . . conducted by the strange inferiority complexes of auburn millionaires."

Beginning 5 February 1951, the *Tribune* and the *Times-Herald* published another series attacking the press in New York and Washington, a series written by William Fulton. The first story, headed "How Globalist Sirens Seduce New York Press," called the *New York Times* and the *Herald-Tribune* "bellwethers for the internationalist line." These papers reflected the prevailing thought of the "bankers and sharp traders of the Wall St. financial district" and were now supporting the Marshall Plan for aid to Europe, Fulton wrote. "When they are not plugging for the U.N., Eisenhower, Dewey and other globists, the papers are busy attacking 'McCarthyism' (Sen. McCarthy's demands for cleaning Communists and perverts out of the state department). . . . Sometimes called 'the Washington Pravda' after the Communist party newspaper in Moscow, the *Washington Post* is chalking up a record for defending Reds and pinkos, slavish devotion to the Truman administration and violent attacks on pro-American members of Congress." Fulton also accused the Washington bureau of the Associated Press of an anti-McCarthy bias. Fulton said that Meyer had been a Republican but had changed parties because President Truman had appointed him president of the International Bank; he said that Meyer's son-in-law, Philip Graham, publisher of the paper, had been one of Felix Frankfurter's "radicals"; that Mrs. Meyer was "a clubwoman who has gone in for social causes"; that Herbert Elliston, the editor, was "British-born"; that Ben Gilbert, the city editor, had been a member of the Young Communist League; and that Alan Barth, the chief editorial writer, was "the leading architect of the *Post's* pinko structure." In another article, Fulton wrote that the *New Yorker* magazine "has been carrying the torch for notorious pinkos" and that some writers for that magazine and for *Time* have been "outright Communists." He also charged that book reviewers for the *New York Times*, the *Herald-Tribune*, and the *Saturday Review of Literature* had panned anti-Communist books and praised pro-Communist authors. Under the heading "Dozens of Left-Wing Writers Carry on Drive for Globalism" Fulton listed columnists Drew Pearson, Walter Winchell, Elmer Davis, Marquis Childs, Harold Ickes, Eleanor Roosevelt, Thomas L. Stokes, Doris Fleeson, Frank Kingdon, Frank Edwards (a radio commentator), and Joseph and Stewart Alsop. The Alsops, he said, "have never quite gotten over the fact they are distant relatives of the late President Roosevelt."

An editorial on 28 April 1951 was based on a report that President Truman read four newspapers each day—the *New York Times*, the *Herald-Tribune*, the *Baltimore Sun*, and the *Washington Post*. "The selection gives a good indication of why he is so frequently out of touch with what the people of the United States are saying and thinking," the *Tribune* said. "There is little wonder that the little chump doesn't realize he's a chump." In an editorial on 4 January 1952, the *Tribune* listed publications which had criticized McCarthy but were never "unkind" to Owen Lattimore, whom McCarthy had called "the architect of our Far Eastern policy." It included the *Post* and the usual others, but also included the *Christian Science Monitor*, the *Minneapolis Tribune*, the *Erie Dispatch*, and the *Providence Bulletin*. On 16 February 1952, the *Tribune* suggested that there was a conspiracy on the part of "the Truman press" to support Mr. Truman's "illegal" entry into the Korean War and to criticize Senator Taft for his criticism of Truman. It suggested that the *Washington Post* was the leader of this conspiracy.

When I talked with him, Willard Edwards said that, without question, the *Chicago Tribune* was McCarthy's "stoutest, most unquestioning supporter." And even though Edwards was a personal friend and journalistic ally of McCarthy, he was sometimes appalled by the enthusiasm of the *Tribune's* editorial writers. "I considered McCarthy a good news source," Edwards said. "I cultivated him for that."

For a while, I functioned as almost a member of McCarthy's staff. I'd go out and investigate things for him. I liked and enjoyed Joe McCarthy. I was never perturbed by the thought that I should check everything he said. Sometimes, when other reporters couldn't get past Mary Driscoll [McCarthy's secretary], I'd make the call and get us in.

But I realized later that he was almost uncontrollable. I'll tell you how I came to know that Joe exaggerated. Some of the staff came to me and asked me to write a speech for Joe. They had a good solid

*case about the infiltration of the National Labor Relations Board—
people with Communist leanings, Communist propensities, etc., all
those words we used those days when we didn't have actual proof
that they were Communists.*

*I did it reluctantly. I deliberately understated it. My lead was: "I
rise to present evidence demonstrating the existence of Communist
leanings among a number of officials of the NLRB." . . . I handed the
speech in. Nothing happened for two weeks, and I called over to ask
what happened. They said, "Joe's working on it."*

*Finally he gave it. His lead was: "I rise to present evidence that the
NLRB is honeycombed with members of the Communist party."*

*That was his great flaw—exaggeration. If the Communists had want-
ed to pick someone to attack them, they couldn't have done better.
It killed anti-Communism for years. It did give the Communist party
a setback, though, which partly compensated for it. Communism hasn't
amounted to much since 1954.*

Edwards remembered first meeting McCarthy in 1948 or 1949 at a
noisy party in the apartment of Ray Kiermas, McCarthy's assistant,
in whose back bedroom McCarthy lived. "Joe had a trick that he liked,
and each newcomer would have to do it," Edwards said. "Joe would
balance a marble on the newcomer's head and tell him he had to
drop it into a funnel stuck under the belt of his pants. Then Joe would
pour warm water into the funnel. He thought that was a great joke.
He never did grow up. He was just a kid on the playground, but he
was the leader, and he never wanted anyone to help him. He wouldn't
take advice. I tried to help him. Edward Bennett Williams [McCarthy's
attorney] tried to advise him, but he wouldn't listen. If he had just
been willing to compromise a little, he could have avoided censure,
but he wouldn't compromise." Jean Kerr, McCarthy's assistant whom
he later married, was "very smart about the press, but she was another
he wouldn't take advice from," according to Edwards. Edwards said
that McCarthy disliked stories about his personal affairs:

*Once he knew something about the scandal about Air Force Sec-
retary Talbott and he decided to give a leak to the New York Times—
to Bill Lawrence, who hated him—and it was a good scoop, played
on page one by the Times. Oh, I was mad. I decided to get back at
him, so I wrote a story about his troubled relations with Jean Kerr
before their marriage, how she rejected him, etc., a real gossip story.
We were in New York when it broke, and the New York Daily News
played it big—"The Troubled Times of Jean and Joe." I avoided him
for a day. He said to me the next day, "You were smart to stay out
of sight—I'd have killed you yesterday." I told him there would be
no more stories like that if he stopped leaking to the New York Times.*

Edwards estimated that in 1953 and 1954 from 40 to 50 reporters were assigned to cover McCarthy daily. Most of the reporters enjoyed him and relations were friendly, but two or three of them disliked him, and McCarthy liked to embarrass those reporters. (Murrey Marder disagreed with this estimate, saying that only about 10 reporters covered McCarthy regularly in those years, representing the three wire services, the *Washington Post*, the *Washington Star*, the *New York Times*, the *Baltimore Sun*, the *Boston Globe*, and Drew Pearson's staff.)

"Phil Potter [*Baltimore Sun*] was one who really detested him," Edwards said. "He was very emotional about it. Phil told me that after that thing about [Secretary of the Army] Stevens's 'chicken dinner,' it literally made him sick to his stomach—he couldn't write the story. But even Phil got along with him personally on a joking basis."[46]

Coverage of McCarthy by the *Baltimore Sun* was as thorough as that of the *Washington Post*. Potter did most of the Washington reporting on McCarthy, but Gerald Griffin, later managing editor of the *Sun*, also covered him there and on the road. "My relationship with McCarthy was, by my choice at least, arm's length," Griffin recalled in a letter.

I found him courteous, affable, and generally obliging in conversation and in answering questions. I had difficulty in keeping up with his campaign travels in 1952—he was speaking in many states in support of candidates he favored—but that was largely because of the secretiveness and suspicious attitude of his staff people. He told me of his schedule when I could see him. Once he invited me to travel with him in his private plane. I declined and told my managing editor I didn't want to feel obligated to McCarthy in any way; the editor agreed, even though it meant that I would miss some of his speeches.[47]

Griffin didn't remember McCarthy attacking the *Sun* or calling it the Baltimore *Daily Worker*. "The *Sun* had no use for him editorially, but in its news columns printed a lot about him."

I myself was influenced by a former managing editor, William E. Moore, who thought that the best way to expose something he disliked was to put it on page one . . . on the premise that sensible people shared his attitude and should know what was going on. I still believe in this, as opposed to the silent treatment. The Sun, I recall, was one of the few newspapers that gave any space to McCarthy's monstrous "charges" of pro-Communism against General Marshall; I thought the McCarthy speech in the Senate was so absurd that the public should know about it. Looking back, I think we were right; how can a dem-

*agogue and a dangerous man be exposed unless his actions and words
are first reported?*

In Griffin's opinion, given the political climate of the early 1950s,
newspapers could not have stifled McCarthy even if they were agreed
on how to deal with him. "I don't recall that any single newspaper
was especially successful in handling him," he wrote.

I liked—and still do—the way the Milwaukee Journal *treated him,
but I remember McCarthy was re-elected in 1952. I think Phil Potter
did as well as any reporter, and better than most, in covering Mc-
Carthy factually. It took facts to bring McCarthy down to earth, and
this, as I saw it, took much more painstaking effort and time to develop—more than most newspapers chose to allow. Yet the newspapers functioned in reporting what McCarthy was doing and
eventually the truth caught up with him. It was a painful process.*

Edwards, the *Tribune* reporter, differed on this point. "The anti-
McCarthy press did more to make McCarthy than anyone else," he
said, "especially the *Washington Post*."

One day I counted 18 articles in the Post *about McCarthy; that
couldn't help but build him up.*
*That was also proved by the press boycott after censure. If the anti-
McCarthy press had been smart enough to play him down, he'd have
been beaten much earlier. There was a real silence after the censure.
McCarthy kept appearing for a while on the Senate floor, but most
of what he said was not even reported.*

Edwards remembers that one day in 1955 William S. White came
out of the press gallery and said to him, "I was just listening to a
speech by Joe McCarthy. It was a hell of a speech." He said he was
going to write a big story about it, but in the *Times* the next day it
was a one-paragraph story—a "shirttail"—on page 47, which indicated
to Edwards that the *Times* had adopted a policy of suppressing news
of McCarthy.

No publication fought McCarthy more tirelessly than the *Progressive*, a monthly magazine founded in 1909 by Robert M. La Follette,
Sr., and published in Madison, Wisconsin. Its editor and publisher
in 1950 was Morris H. Rubin. Like other journals of political opinion,
the *Progressive* had a limited circulation and a long lead time for its
articles. It was read by many who held influential places in politics
and the media, but it never had great public impact.

On two occasions, however, it did break into the national news with special publications that presented an array of facts about McCarthy, and each of these publications had a lasting effect. The first, in the summer of 1952, was *The McCarthy Record*, mentioned earlier, intended to bring out the unpleasant facts about McCarthy before the 1952 election. It was sponsored by a group of Wisconsin citizens of both parties as a nonpartisan effort and bore no visible relationship to the *Progressive*, but Rubin, its editor, was the force behind its publication. It was, at the time, the best single source of information on McCarthy's career, until Rubin produced another more complete, updated study of McCarthy.

The second was published in April 1954 as a special issue of the *Progressive* titled *McCarthy: A Documented Record*. It ran 96 pages and sold for 75 cents. Rubin said that the press run was 180,000 and that all were sold. Its value was as a reference book. "People needed something they could rely on, something that was documented," Rubin said. "They needed facts so that they could answer questions on the local level. Editors, speakers needed it. We made a tremendous effort to make sure everything was right. We were much more thorough than the Woodward and Bernstein [*Washington Post* Watergate reporters] system of two sources. We knew that if McCarthy could have found just one error, he could have discredited the whole thing."[48]

Rubin sent the first copy to McCarthy by registered mail, return receipt requested, with an offer of equal space—96 pages—for a reply. McCarthy never answered, but the receipt came back. When Washington reporters asked McCarthy about the publication, he refused to comment. Rubin held a press conference at the Willard Hotel in Washington to introduce the publication. He expected a dozen reporters, at most, but 40 or 50 came. "I had to send out for more whiskey," he told me. The Eisenhower White House ordered six copies, then 12 more, and one Washington book store called Madison to re-order 500, then again in the afternoon 500 more.

Rubin said that he believed the publication of this documented record was one of the factors in McCarthy's downfall. During the hearings that preceded McCarthy's censure by the Senate, the committee chairman, Senator Watkins, had a copy of the special edition on his desk, he said. Not once, however, did McCarthy attack the publication or its editor. No other opposition publication that McCarthy knew about escaped his attacks. And in Rubin's opinion, this was because of the *Progressive*'s historical connection with the La Follettes. McCarthy never did anything that he thought would offend the former Progressives in Wisconsin, Rubin said.

One effect of the McCarthy affair was to start on the path to journalistic fame a young woman who had never before covered a hard
news story and who has since held a place for two decades as one
of the top political reporters in the country. McCarthyism gave us
Mary McGrory.

Mary McGrory was a cub reporter and feature writer when the
editors of the *Washington Star* assigned her to cover the Army-
McCarthy hearings in the spring of 1954. She knew almost nothing
about McCarthy and she hadn't been following the hearings closely.
That didn't matter; cover it as though you were a drama critic, she
was told by her editor. It was a sound idea; everyone in Washington
who cared about the hearings watched them on television, and there
were no surprises left for the newspapers, especially an afternoon
paper like the *Star*, whose accounts of the hearings appeared in print
24 hours after the event.

Miss McGrory said that she conceived her job as explaining to the
television audience who the people were and what they were like.
"I covered it for 36 days," she said. "I never spoke to McCarthy. I
never interviewed anyone. I wrote around McCarthy. I never took
him head-on. I concentrated on the people—Cohn, Jenkins."[49]

Her stories were irreverent, sardonic, and full of description. "The
star, Senator Joe McCarthy, ploughs his high-shouldered way through
the crowds amid small cheers," she wrote on 23 April 1954. Ray Jenkins, she described as "a big bear-like man with short brown hair and
a forehead furrowed with three deep vertical lines." Mary McGrory
remembered the first time she saw McCarthy, "with his light eyes
under heavy black brows. . . . 'There's a bully if I ever saw one,' I
said to myself."

Coverage of McCarthy in the *Star* up to that time had been thorough,
fair, but conservative, mostly by Cecil Holland, the political reporter.
The paper was solidly Republican, and its editorials, while sometimes
critical of McCarthy, were often critical of his opposition. One of its
columnists, Constantine Brown, was aggressively pro-McCarthy.
Readers were not prepared for Mary McGrory's cheeky reports. "The
readers were just outraged," she said. "We got a lot of mail, and the
editors were besieged, but Newbold Noyes [the editor] kept them all
away from me. It was so vehement, on both sides. Some people said
I had joined Judith Coplon and Alger Hiss, but others said, 'Can we
adopt her? Can we take her out to dinner?' "

The McGrory stories became required reading in Washington, and
she was assigned to cover the Watkins committee hearings on Mc-
Carthy and the Senate debate on censure. From then on, Mary
McGrory covered politics.

It is hard to think of a less likely target for Senator McCarthy than the stuffy old *Saturday Evening Post*, a weekly magazine best known for its fiction—stories of Alexander Botts, the tractor salesman, Octavus Roy Cohen's Florian Slappey, Tugboat Annie, and Ephraim Tutt, the New England country lawyer. It is also difficult to think of a newspaper columnist whom the epithet "pro-Communist" was less likely to fit than Joseph Alsop, the hard-lining, hawkish, passionate advocate of the maintenance of United States military superiority. But these were McCarthy's targets when he rose in the Senate on 8 August 1950 to read a letter he had written to the editors of the *Post*.

What precipitated this attack was an article by Joseph and Stewart Alsop, the brothers who shared the column, in the July 29 issue of the *Saturday Evening Post*, in which the Alsops wrote of the "miasma of fear" which hung over Washington, the mood of suspicion and distrust and the widespread conviction, on the part of both the State Department and the McCarthyites, that telephones were tapped and spies and informers were everywhere. It ended with the familiar Alsop plea to keep the nation strong militarily and to resist the penny-pinching doctrine of the midwestern isolationist Republicans who said that the threat to national security came from within the government rather than from abroad, thus making it unnecessary to spend money for national defense and foreign aid.

McCarthy was only one of several who were blamed for this state of affairs, and only four paragraphs in the article, which ran 10 columns, concerned McCarthy. The story also deplored the effort of Senator Kenneth Wherry of Nebraska, the minority leader, "to elevate the subject of homosexuality [in the State Department] to the level of a serious political issue on the ground that sexual perversion presents a clear and present danger to the security of the United States."

In his letter, McCarthy took particular exception to the line in the Alsop story which referred to "furtive-looking characters" in the senator's anteroom. He saw this as a reference to his office staff, although the article described these people as probable State Department informants rather than staff. McCarthy said that he had one of the "finest and most loyal" office staffs on Capitol Hill and that this "smear" was highly unfair. Most of the letter concerned what he called an attempt to condemn Senator Wherry "for attempting to remove sexual perverts from sensitive positions in our Government." "The article refers to this as 'vulgar' and 'nauseating,' " McCarthy said. "Upon first reading this I could hardly believe my eyes and again checked to make sure it was the *Saturday Evening Post* I was reading."

He went on to say that the Roman Empire had come to an end when the ruling class became "morally perverted and degenerate" and that any intelligence officer would testify that a "moral pervert" in a sensitive position was a security risk because of his susceptibility to blackmail. "I know some of your editorial staff and frankly I can't believe that Senator Wherry's attempt to accomplish the long overdue task of removing perverts from our Government would be considered either 'vulgar' or 'nauseating' to them," McCarthy said. "I can understand, of course, why it would be considered 'vulgar' or 'nauseating' by Joe Alsop."

This insinuation that Joe Alsop, like McCarthy a bachelor, was a homosexual, was underlined in another paragraph in which McCarthy said Alsop had never been in his office and that the only person from the *Post* who had ever been there was a photographer who seemed to be "a fine normal young man." McCarthy could not believe that the Alsops' article represented the thinking of the *Post*'s editorial staff, he wrote. "But at the same time, certainly the *Post* knew what it was doing when it hired a Joe Alsop to write this article for it."

Ben Hibbs, editor of the *Post*, replied to McCarthy by letter on August 10, saying that the Alsops and the *Saturday Evening Post* were against the employment of "traitors and perverts" by the government just as McCarthy was but that they also opposed "wild, unsupported charges such as you are making." Hibbs listed all the things the *Post* had done to expose "home-grown Communists" and said that if McCarthy had read the magazine's editorial page he would have noticed their criticism of the Tydings committee "for its job of whitewashing in the Communist investigation." "We have criticized officials from President Truman on down who have tried to hush up the investigation of Communists in government," Hibbs wrote. Hibbs asked that McCarthy put this letter in the *Congressional Record*, which McCarthy did not do, and ended with a defense of Joseph Alsop: "I'd like to say that I think your insinuations about Joe Alsop ill become a United States Senator. I know Alsop well, and I know he is a man of high character, with great courage and integrity." Stewart Alsop wrote Hibbs on August 11 that he had heard that Hibbs had "cracked back hard" at McCarthy. "I'm glad to hear it," he wrote. "The [McCarthy] letter seemed to me a particularly slimy business—the sly hint that Joe wasn't 'healthy and normal' like Ollie Atkins [the photographer]."[50]

McCarthy wrote again to Hibbs on August 25, a letter which, this time, he did *not* place in the *Congressional Record*, and which contained the most naked threat McCarthy made against any newsman. As usual, he ignored Hibbs's protestations of anti-Communism and said that the Alsops are "numbered among that group which throws pebbles at Communism in general in an apparent attempt to obtain a phony anti-Communist reputation, and then are found in the vanguard of those who try to smear and destroy anyone attempting to expose the really dangerous Communists—the underground Communists who are in a position to do tremendous damage." McCarthy said that he had noticed Hibbs's objections to his "insinuations" about Joe Alsop, and continued:

One of the things I learned early in life back on the farm was that if you start a fight you should not start crying if you get kicked hard where it hurts in return. When Alsop used your publication to describe McCarthy as being a victim of palsy [the story had reported "a continued tremor which makes his head shake in a disconcerting fashion"], which no one else in Washington seems to have discovered, I think he should expect that I may publicly discuss any of his mental or physical aberrations which I see fit.

I might also add that Alsop or anyone else who gets in the way of cleaning the Communists out of government may well get injured.[51]

Hibbs's reply to this, on September 11, was a listing of other antiCommunist articles published by the *Post*, such as Matt Cvetic's "I Posed as a Communist for the FBI." He ended with a less critical characterization of McCarthy's misdeeds:

We have been constantly critical of President Truman's "red herring" attitude on this Communist issue and have urged searching investigations. My own guess is that there are some pinks in the State Department and in other government departments and agencies, and of course they should be found and ousted; but it seems to me that this can be done without besmirching innocent people and without making such broadside charges that people will lose faith in all government.[52]

Over the next four years, the Alsops repeatedly proposed antiMcCarthy articles to the *Post*, but its editors always found reasons for not commissioning such articles "at the present time." The *Saturday Evening Post* published no further articles on McCarthy, and it seems likely that for once he had been successful in intimidating a publication. Joe Alsop, who had pressed these story suggestions with great urgency, wrote me in 1976 that he did not remember whether the *Post* had been intimidated: "Had I been Hibbs, I should not have attempted any crusading," he said. "The old *Post* was just not that kind of magazine. Furthermore, I would guess that about 30 percent of its readers were fairly ardent McCarthyites."

The Alsops continued to hammer at McCarthy in their syndicated column despite the loss of about 20 client newspapers. One particularly vigorous cancellation letter came from Richard Lloyd Jones, publisher of the *Tulsa Tribune*, on 7 November 1952.

We don't have to give any reasons for dropping you, Mr. Alsop [Jones wrote]. I ordered you out as a contributor to our paper. And that is all that is necessary for you to know.

I don't like your stuff.

You are one of those chaps that condemned Joe for telling truths you were not brave enough to face . . .

We are infested with sneaks, liars, corruptionists, traitors and these horrors do not seem to concern you nor the sophisticated journalistic stupids who, calling themselves "liberals," haven't any idea what liberty is.[53]

The Alsops never lost sight of the policy implications of McCarthyism. To them, McCarthy was primarily important as a tool in the hands of the isolationist bloc in Congress. Isolationism was an important part of McCarthy's appeal to Wisconsin voters, and his criticism of the unpopular war in Korea was always well received by Wisconsin audiences. On 18 September 1950, before an American Legion group in Houston, Texas, he had said, "American blood is being used to wash out the blunders of Acheson and his crowd. If Truman keeps him on there won't be any blood left."[54] And speaking at the Lincoln Day dinner of the Council of South Side Advancement Associations in Milwaukee on 13 February 1952, he was applauded when he said that the United States did not have the manpower to fight Communists all over the world: "Let others do it," he said. "We should equip them. Acheson wants American boys to do all the fighting and dying."[55]

Other Republicans considered more respectable than McCarthy were sounding the same theme, of course. Senator Taft, campaigning in the 1952 Wisconsin presidential primary, kept saying "It's a Truman war" and attacking the military draft.[56] So did Everett Dirksen, running for the Senate in Illinois; his theme was that the Administration cared more about aid to Paris, France, than to Paris, Illinois.[57] And Senator Nixon, campaigning in 1952 as the nominee for vice president, told college students they would be drafted if the Democrats were returned to power.[58] McCarthyism was essential to this line of argument; it made it possible to be against Communists at home while ignoring Communists abroad, where the real danger lay. The Alsops belabored this point.

McCarthy never renewed his insinuations about Joe Alsop's sexuality. He frequently assailed him, as he did others, as a follower of the *Daily Worker*'s line, and he regularly referred to him as "Allslop," one of those simulated slips of the tongue with which McCarthy delighted his audiences.

More than one-third of the Alsops' mail from readers during the McCarthy years objected to criticism of McCarthy. Writers of such letters got uncompromising answers. But according to Joe Alsop, the pro-McCarthy mail began to drop off in mid-1953, almost a year before such a trend showed up in the Gallup Poll, and Alsop said he knew then that McCarthy was on his way down.[59]

The Alsop columns were blunt. "What's wrong with McCarthy," they wrote on 25 October 1952, "is simply that he does not play the American political game according to the rules. He cheats. He proceeds on the assumption that the voters are too stupid to prefer the complicated truth to the simple, dramatic lie. So far, moreover, McCarthy has gotten away with playing the American voters for boobs." In his column following McCarthy's major campaign speech in Shorewood in September 1952, Joe Alsop wrote: "Then came McCarthy, with a typical crafty, oily, falsely emotional, contrived speech, including an obvious fabrication concerning his former relations with the late James Forrestal. . . ."

Objectivity was not a goal pursued by many columnists, and the Alsop column never bowed that way. One gets the impression that manipulation of government officials to do what the Alsops considered best for the United States was at least as much their goal as providing information or persuading readers to a point of view.

Alsop has not perceived a change for the better in newspaper practices as a result of the McCarthy period. "I am horrified by what has happened to our business," he told me, in a reference to Watergate. "Independence, honest reporting, hard work, are the qualities that I value in newspapers. I do not value self-dramatization, self-righteousness, and self-appointment to be the moral censors of the nation. . . . All these rules seem to me to have been forgotten in the last years, and I am persuaded that our business will pay a heavy bill for this forgetfulness in the years to come."

The columnist with whom McCarthy feuded most bitterly was Drew Pearson, a flamboyant muckraker whose column was carried by more newspapers than that of any other columnist. Pearson also reached millions of people through his weekly radio and television broadcasts. He was a formidable adversary. Pearson began criticizing McCarthy during the first month of the senator's crusade against Communists in government, and he never let up. For many readers, his column was the only source of anti-McCarthy comment available in newspapers which either favored McCarthy editorially or failed to comment at all.

There is much uncertainty about how it began and exactly what happened, but on 12 December 1950, in the men's cloakroom of Washington's Sulgrave Club, McCarthy either punched, slapped, or kicked Pearson.[60] The "fight" was broken up by Senator Richard M. Nixon. McCarthy had let it be known that he planned to attack Pearson in the Senate, and that was the apparent cause of the brawl. He said that Pearson had said to him, "McCarthy, if you talk about personal things regarding me on the Senate floor, I'll get you," after which, McCarthy told reporters, "I slapped him in the face. I slapped him hard." According to Pearson, the senator kicked him twice in the groin, and Fulton Lewis, Jr., a broadcaster and McCarthy confidant, said that McCarthy had punched Pearson, lifting him "three feet off the floor." Later, in a court hearing, Pearson testified that McCarthy had been "badgering" him, trying to force him to leave the club.[61] He said that he had asked McCarthy, "Joe, how is your income tax case coming along? When are they going to put you in jail?" and that McCarthy had answered, "You take that back," and challenged him to come outside and fight, a challenge he refused. Later, when he was leaving the club, McCarthy came up to him from behind, pinned his arms, swung him around and kicked him in the groin. Then McCarthy kicked him a second time and said, "Take that back about my income taxes."

McCarthy made his heralded attack on Pearson three days later on the Senate floor. He called Pearson a "Moscow-directed character assassin" and an "unprincipled liar and fake" with a "twisted, perverted mentality." Much of his speech was a 10-year collection of diatribes against Pearson by politicians and others who thought they had been maligned by Pearson. He also said that Pearson and the Communists had hounded to death the late James Forrestal, President Roosevelt's Secretary of the Navy, and that David Karr, a Pearson employe, had been a member of the Communist party. He ended the speech by calling upon editors and radio stations to stop carrying Pearson's columns and broadcasts in order to still "this voice of international Communism," and he demanded that citizens boycott the Adam Hat Co., the sponsor of Pearson's broadcasts. "Anyone who buys an Adams [sic] hat," he said, "any store that stocks an Adams hat, anyone who buys from a store that stocks an Adams hat, is unknowingly and innocently contributing to the cause of international Communism by keeping this Communist spokesman on the air."

McCarthy reprinted this speech and two subsequent speeches about

Pearson in a 32-page booklet which he sent to Wisconsin newspaper editors and others. Because the remarks had been made on the Senate floor, he was immune from libel or slander. Pearson sued, nevertheless, on 2 March 1951, asking $5,100,000 in damages from McCarthy and eight other persons, mostly McCarthy employes, charging libel, conspiracy, and assault, the latter charge based on the Sulgrave Club incident.[62] Pretrial hearings in the suit produced many headlines in the next three years, but Pearson dropped the suit in 1954, ostensibly because court officers had been unable to find and serve papers on the necessary witnesses.

On 30 December 1950, the Adam Hat Stores, Inc., announced that it would not continue as Pearson's sponsor.[63] The company's president said that the decision had been made in May 1950 and had nothing to do with McCarthy's call for a boycott of its products. This was confirmed by Pearson, who said that he thought McCarthy might have known of this decision a few days before he called for the boycott and was trying to steal the credit for ending the broadcasts. Generally, however, it was believed that McCarthy's speech had been a factor in the company's decision.

In an obituary column that followed McCarthy's death, Pearson wrote that "the silent treatment" by the press and television after his censure had killed McCarthy. "The exhilarating stimulus of the crowds, of the headlines, of the klieg lights ruined Joe's effectiveness in his earlier days," he wrote. "The exhilarating stimulus of alcohol ruined his effectiveness in recent days. These last three weeks, he had been on a literal whiskey diet. He had been on it before and gone to the hospital—three times in nine months. Once he had kicked a hospital corpsman, had been kept in restraints, had sometimes been out of his mind. . . . I'm afraid Joe wanted to die. He would not have stuck to his diet of whiskey had he wanted to live."[64]

The *Portland Oregonian* was the most conservative newspaper on McCarthy's "left-wing press" list. It normally supported Republicans, although it had supported Senator Wayne Morse, considered a left-wing Republican, until Morse broke with the GOP during the Eisenhower-Stevenson campaign of 1952. "We were very critical of McCarthy from the beginning," said Malcolm Bauer, who with Herbert Lundy wrote most of the anti-McCarthy editorials. "We felt that his accusations were unfounded." Later, Bauer said, they were critical of General Eisenhower for his failure to stand up for General Marshall against McCarthy.[65]

Bauer did not know how McCarthy found out about the paper's editorial position, but McCarthy had visited Portland several times between 1950 and 1952 and might have seen one or more of the editorials. "One editorial slur against his attacks on Reds in government would do it, as far as Joe was concerned," according to A. Robert Smith, who covered state and local politics for the *Oregonian* in those days. "For McCarthy, the division was simple: you are either for me or against me, for freedom or Communism. So I guess there were many of us who might have qualified as left-wingers to Joe, including the good gray *Oregonian*."

I used to live around the corner from Joe on Capitol Hill [Smith wrote to me]. He was a sad sack, basically an irrational person, and the most all-consuming opportunist whose remarks required no rational foundation. I always thought he dreamed up that term left-wing press to explain or dismiss any newspaper which didn't cheer him or dared to criticize his outrageous behavior. It was a tactic to counteract any tendency to thoughtful analysis.[66]

McCarthy never attacked the *San Francisco Chronicle*, although that staunchly Republican paper published 93 anti-McCarthy editorials from 1950 through 1954, according to Ken McArdle, a *Chronicle* editorial writer from 1945 through 1954 and chief editorial writer from 1949 on. McArdle said that the paper's criticism of McCarthy did cost the paper one large advertising account, that of a clothing store called Atkins. The owner came to Charles Thieriot, the publisher, and demanded a change in editorial policy. But Thieriot and the editorial board decided that a change was unthinkable, and Atkins withdrew his advertising for six months. Later that year, toward the end of the Army-McCarthy hearings, Atkins ordered a full page, and the boycott ended.[67]

Time magazine, almost always on McCarthy's "left-wing" list, had been skeptical about his charges from the start. Its first reference to his campaign against Communists in government, on 6 March 1950, followed McCarthy's six-hour Senate speech in which he said there were 81 Communists or party-liners in the State Department. *Time* called this "a wild attempt to decapitate both Harry Truman and Dean Acheson in one horrendous swing" and said pointedly that the senator had refused to name a single name. Two weeks later, reviewing the early testimony before the Tydings subcommittee, *Time* said that McCarthy's accusations seemed to be based on an old list of names "dredged up" in 1947 by the House Appropriations Committee.

On 22 October 1951 McCarthy was the subject of *Time*'s "cover story," a highly editorialized assessment of his campaign to date. It said that he had not given the Tydings committee the name of a single

Communist in the State Department but that this failure had not deterred him. "He bored in, hitting low blow after low blow. He set up a barrage of new accusations which caught the headlines, drawing attention away from the fact that he had not made good on his original charge. He even began to produce some names. But most of the men he has named never were in the State Department." *Time* said that the few persons mentioned by McCarthy who actually were Communists had been exposed earlier by other investigators. "Joe, like all effective demagogues, found an area of emotion and exploited it. No regard for fair play, no scruple for exact truth hampers Joe's political course. If his accusations destroy reputations, if they subvert the principle that a man is innocent until proved guilty, he is oblivious."

The cover story reached a larger audience than had any other printed comment on McCarthy up to that time, and McCarthy's opponents hailed it as a major development. "Bluff, misrepresentation and downright lies have been the theme of the McCarthy story," editorialized the *Grant County Independent*, in Wisconsin, "and *Time* gives it in almost blow-by-blow detail."[68]

On October 31 McCarthy released a letter to Henry R. Luce, *Time's* editor, in which he said that *Time* had joined "the camp-following elements of the press and radio," taking its lead from the *Daily Worker*. He centered on *Time's* charge that he lied about Gustavo Duran, a United Nations employe and one of McCarthy's favorite targets. *Time* had said that Duran, "never a Red, was definitely and clearly an anti-Communist" and that Duran had worked for the United States government in Cuba during World War II tracking down Axis and Communist agents.[69] As proof that *Time's* story was "a vicious and malicious lie," McCarthy quoted from what he said was a memorandum from James Shepley, a Washington correspondent, on 25 April 1947, "which goes much further and ascribes many more damaging activities to Duran than those discussed by me." He demanded that *Time* correct its false statements about Duran and "the many false statements in the story."

Luce replied to McCarthy by letter on November 5, saying that Shepley's dispatch was not published because it had simply transmitted some charges against Duran collected by U.S. Army Intelligence and that further checking had convinced *Time* that there was not sufficient documentation to support the charge that Duran was a Communist agent.[70] This letter crossed with a telegram from McCarthy to Luce, in which the senator threatened to publish the complete *Time* file on Duran. James Linen, *Time's* publisher, replied that *Time's* files are "normally considered to be immune from pilfering and from public use," but that if McCarthy wanted to publish the material, he could not prevent him. McCarthy did publish *Time*'s file material on 14 November 1951 by inserting it in the *Congressional Record*, where it ran for eight pages. In another letter to Luce which McCarthy put in the *Record* at the same time, he quoted a telegram sent to Luce by William Loeb, publisher of the *Manchester Union*, which said that *Time*'s story "for filthy innuendo outdoes anything McCarthy's worst enemies ever accused him of doing." Loeb said that the Communists' "number one target in the U.S. is to destroy McCarthy . . . a man who if not the perfect champion fights effectively for a cause we should all be interested in." The Duran material in *Time*'s file was obviously what Luce had said it was—unevaluated raw material from intelligence files. It does not seem possible that any conclusion about Duran's loyalties could have been made from this material.

On 28 January 1952, in yet another letter to Luce (released to the press), McCarthy threatened to carry his campaign to *Time*'s advertisers. He said that *Time* had failed to correct any of the false statements in its "smear attack" on him. "I am preparing material on *Time* magazine," he wrote, "to furnish all of your advertisers so they may be fully aware of the type of publication they are supporting." This tactic was denounced by publications of every political stripe, from the *Post* to the *Daily News* in New York, and the *Capital Times* to the *Fond du Lac Commonwealth-Reporter* in Wisconsin. *Business Week* said that such a move "could wreck this country's free press as surely as though the government took control."[71] McCarthy was slow in following up this threat and it was not until June, five months later, that his letters began going to *Time* advertisers. On June 16, Linen said that eleven national advertisers had reported getting letters from McCarthy, sent under his congressional frank, urging a boycott of *Time*.[72] The mailing included a copy of the *Time* file on Duran, reprinted from the *Congressional Record*, and an article by Nora de Toledano in the *American Mercury* which argued with *Time*'s story point by point and predicted a flood of cancellations by subscribers. McCarthy said in the letter that the advertisers were "helping to pollute and poison the waterholes of information," that it was more important to "expose a liar, crook, or traitor who is able to poison the streams of information flowing to a vast number of American homes than to expose an equally vicious crook, liar, or traitor who has no magazine outlet for his poison."[73]

Time magazine spokesmen then and later denied that McCarthy's letters had any effect on advertising.

McCarthy sued one newspaper for libel and two years later collected $16,500 in an out-of-court settlement. The paper was the *Syr-*

acuse *Post-Standard*, one of the S. I. Newhouse chain. The *Post-Standard*, a morning newspaper with a circulation of 79,753, never figured in McCarthy's affairs at any other time, but on 9 October 1951 it carried an editorial, "McCarthy and the Davis Incident," which precipitated the suit. The editorial was based on a wire service account of the arrest in Switzerland of a man named Charles E. Davis, who confessed trying to frame John Carter Vincent, then ambassador to Switzerland, with a fake telegram. Davis said that he was acting on orders from McCarthy. The editorial called it "damning in the eyes of all the world to see a Senator of the United States engaged in bribery and stealth of the lowest order." It also identified McCarthy as the perpetrator of a faked photograph in the Maryland senatorial campaign, accused him of accepting $10,000 from the Lustron Corporation for an article on housing which someone else had written, and said he was "a disgrace to the United States."

In the pretrial examination of McCarthy that began in Syracuse on 29 February 1952, Tracy H. Ferguson, the leading attorney for the newspaper, tried vainly to elicit an admission that McCarthy had a direct connection with Davis.[74] McCarthy testified that Davis had asked him for money to pursue investigations for him but that he had given him none. He said that he considered Davis "completely irresponsible and of no value" and that he had given the FBI everything he got from Davis. Ferguson was unable to shake McCarthy on this point, and the inability to prove that Davis was McCarthy's agent was the principal reason for the newspaper's later decision to settle the suit. Nor was Ferguson able to shake McCarthy on any of the other issues raised by the editorial. McCarthy refused to admit that he had directed Jean Kerr, his secretary, to insert the faked photograph of Senator Tydings and Earl Browder, the U.S. Communist party chairman, in the campaign tabloid of John Butler, who defeated Tydings in 1950. He was unable to get McCarthy to admit that anyone else had had anything to do with writing the Lustron article or that there was anything improper about being paid for the article. Ferguson tried repeatedly to get McCarthy to admit that his attacks on individuals in government were similar to tactics used by Communists, but this was a political question, easy for McCarthy, and the senator turned each question into a political speech—his standard speech—without ever answering Ferguson's questions.

Ferguson had obviously been supplied with information from McCarthy's enemies—the most obvious source was Senator Benton—and used the occasion to question McCarthy under oath on charges and past events that might discredit him. He asked about the action of the Wisconsin Supreme Court in censuring McCarthy for running for the Senate while holding a judgeship, and about a speech he once was said to have made in which he claimed to have "ten pounds of shrapnel" in his leg. McCarthy denied that he had ever made such a speech and said that the story was something that "Bennie Wexler" of the *New York Post* had made up. He said that the Supreme Court had first ruled he could run while a judge, then later reversed itself. Ferguson was unable to challenge McCarthy's versions of these events. Ferguson's final strategy, revealed on the second day of the examination of McCarthy, was to argue that similar or worse things had been written about McCarthy in other newspapers and magazines and that McCarthy had failed to sue them. He cited cases in which courts had held that a second libel caused less "mental anguish" than a first libel and therefore was less damaging. In support of this argument he attempted to introduce articles and editorials from *Time* magazine, the *Milwaukee Journal*, the *Washington Post*, the *Christian Science Monitor*, the *Baltimore Sun*, the *Capital Times*, the *St. Louis Post-Dispatch*, the *Raleigh News & Observer*, the *New York Times*, and *Commonweal*, and a cartoon published by the *Tampa Tribune*. "I want to show other publications in words or substance said the same thing about this plaintiff," Ferguson said.

Out of the 21 submissions, McCarthy would admit having read only an editorial from the *Washington Post*, one from the *Baltimore Sun*, a *Time* magazine article, and the cartoon. Ferguson asked, in each case, whether McCarthy had sued the publication; in each case McCarthy's attorney objected to the question and in each case the judge upheld the objection. Objections to Ferguson's reading aloud the "libelous" portions of the articles were also upheld. This part of the examination revealed something of McCarthy's newspaper reading practices. He testified that he regularly read the *Washington Star* and the *Washington Times-Herald* and that he occasionally glanced at the *Washington Post* in the Senate anteroom. Other than that, he read only what his clipping service furnished him from Wisconsin papers. He had seen the *Tampa Tribune* cartoon reprinted in some Wisconsin paper. (I doubt whether McCarthy's reading was as limited as he pretended it to be; there is evidence, from his reactions to newspaper stories, that he read the *Post* regularly, and that he often read the *New York Times* and *Time* magazine, at the least.)

At one point, Ferguson asked McCarthy to read a *Milwaukee Journal* editorial. McCarthy refused. "I can tell it is a usual *Milwaukee Journal* editorial," he said. "It is the usual left-wing smear, and I am not going to sit here and take up my time reading smear articles unless the Court orders me to." McCarthy also refused to read a *Baltimore Sun* editorial. He said a *Washington Post* editorial looked familiar because he had read "substantially the same" in the *Daily Worker.* He said *Time* was guilty of "degenerate lying," and he said that the *Capital Times* had an editor who refused to answer questions as to whether he was "the leading Communist in Dane County." He refused to say whether he considered *Commonweal* and the *Christian Science Monitor* "left-wing smear" papers.

On 14 March 1953, McCarthy announced that the suit had been settled out of court. His statement did not include the amount of the settlement, later learned to be $16,500, but said that the amount was less important than the fact that the paper had agreed to publish a "clarification of the facts" in its editorial column. The publisher had been willing to "correct misstatements that his paper has published as the result of reliance upon information that was in error."[75] The "clarifying" editorial published March 15 stated that the *Post-Standard* wished to correct certain statements "that were written in good faith and in a sincere belief in their truthfulness but which have nevertheless proved to be untrue and unfair to Sen. McCarthy." The newspaper, it said, had relied upon Davis's testimony in the Swiss case but had since found that Davis "is beyond belief and that Sen. McCarthy has not committed any act deserving of criticism in connection with that matter." It was satisfied that McCarthy was not responsible for faking the Tydings-Browder photograph and convinced that acceptance of the $10,000 from Lustron was "on the same plane as the common practice among legislators of accepting fees for speeches and earning other fees from legitimate services." It was the Davis testimony that caused the *Post-Standard* to attribute all these other acts of wrongdoing to McCarthy, the editorial said, concluding, "Inasmuch as Davis on the basis of his record is unworthy of belief we are happy to make these corrections in fairness to Sen. McCarthy, our readers and ourselves."

It seems probable that the *Post-Standard's* editorial was libelous as the law was interpreted in 1953; it had gone far beyond the facts that could be proved. It also seems likely that it would not have been deserving of damages under the law as it has been interpreted since the landmark case of *New York Times Co. v. Sullivan* in 1964 (376 U.S. 254 [1964]). Ferguson shares this opinion. Now the plaintiff would have to prove not just that the facts were wrong but that the editorial was written with malice.[76]

Most of the nation's newspapers, and even most of those on McCarthy's "left-wing" list, supported the Republican party in the 1950s. Most of them also supported McCarthy during the first four years of his campaign against "Communists in government." As long as the people McCarthy was accusing of treason were Democrats, they approved. But when it became obvious, in the early months of 1954, that those being accused of tolerating Communists in government were part of the Republican administration of President Eisenhower, Republican publishers, with the notable exceptions of the publishers of the *Chicago Tribune* and the Hearst newspapers, began to see McCarthy in a new light.

The most spectacular about-face was that of the Scripps-Howard newspapers. On 12 July 1954 the flagship paper of the chain, the *New York World-Telegram*, began a five-part series by Frederick Woltman evaluating McCarthy's performance and finding him "a major liability to anti-Communism." Woltman had a national reputation as an anti-Communist writer and investigator. The *World-Telegram*, in a sidebar story, boasted that he was "the premier Red baiter among American newspaper reporters." The *New York Daily Worker*, the official Communist newspaper, called him "Freddie the Fink." In earlier years, he had been a personal friend of McCarthy. For 16 years he had had the "Red beat" for Scripps-Howard. He had won the Pulitzer prize for national reporting in 1946 for his exposés of Communist infiltration.

World-Telegram readers could not believe that Woltman would turn against McCarthy. Letters from incredulous readers filled the pages of the newspaper for days after the series began. Some doubted that he had really written the stories, and others said that Woltman must have been forced to write them against his will.

In the first story, Woltman wrote that he had spent three months rechecking McCarthy's record since 9 February 1950 and had concluded that McCarthy had played into the hands of the Communists. "He has made the going tougher for the many others who long before had been fighting to stop the spread of communism at home and abroad," Woltman wrote. It was clear from Woltman's stories that the change resulted from McCarthy's attacks on the Eisenhower administration: "He has widened the split in his own Republican party, and demonstrated that, unless he has his way, he's willing to destroy the Eisenhower administration at a time when it's grappling with a world crisis. Now, after 18 months of Republican rule, Sen. McCarthy still is hammering out accusations of treason and espionage in government without producing evidence."[77] Woltman gave McCarthy credit for "helping make the man in the street more security conscious," but concluded that the debit side of his career overbalanced the credit. In an editorial that followed the series, the *World-Telegram* denied that the series represented any change in Scripps-Howard editorial policy, and promised that the newspapers would continue to wage "unrelenting warfare against communism." It seems transparently obvious, however, that Scripps-Howard executives had simply decided that McCarthy was harming rather than helping the Republican party and that it was time to get rid of him. Having the job done by Woltman, the "Red baiter," was a safe way of dumping McCarthy without opening the newspapers to charges of being soft on Communism.

It was an important signal to other Republican newspapers and to Senate Republicans. If so resolute a Commie-fighter as Woltman could turn against McCarthy, it was a safe move for all. Without this switch by Scripps-Howard and other moderate Republican newspapers, it is doubtful that the Eisenhower administration and the moderate Republicans in the Senate could have steeled themselves to the ordeal of censuring McCarthy.

One other development contributed to the creation of a political climate in which it was safe—even prudent—to oppose McCarthy. This was the rise of the medium of television, which McCarthy first "used" as effectively as he had used the press, but which ultimately helped do him in.

6.
Four Crises
In Television

McCARTHY'S RISE to national prominence coincided with the explosive growth of television in the United States. In February 1950, when he spoke at Wheeling, there were only 98 television stations and 3,700,000 receivers, and radio was by far the most prevalent form of broadcasting; there were 2,029 stations and 83 million receivers; 94 percent of American families had at least one radio in the home. But people were buying television sets as fast as they could get them, and by the end of 1950 there were 10 million sets and 106 stations in 65 cities. By the end of 1954, the year that McCarthy's appearances on the television screen became more important than the reporting of his activities by newspapers, there were 35 million sets in operation, and with 413 stations in 273 cities, television coverage extended to all but the most remote corners of the nation.[1]

McCarthy's propaganda techniques had forced newspapers and wire services to reexamine their practices and to make greater use of interpretive reporting. His effect on television was equally important, and his aggressive efforts to use the new medium for his own ends forced networks and stations into major policy decisions.

The broadcasting media were ripe for manipulation. In 1947 three former FBI agents had begun publication of a four-page weekly newsletter called *Counterattack: The Newsletter of Facts on Communism*.[2] The agents collected lists from government, congressional, and legislative sources and published "citations" of the "front" connections or activities of prominent citizens. A "front," by their definition, was

176

any organization that "helped Communism." Their lists went far beyond the attorney general's list of subversive organizations; in 1948 *Counterattack* published a list of 192 organizations it considered "fronts," only 73 of which were on the attorney general's list. At first the publication was directed to businessmen in general, but it gradually came to concentrate on broadcasting, a target in the public eye. *Counterattack* not only listed names; it also urged people to complain to broadcasting companies and to sponsors of programs so as to drive the persons "cited" out of their jobs and out of broadcasting. People did complain, and performers were dropped from programs because they were "controversial." For the publishers of *Counterattack*, who also offered to investigate program talent for sponsors, it was a profitable business; other groups entered the field, some for profit and some for the sake of wielding power.

On 22 June 1950, American Business Consultants, the publishers of *Counterattack*, issued a 215-page book called "*Red Channels: The Report of Communist Influence in Radio and Television.*" As perpetrators of this infiltration it listed 151 persons—actors, actresses, writers, musicians, playwrights, directors—some of the best-known and most-respected people in the industry. The editors did not say that everyone listed was a Communist, only that they had helped advance "communist objectives." Everyone on the list was affected by the publication; not all of them lost jobs, but many did. Some went to Europe; one committed suicide. Networks and advertising agencies, seeking to avoid further attacks, established their own "security" departments to screen out "controversial" persons; the blacklist was institutionalized.

McCarthy's principal benefit from this disarray was in the gift of free time on the air, but he also made sporadic forays into the affairs of broadcasting, seemingly intended to keep the medium on the defensive. "We have a vast number of Communists in press and radio," he said in a radio interview on 18 May 1952, citing Louis Budenz, former editor of the *Daily Worker*, as his source.[3] On June 30, the magazine *Broadcasting-Telecasting* warned its readers, "Don't kiss off request of Sen. Joseph McCarthy for list of State Dept. contacts with radio-TV newsmen." On July 5 McCarthy introduced legislation to ban the showing of films written by supporters of "Communists and Communist-fronts."[4] In October he threatened to ask the Federal Communications Commission to revoke the license of KING-TV, Seattle, after that station had refused to broadcast a prepared speech unless he deleted statements that the station's attorneys considered libelous, but he did not actually file a complaint.[5] In December he announced that as chairman of the Senate Committee on Expenditures in the Executive Department he would investigate the FCC, presumably for Communist influence, but this, too, failed to happen.[6]

He continued to harass the FCC in 1953, however, over the assignment of television licenses in Wisconsin, trying to switch Channel 10 in Milwaukee from educational use to commercial so that it could be assigned to the Hearst Corporation, publishers of the *Milwaukee Sentinel,* the largest paper supporting him in Wisconsin,[7] and trying to prevent the assignment of a UHF channel in Milwaukee to Bartell Broadcasters, a Madison group that included persons active as Democrats. *Broadcasting-Telecasting* said on June 8, referring to the Bartell firm, "They're on McCarthy's list and his staff investigators already have been on the job." On June 15 the magazine reported that McCarthy had introduced a bill to require radio and television stations to keep recordings of all broadcasts. McCarthy explained that "disc jockeys" could indulge in libel and slander because they were not recorded. "It seems Joe McCarthy just can't keep his nose out of the broadcasting business," editorialized *Broadcasting-Telecasting* on June 22. "This is sheer nonsense. This smacks of censorship, even thought control." On July 20 the magazine reported that McCarthy's bill was getting "the slow brush-off," and that was the last heard of the matter. On September 14 the magazine quoted a story in the *New York Times* saying that McCarthy was planning a weekly television show, privately sponsored, in which he would attack Democrats. This never materialized.

McCarthy's first appearance on national television appears to have been during the Tydings subcommittee investigation of charges made by him at Wheeling and on 20 February 1950 when he talked of "81 cases"on the Senate floor. These hearings had begun on March 8, and were broadcast on 6 April 1950 by NBC and CBS on the occasion of testimony by Owen Lattimore, a consultant on Far Eastern affairs whom McCarthy had called "the top Soviet agent" in the United States. The fact that the hearing was televised was unusual enough to warrant a two-column headline in the *New York Times.*

Radio was still the more important broadcast medium in 1951, however, and in August of that year McCarthy demanded free time to answer the radio speech of President Truman in which the president had warned that "scaremongers with rotten motives" were stirring up public hysteria with irresponsible charges about Communists infiltrating government. McCarthy said that although Truman had not mentioned him by name, news stories and radio reports had identified him as the target of Truman's attacks. Free time was offered—the very next day—by the National Broadcasting Company, the Columbia Broadcasting System, and the Mutual Broadcasting System.[8]

Mutual's offer was for an appearance on a regular weekly radio program, "Reporters' Roundup," in which the visitor of the day was interviewed by a panel of reporters. McCarthy appeared frequently on such programs, and often squabbled with the reporters, talking through their questions and bullying them as he sometimes bullied senators. He appeared on "Reporters' Roundup" on 13 September 1951, and part of his "reply to Truman" was an attack on the press. One of his questioners was Philip Dodd of the *Chicago Tribune*. The transcript of the program shows Dodd asking soft questions:

DODD: Senator McCarthy, in a general way, do you have any comment on the way the press has covered the story of your activities to unearth Communism in the government?

McCARTHY: Oh I think the press as a whole is not bad. I might say as you know Louis Budenz has named 400 members of the press and radio—gave their names to the Justice Department, to the Committee, as men who are members of the Communist party, who follow the Communist line.

This was standard McCarthy fare, repeated hundreds of times that year. What followed would invariably explain that the Communist *Daily Worker* laid down the line, and all these other "*Daily Workers*"—the *Washington Post, Milwaukee Journal,* and so on—followed that line faithfully. Dodd's next question implied acceptance of the truth of the Budenz charge and set up McCarthy's reply.

DODD: How do you think that 400 would have received instructions from the Communist party?

McCARTHY: Very simple. That's been set forth in detail by witnesses. They receive their instructions from the Daily Worker.[9]

Each week McCarthy sent out phonograph records from his Washington office to radio stations in Wisconsin. One of them went on 21 June 1951 to WBEV, in Beaver Dam. On this record, an interviewer pretending to be a reporter said, "I see the reaction of the left-wing press to your speech on General Marshall was just what you predicted it would be." McCarthy responded that the "Communist *Daily Worker*" had attacked him with "two vicious editorials," and that "the camp-following elements of the press" had "fallen in behind like trained seals, all shouting 'smear.'" None of the "camp-following press" had said that a single word or phrase in his speech was untrue, McCarthy said. "Bob White," the interviewer, then remarked that "the latest smear on Senator McCarthy" was by Drew Pearson and the *Milwaukee Journal* in regard to McCarthy's military record. Pearson had written that McCarthy saw no combat service, the interviewer said, but he did not say what the *Journal* had published. He read excerpts from several letters from military figures commending McCarthy's service. "I think it's a waste of time proving Pearson is a liar," McCarthy responded. "That's too well known. It's also a waste of time proving that my friends at the *Milwaukee Journal* and the *Capital Times* will do almost anything whenever I attack and step on the toes of the Communists and the dupes and stooges of the Kremlin. For some unknown reason they scream very, very highly." McCarthy then repeated his taunt that William T. Evjue, editor of the *Capital Times*, had once called his own city editor, Cedric Parker, a Communist, an issue that McCarthy had first raised in 1949. And he said that the *Journal* had two editorial writers who had contributed to the Alger Hiss Defense Fund.[10]

Radio stations in Wisconsin used such propaganda offerings from congressmen routinely, and reporters often encountered people in rural areas who had absorbed this kind of message. McCarthy, like President Nixon 25 years later, sought opportunities to bypass the press and speak directly to the public, eliminating the possibility of interpretation and analysis. He did this first through radio and then through television, and he proved to be more successful than anyone except incumbent presidents in forcing the networks to give him free time. McCarthy's "Alger, I mean Adlai" speech in Chicago on October 27 was his most notable television appearance of 1952. He appeared on a number of panel shows that year, and he got into brawling arguments with his questioners on at least three of them—Dumont's "Author Meets the Critics," ABC's "Hot Seat," and NBC's "Meet the Press." And there was the fiasco at KING-TV in Seattle, described in chapter 4.

The Republican landslide of 1952 made the Republicans the majority party in the Senate and installed McCarthy as chairman of the Senate's Committee on Government Operations and of its Permanent Subcommittee on Investigations. In this role he began a prolonged investigation of subversion in the Voice of America, the international radio outlet of the State Department's International Information Administration, predecessor of the United States Information Agency. These hearings were carried intermittently on television by one or another of the networks and gave McCarthy his first opportunity to appear regularly. The hearings often became sensational, as Voice employes accused co-workers and superiors of disloyal attitudes and actions. What viewers saw, for the most part, was McCarthy bullying a series of defiant or cringing bureaucrats, mocking their protestations of innocence and sneering at their declarations of hatred for Communism. Marya Mannes, writing in *The Reporter* on 31 March 1953, said this about the Voice of America hearings: "To them [the viewers] these hearings, like any peep show, are a degrading experience, degrading to themselves, degrading to justice, degrading to government. Since they confuse instead of clarify, and prejudice instead of inform, it is hard to see what service they perform for the American public or for good government."

The public hearings began Monday, 16 February 1953, in Washington, after a series of closed hearings in New York.[11] McCarthy said that the committee would investigate "mismanagement and subversion" in the agency. The mismanagement charge was the result of an argument between engineers about the best location of transmitters and turned out to be of little public interest. The charges of subversion related to programming, and this became an argument about how to make propaganda, with McCarthy and his accusatory witnesses taking the position that anything less than denunciation of Communists and praise for anti-Communists was subversive. Those defending themselves against the charges argued that a more subtle approach might be more effective and that pro-American or anti-Russian statements by Americans known abroad as pro-Communists might impress listeners in the Iron Curtain countries. The committee paid little attention to the arguments for these refinements.

This was a period when the Eisenhower administration, and particularly Secretary of State John Foster Dulles, was trying desperately to appease McCarthy, hoping that he would develop loyalty to the new Republican administration. During the first week of closed hearings, the State Department reacted by demoting one Voice of America official, recommending discharge of another, and firing three low-level employes. On February 18 the director of the agency, Wilson M. Compton, admitted "waste" in regard to the radio transmitters and resigned. One day later, the State Department told the McCarthy committee that it had ordered the Voice to use no material by Communist or "controversial" authors. McCarthy replied with a demand that all books by Howard Fast, a "controversial" author who had pleaded the Fifth Amendment when asked by the committee whether he was a Communist, be removed from the shelves of Voice of America libraries.

The television cameras first appeared at the hearing on February 19, as committee members and staff questioned Voice employes about editing decisions which other employes had said were intended to water down the anti-Communist message of the broadcasts. One of those who made such accusations was a Nancy Lenkeith, and

McCarthy displayed a surprising delicacy as she approached a point in her testimony in which she said that one of her superiors in the agency had invited her to join a commune in Rockland County, New York. McCarthy halted her testimony to say that he had heard it earlier in a closed hearing and that it should not be repeated because "children might be listening on television." The testimony, the *New York Times* reported the next day, involved derogatory remarks about religion and a mention of "free love."

William S. White noted in a column in the Sunday, February 22, *New York Times* that the Republicans were finding out that McCarthy hadn't changed at all and was going to be as annoying to them as he had been to the Democrats. White said, however, that Republican senators were loyal to McCarthy because they owed him so much— "by objective standards he seems to have had a hand in the election of at least eight Republican Senators in the last two years." The administration could not depend on Senate Republicans for any help in controlling McCarthy, he said. On February 23, the administration announced that Robert L. Johnson, president of Temple University, would head the Information Administration. McCarthy's contemptuous response was that his investigation would continue for a long time. The next day, the State Department suspended Alfred H. Morton, chief of the Voice broadcasting service, because he had disagreed on the use of statements by Howard Fast. The next day Morton was reinstated but reprimanded for "bad judgment."

These hearings marked McCarthy's debut as a television producer. After rehearsing the witnesses—friendly or hostile—in closed session, he arranged for the testimony he wanted the public to see and hear to come up during the two hours a day that the hearings were covered by television. Reed Harris, acting director of the Information Administration at the time he appeared, had been questioned in closed session before he made a two-day appearance before the committee. Charges against Harris on the basis of actions affecting the Voice of America were trivial; he had been accused of cutting back on broadcasts in Hebrew to Israel, for budget reasons, he said. McCarthy spent little time on this.

The real reason Harris was there was that he had written a book when he was twenty-one, *King Football*, an attack on the commercialism of college football, dashed off in three weeks after Harris had been expelled from Columbia University because of something that appeared in the school newspaper while he was editor. But the parts that McCarthy read aloud with malicious satisfaction concerned "free love" and the right of professors to teach atheism and Communism, as Harris groaned, "But that was 21 years ago, Senator!" McCarthy declared that Harris had never been cleared for loyalty and security, and when Harris testified that he had been cleared six or seven times, including two full field checks by the FBI, McCarthy hinted that his staff would prove otherwise. Repeatedly, Harris would declare his hatred of Communism while McCarthy looked away and talked with aids and then would interrupt to say, "Which question are you answering?" or "Try to answer my question." Over and over again he went back to the purple passages of *King Football*. It was show business, and McCarthy played the part of the inquisitor with obvious pleasure as Harris squirmed before the cameras, alternately defiant and apologetic. A year later, a film clip of this interrogation became the most dramatic segment in Edward R. Murrow's celebrated documentary on McCarthy.

On March 4, the second day of Harris's testimony, the hearing was being televised by the ABC network. McCarthy and the network agreed that the hearing would begin at 10:30 A.M. and recess at 12:30 P.M. so that the network could inform stations in advance when to resume local programming. Harris had complained that the previous day's television coverage had been unfair to him, and McCarthy announced at the beginning of the day's testimony that television coverage would continue through Harris's rebuttal. Other witnesses, however, most of them hostile to Harris, took up so much time that it was 11:50 before Harris took the stand. At 12:23 McCarthy interrupted to announce that he understood that television coverage would continue past the 12:30 cutoff. Harris continued to testify, ending his statement at 1:07 P.M. ABC, however, cut off the hearing at 12:30, as scheduled, and switched to a commercially sponsored giveaway show for housewives. Coverage continued only on WMAL-TV, the Washington, D.C., ABC outlet. The network's explanation was that McCarthy's announcement that the hearing would continue past 12:30 had come too late for them to make the technical arrangements to continue.

Jack Gould, *New York Times* reporter and critic, expressed the opinion that if television was so inelastic that it could not cope with unforeseen developments, it should not undertake live coverage of such serious matters as McCarthy's investigations.

By the same token Senator McCarthy is setting a frightening precedent by bargaining with the broadcasters in the matter of time allotments. If he agrees in advance to recess a hearing on cue, then he must do his share to see that all witnesses have their hour upon the stage. Under these circumstances he is not just an investigator but also a television director. The tyranny of time is always a problem in broadcasting. But this tyranny must not be extended to a deadly serious inquiry where men's reputations are at stake and national policy is in the balance.[12]

Gould did not suggest in either of the two columns he devoted to this event that McCarthy had delayed the hearing deliberately to cut off Harris's rebuttal. But if McCarthy had done it deliberately, it would have been consistent with his manipulation of events in relation to newspaper and wire service deadlines in order to obtain maximum publicity for his side of an argument. McCarthy paid similar attention to television's deadlines. According to Ben H. Bagdikian, a reporter for the *Providence Journal* in the fifties, "McCarthy used to bring his witnesses out of closed hearings each day in time for the noon news and the six o'clock news. He was one of the first to catch on to the uses of the new media. He was so blunt about it that he'd cut off the witness abruptly once the deadline passed."[13]

McCarthy's attack on Adlai Stevenson on the eve of the 1952 election was the first of four television events that stand as milestones in the last three years of McCarthy's career as a major figure in American politics. The second of these took place on 24 November 1953, and it is notable not so much for its impact on viewers as for what it told the president and the eastern Republicans about the possibility of co-existing with or appeasing McCarthy. The controversy began with a charge by Attorney General Herbert Brownell, in a speech November 6 in Chicago, that President Truman had promoted Harry Dexter White, an assistant secretary of the treasury, to a "high and sensitive post" after he knew that White was a Communist spy.[14] This was part of an attempt by the Eisenhower administration to co-opt the Communists-in-government issue.

Truman denied the charge in a speech broadcast nationally on November 14 from Kansas City, Missouri, and then said, in the last paragraphs of the speech:

It is now evident that the present Administration has fully embraced, for political advantage, McCarthyism. I'm not referring to the Senator from Wisconsin—his only importance is that his name has taken on a dictionary meaning in the world. And that meaning is corruption of truth, the abandonment of our historical devotion to fair play.

It is the abandonment of "due process" of law. It is the use of the big lie and the unfounded accusation against any citizen in the name of Americanism and security. It is the rise to power of the demagogue who lives on untruth; it is the spread of fear and the destruction of faith in every level of our society.[15]

Early the next day McCarthy demanded free time, saying that he had found the former president's description of McCarthyism "very unflattering." The ABC network immediately offered him a half-hour on November 23, a Monday night. NBC subsequently offered 15 minutes on the 24th, an offer which McCarthy rejected as "not adequate." But by the end of the week ABC, CBS, and NBC had agreed to give him a half-hour on radio and television on November 24. The Mutual radio network also offered time. On November 23, McCarthy threatened to complain to the Federal Communications Commission— where he was thought to have friends—about any radio or television station that had carried Truman's remarks and that might fail to carry his.[16] Some stations had refused to carry McCarthy's attack on Stevenson, but there was no report of any station failing to carry the November 24 speech.

McCarthy did criticize Truman. He said that the former president had helped not only Harry Dexter White but also many other suspected Communists or fellow travelers, that the Truman administration had "crawled with Communists," that it had "sold out the nation to its enemies" with high taxes and the military draft as the result. But McCarthy also disagreed with President Eisenhower, who had been saying that the record of his administration and of the Republican party would be the issue in 1954 and that Communism would not be an issue. "The raw, harsh, unpleasant fact is that Communism is an issue and will be an issue in 1954," McCarthy said, which made McCarthy, rather than the president, the central issue in the election. He said that "Democrat office seekers" were saying that McCarthyism was the issue. "In a way, I guess it is, because Republican control of the Senate determines whether I shall continue as chairman of the investigating committee. Therefore, if the American people agree with Truman, they have a chance to get rid of me as chairman of the investigating committee next fall by defeating any Republican up for election."[17] (The Senate at that time was evenly divided, with the vice president as the tie-breaking vote that enabled the Republicans to organize the Senate. A loss of one seat would tip the balance to the Democrats.)

McCarthy said that the administration was doing a better job of getting rid of Communists than the Truman administration had but that there were "a few cases where we [Republicans] struck out." One, he said, was the case of John Paton Davies, "still on the payroll after 11 months of the Eisenhower Administration." McCarthy's discussion of the Davies case was a transparent distortion of the facts that particularly annoyed aides in the White House. One such aide, according to James Reston, had called the speech "a declaration of war against the President,"[18] and that is the way it was interpreted by editorial writers and columnists all over the country. The *Washington Post* commented:

In his intemperate reply to former President Truman, Senator McCarthy talked as though he thought he is the Republican party. The Senator was not content with his distorted attempt to identify Mr. Truman with communism. He tried also to lay down the law for the Eisenhower Administration, to tell the Administration whom it must fire from the Government and what its foreign policy must be.[19]

The *New York Herald Tribune's* comment was:

The speech was noteworthy chiefly because he took advantage of the free time offered him on the air to issue something very close to a challenge to the whole Republican administration. . . . The Senator from Wisconsin had not before shown his hand so clearly. If this speech is to be a criterion, he is following a personally ambitious course—one which, if unchecked, could wreck the Republican party and bring great harm to the country.[20]

Marquis Childs, the political columnist, wrote that McCarthy had declared the formation of a new political party.

Nor was he beseeching anyone to join the McCarthy party. He showed an arrogant strength. If President Eisenhower and the rest of the Republicans care to join up, then that is all right. But McCarthy means to make sure that the election next year is fought over Mc-Carthy.[21]

McCarthy's speech probably helped speed his ultimate comedown by making it clear to more of the moderate Republicans that appeasement was useless, but once again it was a tactical victory for McCarthy, through his manipulation of the media.

Brownell's attack on Truman had been part of a White House plan to pre-empt the issue and to shift the arena for anti-Communist investigations from McCarthy's committee to that of Senator William Jenner of Indiana, a McCarthy henchman who apparently was willing to help undercut his ally if it moved the television cameras to his internal security subcommittee of the Judiciary Committee, which it did, briefly, when Brownell and J. Edgar Hoover went before Jenner's committee to testify about Harry Dexter White.[22] The tacticians behind this scheme told reporters that they had expected it to make McCarthy, not Truman, angry, although such naïveté seems hard to imagine. And then when Truman did respond, the Eisenhower strategists didn't think to ask for time to answer him; they let McCarthy make the request. It was an inept performance on the part of the White House and a setback in the competition with both McCarthy and the Democrats. The mail that poured in came from McCarthy supporters who said it all proved that McCarthy was right, and from independent voters who were shocked that the Eisenhower administration would employ the tactics of McCarthy.

In Jack Gould's opinion, the television networks had exercised remarkably poor judgment in giving free time to McCarthy, more time than Truman had used—30 minutes to Truman's 20. "By meekly submitting to Mr. McCarthy's demand the broadcasters are now in hot water on all fronts. Staff members of the White House are reported to feel that, after the Truman and McCarthy broadcasts, the Eisenhower Administration is now a two-time loser on TV."[23]

McCarthy won the first skirmish of 1954 in his increasingly open challenge of President Eisenhower for the leadership of the Republican party, and he did it again through the medium of television. He had been investigating the army in the fall of 1953, constantly pressing for access to confidential loyalty files, and in December he found a "case"—that of the "pink army dentist." Irving Peress, a dentist from the Bronx, had been drafted and commissioned in October 1952 and promoted to major a year later under the automatic provisions of the law. A month later, someone in the army discovered that Peress had declined to answer questions about his political beliefs, and the adjutant general ordered him discharged within 90 days. McCarthy then called Peress before a closed hearing of his subcommittee, and Peress refused to answer questions about his politics, pleading the Fifth Amendment. He then applied for an immediate discharge, and the Department of Defense granted it.

"Who promoted Peress?" became McCarthy's slogan, and in Wisconsin this question appeared on bumper stickers. McCarthy called before his committee Brigadier General Ralph W. Zwicker, the commandant at Camp Kilmer, New Jersey, where Peress had been stationed, and demanded the names of all officers who had been involved in Peress's promotion and discharge. General Zwicker, on advice of the army counsel, John G. Adams, refused to answer. McCarthy, irate, told the general that he was "not fit to wear the uniform" and said that he "did not have the brains of a five-year-old."[24]

President Eisenhower was indignant about this affront but, as usual, was torn between those who wanted him to take a strong stand against McCarthy—to fight him in the open—and those who feared a break with the McCarthy wing of the party. He decided to make a statement, however, which the press took to mean that he was finally going to denounce McCarthy. "It was newspaper reaction which finally convinced the President early last week to take a firm stand against McCarthy," Drew Pearson wrote. "And on Monday, two days in advance of his Wednesday press conference, he gave orders to have a strong statement prepared." Pearson reported, however, that in the interim, when McCarthy appeared to be conciliatory, the statement was watered down, and when it was delivered on March 3 it did not even mention McCarthy.[25]

James Reston described the statement as something that "sounded like a diplomatic note on the principles that should govern the relations between the legislature and the executive under the United States Constitution."

His theme was that the Representatives of the Congress and the Executive should attend to their own business and cooperate with one another; that the Army was brave, loyal and anti-Communist, including Brig. Gen. Ralph W. Zwicker . . . and that it was unfortunate when the Government was diverted from the grave problems of the world by unnamed individuals who used unfair tactics in unidentified incidents.[26]

Reporters tried to get Eisenhower to say more, but in vain. McCarthy, who had expected stronger criticism, replied to the president on television without knowing what Eisenhower had actually said. In his same March 4 column Reston wrote:

Less than two hours after the President's press conference, the Senator, by prearrangement with the magic lantern people, appeared in Room 155 of the Senate Office Building. There he read out his statement, stopping every sentence or so to give the cameras time to get a new angle. As a result, the McCarthy image and melody lingered on the TV screens tonight long after the President had gone to bed.

McCarthy said that Peress was "the sacred cow of certain Army brass" and that he had established beyond doubt that "certain individuals in the Army have been protecting, covering up, and honorably discharging known Communists. . . . If a stupid, arrogant or witless man in a position of power appears before our committee and is found aiding the Communist party he will be exposed. The fact that he might be a general places him in no special class as far as I am concerned." His final patronizing dig was aimed directly at the president. "Apparently the President and I now agree on the necessity of getting rid of Communists," he said. "We apparently disagree only on how we should handle those who protect Communists."[27] Reston's comment was:

> The Senator's statement was a perfect illustration of his mastery of mass communication techniques. He knows the importance of timing and of violence, and of brevity in a political fight, and he demonstrated all this today.
>
> In the first place, he produced his statement soon enough after the President's to insure that it would be displayed alongside the President's. He concentrated on getting it out on television, but as soon as it was finished he gave it to the press association reporters so they could get it on the wires in a hurry.
>
> Under these circumstances the statement had to be included in the news stories of the President's conference, for it ran directly counter to several points made by the President.

Once again, McCarthy had won the publicity battle and poor Mr. Eisenhower ended up disappointing his liberal supporters and angering the wing of the Republican party that tolerated no criticism of McCarthy.

Willard Edwards of the Chicago Tribune did not regard McCarthy's precipitate action as a triumph. Edwards, like many Senate Republicans, was trying to prevent an open break between McCarthy and the president.

> Every expert in Washington had predicted that Eisenhower was going to tear McCarthy's head off [Edwards said in an interview]. I went to Ike's press conference—I sat next to Joe Alsop—and we listened with bated breath. Ike started reading his statement, and it become obvious that he was going to be very mild. Joe Alsop stood up and said in a loud voice, "The yellow sonofabitch!"
>
> I raced back to Capitol Hill to tell McCarthy what had happened, but I got to his office too late. He had the AP advance story saying that Eisenhower was going to blast McCarthy, and he thought Ike was going to rip him apart and he had released a statement. I got him to put out sort of a correction, but it was too late. That was the day that began the fall of Joe McCarthy. He got calls from two Cabinet members and several other high officials, all supporters of his, who said, "We're all through with you."[28]

As a result of Edwards's advice, McCarthy sent a "correction" to the wire services, telling them to delete the word "now" from his statement that apparently he and the president now agreed on the necessity of removing Communists from government. He said the word was creating a false interpretation, "never intended and completely un-justified."

McCarthy's abuse of General Zwicker cost him a valuable defender, the influential and popular radio news commentator H.V. Kaltenborn, of NBC. On the radio and in a newspaper column published March 1, Kaltenborn said that he had enjoyed defending McCarthy against the emotional attacks of his friends and that during the Truman administration something like McCarthyism had been necessary. But it was not necessary now, with the Eisenhower administration "cleaning out the few remaining Reds with commendable, quiet efficiency." Kaltenborn wrote:

McCarthy has too often hit below the belt. Even a good fighter sometimes misplaces a punch in the heat of battle, and McCarthy is fighting a gang of unscrupulous traitors who will use any means to achieve their ends. Yet McCarthy uses the same bludgeon to hit an honorable Army general that he swings at a treacherous Communist.

He has become so vindictive in fighting his battle that he treats as an open enemy anyone who is not on his side in any attack he chooses to make. He is constantly using improper means to achieve what may or may not be a proper end. He has become completely egotistical, arrogant, arbitrary, narrow-minded, reckless, and irresponsible. Power has corrupted him.[29]

On Sunday, March 7, speaking in Miami, Florida, Adlai Stevenson described the Republican party as "divided against itself, half McCarthy and half Eisenhower." The speech was broadcast on NBC and CBS. McCarthy, who happened to be in Miami, immediately demanded free time, basing his request on the unflattering use of the word *McCarthyism* as he had the year before when he was given time to reply to Truman. "I have no doubt," he told reporters in Miami, "but what they [the networks] will give it to me."

For the first time, they did not. The networks (NBC and CBS) quickly offered time to the Republican national committee. Leonard Hall, the Republican national chairman, after consulting the White House, announced that Vice-President Nixon would make the reply. McCarthy insisted that he, too, was entitled to reply, because Stevenson had attacked him personally. NBC and CBS rejected his demand, and McCarthy threatened to take them before the FCC or into the courts. At a press conference in New York on March 9, he refused to talk to their representatives and he turned his back on their cameras. He said that the networks' decision was "completely immoral" and "arrogant": "I think both networks were completely dishonest to put out the Stevenson speech, blasting the devil out of me, as a public service, and then not giving me the courtesy of time to reply. I want nothing to do with either NBC or CBS."[30]

Variety, the show business weekly, reported on March 10 that Washington lawyers believed that NBC and CBS had the law on their side in refusing McCarthy time to answer Stevenson. It said that the equal time provision in section 315 of the communications act provided only that equal time should be made available to rival candidates in an election campaign; McCarthy was basing his demand on a 1949 FCC policy report on editorializing by broadcast licensees which said that broadcasters must offer "balanced" presentations of controversial issues. *Variety* quoted McCarthy as saying, "I am delegating no one to answer the attack made upon me. Everyone knows the FCC rules provide they must give me time, otherwise it is completely dishonest and unfair."

Jack Gould advised the networks to "hold resolutely" to their refusal of time for McCarthy. "If they bow on this issue of principle," he wrote on March 10 in the *New York Times*, "their networks no longer will be their own." Gould said that the offer of time to the Republican national committee and the selection of Nixon met the basic test of impartiality, fairness, and common sense.

To accede to the Senator's threats only will reduce political discussion on the air to the point of complete chaos or lead to its drastic curtailment. Either eventuality would make a tragic mockery of freedom of the air.

If Senator McCarthy must be given free time whenever a Republican or a Democrat speaks of him unfavorably, he would be on the air more often than any other person. Under the Senator's concept of equal time he, in effect, would dominate the airwaves. That's the critical issue for broadcasting and nothing's to be gained by not facing it.

The *New York Herald Tribune* also praised the networks for holding firm. "Mr. McCarthy's ability to insult and calumniate those who oppose or criticize him is well known," its March 11 editorial said. "By refusing to be bullied, the broadcasters will assure their own future and help to guarantee America's." And *Variety* commented in its March 17 issue, "Until very recently the networks have exhibited little inclination to stand up to McCarthyism." Bob Considine, an International News Service columnist, however, wrote that the position of radio and television was precarious because they were "wards of the FCC." Their decision on McCarthy might be "a basic cause for extreme migraine."[31]

McCarthy's only offer of free time came from the Mutual Broadcasting System, which had not carried Stevenson's speech, and the offer was for a spot on the March 11 radio program of Fulton Lewis, Jr., a news commentator and McCarthy supporter. But events crowded in so thickly that by the time McCarthy appeared on this program, four days after the Stevenson speech, he had two more formidable critics to answer.

One was Senator Ralph Flanders, a Vermont Republican, who rose in the Senate on March 9 to accuse McCarthy of deserting the Republican party and to ridicule his hunt for Communists. "He dons his warpaint," Flanders said. "He goes into his war dance. He emits his war whoops. He goes forth to battle and proudly returns with the scalp of a pink Army dentist. We may assume that this represents the depth and seriousness of the Communist penetration in this country at this time."[32] *Variety* reported on the 17th that Flanders had been "hauled off before the cameras to film some of the choicer fragments of his speech" and that these fragments on the evening news shows had been viewed by President Eisenhower, who then issued a statement praising Flanders's speech, his boldest move against McCarthy thus far. "Ike saw it on TV, he didn't read it," *Variety* said.

The other critic was Edward R. Murrow, television's most respected figure, who—also on March 9—presented on his popular "See It Now" weekly program a documentary which provided, through skillful film editing, a devastating critique of McCarthy and his methods. Nothing like it had appeared on television. McCarthy's world was beginning to fall apart. His favorable rating in the Gallup Poll, which had reached 50 percent, fell to 46 percent; it never went up again. On March 11 Irv Kupcinet, a *Chicago Sun-Times* columnist, reported that even the "so-called isolationist wing" of the Republican party, composed mostly of midwesterners, was cooling off on McCarthy. One of them, Kupcinet reported, said that McCarthy had taken a beating, mentally and physically, and needed "a rest—a long rest."

The "See It Now" broadcast, produced for CBS by Murrow and Fred W. Friendly, was the beginning of the third of McCarthy's television-related crises. The story of the broadcast has been told many times and in great detail, most notably by Alexander Kendrick, Murrow's biographer, and by Friendly.[33] This program, along with the climactic ending of the Army-McCarthy hearings, are among the things many of us remember best of the McCarthy period; for some, they are almost the only things remembered.

Murrow began the program by announcing that McCarthy would be offered equal time for a reply. The technique employed was to show a film clip of McCarthy issuing one of his half-truths or distortions, followed by Murrow's recitation of the truth—that a barn in

Lee, Massachusetts, for example, had nothing to do with Adlai Stevenson, although McCarthy had seemed to say that the barn proved that Stevenson was tied in with Communists. The program showed McCarthy giggling as he chortled over the feigned slip of his tongue— "Alger ... I mean Adlai"—in the election eve speech in 1952. It showed McCarthy telling General Zwicker that he was unfit to wear the uniform, and it showed the bullying of Reed Harris, to great effect.

Using a pile of newspapers as a prop, Murrow pointed out that although McCarthy had said that only the "left-wing" press opposed him, every newspaper in the big pile had criticized the senator for his rudeness to Zwicker. As he leafed through the papers, viewers saw the *Chicago Tribune*, which had, indeed, criticized McCarthy on this issue. In the editorial with which Murrow ended the show, he said that McCarthy's primary achievement had been to confuse the public about internal and external threats of Communism.

This is no time for men who oppose Senator McCarthy's methods to keep silent, or for those who approve. We can deny our heritage and our history, but we cannot escape responsibility for the result. There is no way for a citizen of the republic to abdicate his responsibilities. As a nation we have come into our full inheritance at a tender age. We proclaim ourselves—as indeed we are—the defenders of freedom, what's left of it, but we cannot defend freedom abroad by deserting it at home. The actions of the junior senator from Wisconsin have caused alarm and dismay amongst our allies abroad and given considerable comfort to our enemies, and whose fault is that? Not really his. He didn't create the situation of fear; he merely exploited it, and rather successfully. Cassius was right: "The fault, dear Brutus, is not in our stars but in ourselves."[34]

This was a relatively mild editorial statement, hardly critical of McCarthy; it was almost defensive, a justification for making such a program. It was not nearly as strong as the editorials that had appeared regularly in some newspapers for four years.

In some ways the most remarkable thing about the program was that it was so late. Even the conservative Republican newspapers had begun to turn on McCarthy as it became apparent that he was willing to fight President Eisenhower in the same way he had fought President Truman. But television had been so cowed by the Red-baiters, the blacklisters, and the fearful sponsors that Murrow's cautious courage seemed heroic. Eric Sevareid, the CBS television commentator, said in a special broadcast in January 1978 that Murrow's program was effective, took a lot of courage, "but it came very late in the day. ... The youngsters read back and they think only one person in broadcasting and the press stood up to McCarthy, and this has made a lot of people feel very upset, including me, because that program came awfully late. Coincided with the Army charges against McCarthy."[35]

Sevareid said that other broadcasters—he named radio commentators Elmer Davis and Martin Agronsky—had criticized McCarthy much earlier, and that Agronsky had lost many of his sponsors as a result. Agronsky, who is still active as the moderator of a television news program, confirmed this.[36] He said that in 1953 he was doing a 15-minute program each morning from Washington for ABC, half news and half commentary. The program was sponsored locally in each city, and his income and that of the local station and the network was dependent on the number of sponsors. At his peak, he had about 120 sponsors. "In my commentary, I followed the McCarthy thing very closely," he said, "along with the House Un-American Activities Committee, the Hollywood 10, and all that. As a result, some sponsors got scared. A customer would go into a department store and say, 'Why have you got this Commie on the radio? I won't buy any underwear from you.' I began to lose a lot of sponsors. Then I discovered there was more to it than that."

One day Agronsky ran into G. David Schine, McCarthy's aid, outside the senator's hearing room. "How's your sponsorship going?" Schine asked. Agronsky said everything was fine. "Who's your sponsor in Houston?" Schine asked. Agronsky said he didn't know. "Are you sponsored in Houston?" Schine persisted. "What's the point of all this?" Agronsky asked. "It's just something for you to keep in mind," Schine said. "Then I discovered that the sponsor in Houston had dropped me," Agronsky said. "He did it after McCarthy appeared there to make a speech. McCarthy was doing this to my sponsors everywhere he went. I think he had his staff telephoning them, too." Agronsky lost more than half of his sponsors, to the point that neither he, the stations, nor the network were making money on his broadcasts. At a meeting of ABC affiliates in Chicago, the stations complained to Robert Kintner, the ABC president, about Agronsky's comments on McCarthy and demanded that he be fired. "Some friends in Chicago told me about this," Agronsky said, "and when Kintner called me from New York the next day to ask me to come up to see him, I thought I might as well clean out my desk."

In New York, Kintner told Agronsky that some affiliates had said that the senator was a great patriot and was being treated unfairly. "They suggested I should talk to you about the way you're reporting McCarthy," Kintner said. "Are you going to change?" "No," said Agronsky. "That's what I thought you'd say," Kintner said. "Keep it up." In Agronsky's opinion, Kintner was one of the great men in broadcasting. "He was the first guy in the business to understand that there is a value in news that brings prestige to everything else a network does."

Jack Gould told me that Murrow knew that his criticism of McCarthy was late. Gould had had lunch with Murrow shortly after the McCarthy broadcast and told him that he was regarded as a hero in many quarters. "My God," Murrow said. "I didn't do anything. Scotty Reston and a lot of guys have been writing like this, saying the same things, for months, for years. We're bringing up the rear." "But we both overlooked the fact that TV was hotter than a pistol," Gould said. "We didn't realize how much impact it had."[37]

One of the reasons for the program's impact was that it was Ed Murrow saying these things. Like Eisenhower, who "brought the boys home" from World War II, Murrow was a war hero, a symbol of victory and the happy unity of national purpose that was dissipated in the anxious postwar period. Murrow was the one who brought the war news each night on the radio from London, a part of everyone's life. In the public eye, this was no mere politician. CBS reported that it received more than 12,000 telephone calls and telegrams in the 24 hours after the broadcast, and the messages favored Murrow's point of view by 15 to 1. CBS affiliates all over the country contributed similar reports.[38] The March 17 *Variety* reported that "all TV" was proud of the Murrow show and that both NBC and ABC had actually named CBS as they gave the network credit, an unprecedented event. "Murrow has now attacked head-on the one-man-myth and pointed up its factual inconsistencies and dubious logic."

In McCarthy's response to Murrow on March 11 on the Fulton Lewis, Jr., radio show, he hit back at Stevenson and Senator Flanders as well. "I may say, Fulton," McCarthy said, "that I have a little difficulty answering the specific attack he [Murrow] made, because I never listen to the extreme left-wing, bleeding-heart element of radio and television." McCarthy then read from a copy of a story that had appeared in the *Pittsburgh Sun-Telegraph* 18 February 1935. It was headlined "American Professors Trained by Soviets Teach in U.S. Schools," and listed the names of American educators, many of them presidents of universities, and of Murrow, an assistant director of the Institute of International Education. The Institute was an advisory group to a short-lived educational exchange program, backed by prominent foundations, between the United States and Russia. McCarthy called the participants American advisers to Communist propaganda schools. "This may explain why Edward R. Murrow week after week feels he must smear Senator McCarthy," he said. "Maybe he is worried about the exposure of some of his friends—I don't know."

Murrow had said, in his narration of the documentary, that Mc-Carthy had been lying when he claimed that the American Civil Liberties Union had been on the attorney general's list of subversive organizations. McCarthy, on the radio program, said that Murrow was lying, because the ACLU had been listed as subversive by the un-American activities committee of the California state senate.

Most of McCarthy's remarks that night were addressed to Stevenson's arguments, and particularly the statement that only one alleged Communist had been dismissed from government because of McCarthy's investigations. McCarthy said that he had a long list of Communists exposed by his committee and dismissed from government. He named three: Edward Rothschild, a bookbinder at the Government Printing Office; Doris Powell, a New York employe of the army's quartermaster corps, and Ruth Levine, who had been employed not by the government but by a company in New Jersey that had a government contract. McCarthy obviously thought it more important to answer Stevenson than Murrow, and in this he reflected the emphasis placed by newspapers on the several McCarthy-related stories that were breaking almost at once. The attack by Flanders, the first instance of a prominent Republican attacking McCarthy openly, got the top play in most newspapers. The Murrow story did not appear in the *New York Times* on March 10, the morning after the broadcast. On March 11, there were two McCarthy stories on page one—President Eisenhower, at his press conference, praising Flanders, and McCarthy, at his press conference, saying that the Republican party was being harmed by a few Republicans "who want to be heroes in the eyes of the left-wing press," meaning Flanders, of course, and perhaps Eisenhower. McCarthy said he was going to continue his "barn-cleaning" despite such attacks.

The Murrow story appeared March 11 on page 19 of the *Times*. On March 12, McCarthy made page one with his Fulton Lewis, Jr., radio rebuttal, but Murrow's reply to that—an explanation of his role on the exchange advisory committee—was reported on page eight of the March 13 paper. In the *Washington Post*, the Flanders attack was the banner headline on March 10. An Associated Press story on the Murrow program appeared on page six. Newspaper attitudes toward television in 1954 were still ambivalent. The question of whether what happened on television was really news was debated by editors all over; in general, they felt that a speech on television was less newsworthy than a speech to a live audience. This attitude probably affected the play of the Murrow story.*

---

*In Jack Gould's opinion, the *New York Times* was slow to recognize what was seen on television as news. This began to change when the publisher, Arthur Hays Sulz-

McCarthy did not accept Murrow's offer of equal time immediately. First he asked that William F. Buckley, Jr., who was willing, be allowed to speak for him, but Murrow said that time was open only to the senator. Eventually McCarthy accepted, but for some time the date of his appearance was in doubt. In a speaking tour of the Midwest, he reiterated the charges against Murrow that he had made on the Fulton Lewis, Jr., program. Murrow, in the meantime, had defended himself—on his radio program—against McCarthy's charge about his service on the advisory council for the summer session at Moscow University, by pointing out that other eminent Americans, including Republicans, had served on the same board. This was, of course, a perfectly good argument, and many people used it, but McCarthy never paid any attention to it and always managed to make this kind of answer seem to be a partial admission of guilt, as though not only the target but the other "respectable" types were all Communist dupes, at the least. Guilt by association was valid; innocence by association did not work.

McCarthy's reply to Murrow came on the "See It Now" program of April 6 in the form of a film (made by Fox Movietone News) rather than a studio appearance. This was fair enough, considering the artistry that had gone into the Murrow program. It was a crude production, however, and differed from a studio appearance only in the presence of maps on the wall and a pile of documents on the table. McCarthy made no actual reply to Murrow; instead, he attacked, first with a range of insinuations and distortions as ingenious as those he had employed in his hatchet job on Adlai Stevenson in 1952. He said that Murrow "as far back as twenty years ago was engaged in propagandizing for Communist causes," and that his broadcast had "followed implicitly the Communist line laid down in the last six months not only by the Communist *Daily Worker*, but by the Communist magazine *Political Affairs*, and the National Conference of the Communist Party."[39] He said that Murrow had been a member of the Industrial Workers of the World (a group on the Attorney General's list of subversive organizations), that Harold Laski, whom McCarthy called a "Communist propagandist," had dedicated a book to Murrow, and that Owen Lattimore, McCarthy's longtime target, had mentioned Murrow favorably in one of his books. He retold the story of Murrow's

---

berger, watched the 1952 inaugural ceremonies on television and called the national desk to say that the *Times*'s lead story did not contain what he had seen. He gave orders that Gould's summary of things seen on television be interwoven throughout the main story, and from that time on the *Times* covered television as news. It changed Gould's role from critic to reporter. (Gould interview, 24 September 1976.)

connection with the Institute of International Education and the teacher exchange with Russia.

Murrow, replying the same night, said that he had never been a member of the Industrial Workers of the World, that Laski was a Socialist rather than a Communist and that his dedication was the result of appreciation for Murrow's wartime broadcasts from England. He said that he had never met Lattimore.[40] "Senator McCarthy's reckless and unfounded attempt to impugn my loyalty is just one more example of his typical tactic of attempting to tie up to Communism anyone who disagrees with him," Murrow said. "I now join the distinguished list upon which already appear the *Washington Post*, the *Milwaukee Journal*, *Time* magazine, *Commonweal*, the *Christian Science Monitor*, and General Marshall, among others."[41]

The speech was analyzed in the *Washington Star* on April 11 by Cecil Holland, who wrote that the Murrow attack was the best illustration of McCarthy's techniques.

> ... *Senator McCarthy ranged far and wide, painting the dangers of Communist conquest which had no discernible connections with Mr. Murrow. But the account was presented with such feeling and was so interwoven with references to Mr. Murrow by name—and to "the friends of Edward R. Murrow" and "the Murrows"—that an unwary television viewer might have reached the conclusion that the CBS commentator in some fashion not quite clear was responsible for the Communist conquests of Eastern Europe and the downfall of China.*

An April 12 editorial in *Broadcasting-Telecasting* called McCarthy's presentation "savage, cynical and irrelevant." It demonstrated the utter futility of the "equal time" policy, the magazine said.

> *The lesson is to establish definite ground rules at the outset, to make it clear to the parties and the public alike that the use of equal time must be confined to the issues which precipitated the demand for it. The alternative is to let the principle of equal time go by the board and to permit the give-and-take to degenerate into personal vilifications of which the McCarthy performance must be regarded as an unwholesome classic.*

Jack Gould wrote that Murrow would suffer temporarily, because when that much mud is thrown at anyone "it is futile to expect that all of the debris can be wiped from the public mind." But in the long run McCarthy would be hurt by what he did, Gould predicted:

In his anxiety to still Mr. Murrow's voice and drive it from the air, the Senator more effectively confirmed the commentator's thesis than the commentator did. Mr. Murrow only reported as best he could on the use of innuendo, insinuation, the half-truth and the frantic smear. The Senator, on the other hand, gave the expert's own authorized version. It may take a little time before the Senator realizes he was had.[42]

Fox Movietone News charged McCarthy $6,336 to make the film, and McCarthy tried to use the bill to create bad blood between Murrow, CBS, and the Aluminum Company of America (Alcoa), sponsor of "See It Now." On April 23 he announced that he was going to send the bill to Alcoa; the company announced that it would not pay. An Alcoa spokesman said that since CBS had furnished the program as a package, for a set price, CBS was responsible. McCarthy sent the bill to Alcoa anyway, with the comment that since his performance contributed to the advertising of Alcoa products, the company should pay. On May 4 Alcoa mailed back the bill. On May 10 the bill was received by CBS. In Gould's opinion, McCarthy was within his rights in forcing CBS to pay. He was not answering a political speech but a show, and he had a right to reply with a show of his own.[43] Frank Stanton, CBS president, paid the bill but said that normally there was prior agreement about the use of outside facilities if the network was to pay. However, he said, that policy had not been enunciated by CBS before McCarthy's action, and CBS believed that "it would not be proper to refuse to reimburse Senator McCarthy on this ground."[44]

The aluminum company renewed its contract for "See It Now" in November 1954, despite what the company's president called "some uneasy moments." It dropped the program in July 1955 but insisted that the McCarthy episode had nothing to do with the decision. Gould called Alcoa's performance under fire an example of corporate courage that was highly unusual in broadcasting:

Alcoa was subjected to intense pressures—political, economic and emotional—to withdraw from sponsorship [Gould wrote]. For a commercial concern not accustomed to the stresses and strains that are part of life in journalism, the experience could hardly have been a pleasant one. More than one sponsor has collapsed under a mere fraction of the pressure experienced by Alcoa. But Alcoa did not panic. . . . When it came time to renew the program's contract after the McCarthy incident officials of Alcoa did not hint to Mr. Murrow that he should go easy on controversial matters.[45]

Questions have been raised, however, about the techniques employed in the show, the kind of film editing that drew this enthusiastic
response from Barry Gray, a New York radio news commentator: "On
Tuesday night he [Murrow] drew that sword and set to work master-
fully on Joe McCarthy and Joe was killed. Ed Murrow, CBS's ace, did
something so simple no one had thought of it. *He let McCarthy dev-
astate McCarthy.*"[46] But John Cogley, a television critic, argued that
the program was unfair to McCarthy because it relied on pictures
rather than a spoken text. "Television is dynamite. Both CBS and NBC
have tried to present both sides fairly. I am sorry to say I truly believe
the Edward R. Murrow show has set a potentially dangerous precedent which those who are now applauding it may find good reason
to regret in time to come."[47]

Gilbert Seldes, the *New Republic*'s critic and a foe of McCarthy,
said that the producers were wrong in calling the program a report
when it really was an attack followed by an editorial appeal for action.
Seldes said that "in the long run it is more important to use our communications systems properly than to destroy McCarthy."[48] Gould's
comment was that as a work of craftsmanship, the program was "a
masterly performance." It used McCarthy as the principal witness
against himself and showed how he used half-truths to "persecute
rather than investigate." But, he wrote,

*what was frightening about Mr. Murrow's broadcast—and Mr. Mur-
row many times has philosophized on this point himself—was this:
what if the circumstances had been different? What if the camera and
the microphone should fall into the hands of a reckless and demagogic
commentator? If Mr. Murrow with his firm and measured presentation
can overnight stir up strong public reaction, what could the hypnotic,
reckless and charming firebrand achieve in like time? The persu-
asiveness of television for good must not blind us to its like potential
for bad.*[49]

John E. O'Connor, a historian at the New Jersey Institute of Technology, recommended in a recent article that the Murrow-Friendly
film be shown to students as a prime example of a certain kind of
visual communication. He wrote:

*But in the process of putting together the film clips to show the
Senator in the worst possible light, Murrow seems to have fallen into
some of the same techniques used by the man he was exposing. Sec-
tions of McCarthy's speeches were taken out of context, and certain
sequences seem to have been included more because of the expression*

on the senator's face or the tone of his voice—at one point a silly little laugh makes him appear to be insane—rather than the substance of what he had to say. Other sequences—his response to a testimonial dinner, for example, where he sputters and shuffles his feet for a minute or two before admitting to be speechless—seemed to have been included primarily to embarrass McCarthy. They tell us nothing of the methods he used or of the real dangers his movement represented. The fact that the film has been credited with helping to turn public opinion against the senator just a few weeks before the commencement of the Army-McCarthy hearings makes it all the more interesting.[50]

The question raised by these critics is still with us: What techniques are fair in making documentaries? There is common agreement in the television industry that it is proper that a documentary express a point of view—that it take sides. But there is no agreement on how far a film-maker can go in editing to make his point, and an argument about these techniques has been at the heart of every controversy about documentaries in recent years. A reporter whose product appears in print makes the same kind of decisions—what to use, what to leave out, what point to select as a lead, how to say what it means. But the reader knows these things are being done, and he reads skeptically. The illusion of film makes it appear that the viewer is seeing truth, and trickery in this medium is reprehensible. If someone reading a newspaper story is told that a politician's answer to a question is a silly or a slanderous one, he may suspect that the reporter left something out or doctored the answer somehow. But a politican answering a question on television in a foolish way may really be answering another question that is never asked on the air; this is not an unusual practice among film-makers. And the viewer *knows* that the politician uttered that silly answer; he saw it.

Senator Benton provided an example of this kind of editing when he appeared on television in May 1952 to explain why he had refused to testify at a pretrial hearing in McCarthy's libel and slander suit against him when McCarthy had brought a tape recorder to the hearing. Benton played a tape which said, "A veteran court reporter said he knew of no instance where a voice recording was used in District Court to report testimony taken under court auspices." He had a technician delete the phrase "of no instance," and played it back: "A veteran court reporter said he knew where a voice recording was used in District Court. . . ."[51] If McCarthy had chosen to answer Murrow with a sophisticated analysis of the program's techniques instead of a transparently distorted effort to impugn the commentator's patriotism, he might have come out ahead in the exchange. But if he had done that, he might have had to admit the possibility that many of his own accusations were the product of a similar kind of machination.

If a survey were taken now on the question of what single factor was most important in bringing McCarthy down, the answer given by most people would probably be the Army-McCarthy hearings. Not many would remember how the hearings came about or what the argument was, but they would remember McCarthy's display of bad manners and the dramatic climax when Joseph Welch, representing the army, took advantage of a loss of emotional control to show up McCarthy before a watching nation as a sadistic bully. This was McCarthy's fourth and last television crisis.

The Army-McCarthy hearings arose out of McCarthy's investigation of subversion in the army, but they were not an extension of those hearings. They followed the Peress case, the Zwicker incident, McCarthy's humiliation of Secretary Stevens, and his defiant televised press conference that upstaged President Eisenhower's conference. The administration had decided that it was time to take a stand against the senator. Action was in the form of a report issued by the army, charging that McCarthy, chairman of the Permanent Subcommittee on Investigations, the subcommittee's counsel, Roy Cohn, and its executive director, Francis Carr, had sought by improper means to obtain preferential treatment for Private G. David Schine, the committee's former "chief consultant," who had been drafted by the army. McCarthy had countercharged that the army had released the list of improper actions "to force a discontinuance of further attempts by that committee to expose Communist infiltration in the Army."

McCarthy and Cohn had been trying to secure special treatment for Schine ever since the young man had been first called by his draft board in July 1953. First they tried to arrange a commission, but Schine was a college dropout and all three branches of the military turned him down. Cohn proposed to General Walter B. Smith that Schine should be recruited by the Central Intelligence Agency, which McCarthy had proposed to investigate. Schine suggested himself as a special assistant to the secretary of the army, and Cohn proposed that Schine be assigned to check the textbooks of the U.S. Military Academy for subversive influences. Nevertheless he was drafted, but he was not forgotten. Cohn repeatedly called the commander at Fort Dix, New Jersey, where Schine was stationed, the army's general counsel, and the secretary of the army himself, to scold them for their treatment of Schine. As a result, Schine was given 16 passes in a period in which other enlisted men got three, and he was excused from drill to place or answer 250 long-distance telephone calls. Reports of Cohn's activity began to reach newspapers in December 1953, and by early February 1954, Democrats were demanding a report from the army on the matter, while the administration was still hoping to avoid a showdown with McCarthy. But on March 11, the day that McCarthy appeared on the radio program of Fulton Lewis, Jr., to answer the criticism of Stevenson, Flanders, and Murrow, the army filed its charges.

Republicans in the Senate first tried to avoid doing anything at all about the army's report, but the pressure for hearings was strong; the story drew a banner headline in almost every newspaper. Next there was backroom skirmishing about which committee would hold hearings; finally the McCarthy subcommittee voted to investigate its own chairman and Roy Cohn, its chief counsel. Senator Karl Mundt (Rep., S.D.) reluctantly agreed to act as chairman. McCarthy, a witness, demanded and received the right to cross-examine witnesses, a right he had regularly denied other witnesses who appeared before the subcommittee. He fought to remain a member of the committee but was overruled; he then appointed Senator Henry Dworshak of Idaho, a supporter, as his substitute. McCarthy nevertheless dominated the hearings.

Newspapers carried hundreds of stories about these hearings; a book has been written about them alone, and they have been described minutely in a dozen other books; a motion picture based on the hearings has been shown nationally.

During the three weeks before the start of the hearings, McCarthy pretended that he was not involved, pretended that the case involved only John Adams, the army counsel, and Cohn. But when television coverage began on April 22, he could not resist the lure of the cameras. He took over, questioning each witness longer than any other member of the committee, constantly interrupting to gain the floor by raising irrelevant points of order. As Reston reported it,

There were differences of opinion here tonight about whether this was a prudent tactic. Some observers thought it was, mainly because it cast him in his familiar setting as the belligerent fighter against communism—tough, agile, forever ready to do battle with anybody who says anything detrimental to him. . . .

The general view . . . is that this was not smart, from his own point of view, but that he could not help it. When the red lights of those TV cameras go on, the Senator automatically produces sound.[52]

Gould reviewed the first day's hearing as drama, and predicted that if it ran the expected two weeks it was going to wreck housekeeping routines in many homes. (Actually it ran more than six weeks.) He said that it was much like other television shows, but different in that no one knew how it would end. "The absorbing attraction is to follow the testimony as it goes first one way and then another, as first the Army and then Senator McCarthy make their points. On TV it is the drama of unrehearsed actuality unfolding for everyone to see at home."[53] On the first day, NBC, ABC, and Du Mont carried the hearings live, and CBS offered a film summary at 11:30 P.M. In the East, the hearings began at 10:30 A.M. and ran until 4:30 P.M. On the third day, however, NBC dropped its live coverage because it was losing revenue from its usual daytime programs. ABC and Du Mont, neither of which had many daytime commitments, continued the live broadcasts. The hearings scored a rating of 9 to 12 on the Hooper scale, according to Gould, about the same as the Arthur Godfrey show and one called The Big Pay-Off. Gould said that this rating had been compared adversely to the 32 scored by Senator Kefauver's crime committee hearings in 1951, but that this comparison was unfair because there were no other programs competing with the crime hearings, which had a sensational cast of "underworld big shots." But some were saying that it meant people were tired of the hearings, and others that it meant people were bored with television itself, Gould wrote.[54]

NBC's withdrawal was significant because it eliminated live broadcasts to the western half of the United States and to other cities without ABC or Du Mont television stations. There were many protests, and Senator Mundt, the chairman, said that he had received "a deluge of telegrams" accusing the committee of halting the broadcasts. He said that protests should be directed to the broadcasting companies.[55] NBC explained that it had lost $125,000 in advertising revenues during the two days it had carried the hearings live; the network did not say how many protests it had received but said they were "much fewer than expected."

Editor & Publisher, the newspaper trade journal, reported that newspaper coverage of the hearings broke all records for coverage of congressional committees. The first hearing was covered by 120 reporters, three television crews, 12 fixed and three roving newsreel cameramen, and 36 still cameramen. Each wire service assigned four reporters. About 30 temporary wire circuits were set up to serve 33 teleprinters and eight Morse code tables.[56]

Secretary of the Army Stevens, the first witness, was still on the stand after seven days of testimony, and senators, particularly the Republicans, were thinking of ways to end the spectacle. This was still a preliminary; the main event was to be McCarthy in the witness chair. There was no indication when that might take place. The *New York Times* reported that Republicans were going to propose curtailment or elimination of television coverage at the next executive session of the subcommittee. Senator Charles Potter (Rep., Mich.), a subcommittee member, said that he did not know whether he would vote to cut television coverage but that "if hearings were not televised, they would be expedited materially." Senator Dworshak said that a cutback would help, "if only by discouraging some who otherwise might want to use what should be a news medium for publicity purposes."[57]

Ratings had slipped only a little. In New York it was 9, meaning that 9 persons out of each 100 having sets were watching the hearing. In Boston, it was 18. And a reduction in the hours that the hearing was covered by a New York radio station, WNYC, brought such a flood of protests that the station restored full coverage. Jack Gould observed that the networks had never before been confronted with the problem presented by an investigation that could run for weeks and months and cost millions in lost revenues. He wrote:

The current inquiry has exposed a fundamental journalistic weakness in television. It is not that television cannot technically cover the hearings as long as they last; it can. The problem is to what extent economics will allow it to do so. . . . The public, too, has an enormous financial investment in television through the purchase of sets, and, in exchange for supporting advertisers the year round by purchase of products, they have every right to expect full coverage of important public events.[58]

By May 5 McCarthy and Cohn had expanded their countercharges, claiming that the army had sought to halt the investigation of subversives at Fort Monmouth, New Jersey, by holding Schine as a "hostage" and that army officials had tried to blackmail McCarthy by threatening publication of the report of Cohn's activities on behalf of Schine.

In St. Louis, Missouri, the *Post-Dispatch* became a television sponsor. There the hearings were being carried live by the Du Mont affiliate, and the coverage was becoming a financial burden to the station; the newspaper sponsored the live coverage as a public service. The *Inquirer* did the same thing in Philadelphia.

On May 11 the Republicans made an effort to shunt the testimony into executive session. But Mundt had promised to continue public hearings unless both principals agreed to a cutoff. McCarthy agreed but the army did not; Adams said that only his side had testified so far, and it was fair that the public hear the opposing witnesses, too. Mundt lived up to his word and voted with the three committee Democrats to continue hearings, and on they went. Gould put it into perspective:

No viewer who has sat in front of his screen could be unaware of television's tremendous role in the hearings—politically, educationally and socially. As the principals in the investigation themselves have observed so often, it has been the television audience which has constituted the real jury. Whatever the viewer's personal political predilections, he has been his own eye-witness, reporter and judge.[59]

This comment was all the more apt because the committee came to no immediate conclusion; the hearings simply ended. All that was left was the image, the effect on the minds of viewers. The most vivid image was that of the confrontation June 9 between McCarthy and Joseph Welch, the Boston lawyer who served as the army's special counsel. Michael Straight, in his book-length report on the hearings, sets the scene thus:

Was McCarthy maddened by Welch's taunting of his assistant [Cohn]? It was evident that the Senator had waited a long time for this moment. He had come to hate Welch, not because of any single remark made by the Army counsel, but because he had won the sympathy and admiration of the nation, something that on this stage at least McCarthy wanted for himself alone. He hated Welch further and found it necessary to destroy him because of his spirit of ironic comedy. There was no room in McCarthy's world for such a spirit. . . .[60]

Welch had told Cohn that if he knew of a Communist or a subversive in a responsible post it was his duty to report it immediately. McCarthy broke in. Mundt asked him if he had a point of order, to which McCarthy replied:

Not exactly, Mr. Chairman, but in view of Mr. Welch's request that the information be given at once if we know of anyone who might be performing any work for the Communist Party, I think we should tell him that he has in his law firm a young man named Fisher . . . who has been for a number of years a member of an organization which was named, oh, years and years ago, as the legal bulwark of the Communist Party. . . ."

The reference was to Frederick Fisher, who had joined the National Lawyers Guild as a student at Harvard. In 1954, Fisher was secretary of the Young Republican League in Newton, Massachusetts. Mc-Carthy grinned as he went on, his voice heavy with sarcasm:

... I have hesitated about bringing that up, but I have been rather bored with your phony requests to Mr. Cohn here that he personally get every Communist out of government before sundown. Therefore we will give you the information about the young man in your own organization. I am not asking you at this time to explain why you tried to foist him on this committee. Whether you knew he was a member of that Communist organization or not I don't know. I assume you did not, Mr. Welch, because I get the impression that while you are quite an actor, you play for a laugh, I don't think you have any conception of the danger of the Communist Party. I don't think you would ever knowingly aid the Communist cause. I think you are unknowingly aiding it when you try to burlesque this hearing in which we are trying to bring out the facts, however.

Welch asked Mundt for permission to speak on a point of personal privilege. Mundt granted it. As Welch began, McCarthy turned away and began to talk to one of his aids. Welch asked for his attention. "I can listen with one ear," McCarthy said. "This time," said Welch, "I want you to listen with both." He began again, and once again McCarthy interrupted, telling the aid to get the news story showing that Fisher was a member of the Lawyers Guild. Welch began again, saying, "Until this moment, Senator, I think I never really gauged your cruelty or your recklessness." He then told the hearing that Fisher was a Harvard law graduate who was starting what promised to be a brilliant career, and that James St. Clair, Welch's first assistant in the hearings, had picked Fisher as a second assistant. Welch had asked St. Clair and Fisher if there was anything in their backgrounds that might be a source of embarrassment in the case, and Fisher had said that he had once belonged to the Lawyers Guild for a few months.

So, Senator, I asked him to go back to Boston. Little did I dream you could be so reckless and so cruel as to do an injury to that lad. It is true he is still with Hale and Dorr. It is true that he will continue to be with Hale and Dorr. It is, I regret to say, equally true that I fear he shall always bear a scar needlessly inflicted by you. If it were in my power to forgive you for your reckless cruelty I would do so. I like to think I am a gentle man, but your forgiveness will have to come from someone other than me.

McCarthy had been reading a paper, or pretending to read, while Welch spoke. Now he said that Welch had no right to speak of cruelty, because he had been "baiting Mr. Cohn here for hours." He began again to go over Fisher's record. Welch spoke: "Senator, may we not drop this? We know he belonged to the Lawyers Guild, and Mr. Cohn nods his head at me." Welch turned to Cohn. "I did you, I think, no personal injury, Mr. Cohn," he said, and Cohn agreed. "I meant to do you no personal injury, and if I did I beg your pardon." Welch turned back to McCarthy. "Let us not assassinate this lad further, Senator. You have done enough. Have you no sense of decency, sir? At long last, have you no sense of decency?"

Cohn was shaking his head at McCarthy, as if to say, let it be. But McCarthy ignored him and plunged on, asking Welch if he had not brought Fisher to Washington. "Mr. McCarthy," Welch said, his voice full of scorn, "I will not discuss this with you further. You have sat within six feet of me and could have asked me about Fred Fisher. You have brought it out. If there is a God in heaven it will do neither you nor your cause any good. I will not discuss it further. I will not ask Mr. Cohn any questions. You, Mr. Chairman, may, if you will, call the next witness."

There was silence, and then the room rang with applause. Welch walked from the room, and reporters followed him. McCarthy looked confused, deserted. He held out his arms, palms upward, as if to say, "What did I do?" Cohn, writing in 1968, described the moment:

The blow was terribly damaging to Senator McCarthy. He was pictured before the nation as a cruel man who deliberately sought to wreck a fine young lawyer's life. . . . It was pure nonsense, of course, and I suspect Joe Welch knew it. . . . the whole story had run in the New York Times *two months previously. . . . [but] Welch, with his superb instinct for drama, knowing a good thing when it came his way, played the scene for all it was worth.*[61]

James Reston, summing up the effects of the hearings in the 30 May 1954 *New York Times*, said that McCarthy, on television, had "demonstrated with appalling clarity precisely what kind of man he is."

One cannot remain indifferent to Joe McCarthy in one's living room. He is an abrasive man. And he is recklessly transparent. The country did not know him before, despite all the headlines. Now it has seen him. It has had a startling but accurate presentation of his ideas, his tactics, his immense physical power, and it is at least basing its judgments now on firsthand observations. The things that have hurt him and cost him support are his manner and his manners. People are still clearly divided on the substance of his charges and the counter-charges between him and the Army, but on one thing there seems little division: the Senator from Wisconsin is a bad-mannered man.

Reston wrote that McCarthy had lost strength where he needed it most, among respectable, moderate, anti-Communist Republicans. He predicted that the loss would be enough to turn the Republicans in Washington against McCarthy, and this proved to be true. The broadcasting of the hearings made it possible for the Senate to consider censure.

"That coverage did McCarthy in," Jack Gould said recently. "People started to laugh at him. He became a joke, then a bore. He got tiresome. You can blame TV for a lot of things, but that is to its credit." Gould said that ABC and its president, Robert Kintner, had never been given sufficient credit for broadcasting the hearings. In addition to whatever it lost in revenue, ABC had had to pay $50,000 a week to rent transmission facilities for the broadcasts. It fed a network of 50 stations regularly and up to 79 at certain times, and the Du Mont network fed 10 stations. But the decision to broadcast the hearings was a turning point for ABC, which had lagged far behind the other networks; after this, ABC was in competition.[62]

Television coverage created new problems for newspapers, too, because viewers could, and did, compare what they had seen with what appeared in the paper the next day, and they were often critical. The Associated Press got so many complaints that Alan J. Gould, executive editor, found it necessary to defend AP coverage in the newsletter distributed to newspaper clients. Gould said that no two observers ever saw things alike and that this was especially true when observers were partisan, as they were in this instance. He said that many had complained that on television, McCarthy did not appear to shout or roar, as a number of AP stories had reported. He said that a "roar" in the hearing room was toned down in the TV control room so that viewers heard a different sound.[63] Most of the complaints received by newspapers and the AP were from McCarthy supporters. McCarthy himself said, on May 11, that television had led to "more accurate news reporting than he had ever seen on a hearing in which he was involved."[64]

Editor & Publisher reported that editors estimated that the Associated Press had moved more than a million words over the wires in the 36 days of the hearings. The *Chicago Tribune* said that it had carried 10 to 12 columns of news about the hearings a day; the *San Francisco Chronicle*, that it had printed 16 columns a day for the first week and three or four columns a day after that; the *Boston Post*, that the story was on page one from April 22 to June 18 and that on 38 of those 53 days it was the paper's lead story; the *Washington Star*, that it carried 430 columns all told, including 355 columns of news, six columns of editorials, and 16 columns of letters. Southern newspapers reported less-extensive coverage, corresponding in practice to the early stages of McCarthy's campaign. The *Atlanta Constitution* reported two columns at the beginning and a column and a half later; the Phoenix *Arizona Republic* used three to four columns a day; the *Dallas News* reported four columns a day. Only the *New York Times* carried the running transcript of the hearings—7,424 pages—throughout the hearings.[65]

In August, the Senate began consideration of a resolution that called for censure of McCarthy for violation of due process and Senate procedure. Senator Arthur V. Watkins (Rep., Utah), chairman of a special six-man committee set up to consider the resolution, ruled that television, radio, and newsreel cameras would be barred from the otherwise public hearings.

The Columbia Broadcasting System made television history on August 26 when it broadcast a network editorial appealing for permission to cover the censure hearings. On a national radio and television hookup, Frank Stanton, president of CBS, asked listeners for support "in our efforts to lift the curtain of silence that has descended on the forthcoming hearings." Stanton said that he believed the ban on television resulted from confusion and misunderstanding arising from the fact that radio and television coverage was still something of a novelty. One argument, he said, was that radio and television created a circus atmosphere that caused participants to misbehave, robbing the hearings of a judicial atmosphere. But these are legislative, not judicial, proceedings, and the people have a right to see them, he argued. Stanton said that the other argument against broadcasting coverage was that it was "obtrusive, noisy and disturbing," but that there were many other distractions, and the addition of radio and television would make it no more confusing.[66]

The American Civil Liberties Union said in a telegram to Watkins that the public's right to be informed could not be met unless all mass media were accorded equal treatment, and the Radio-Newsreel-Television Working Press Association of New York told Watkins that the association resented the implication that these media were "second-class members of the United States press."

CBS made time available to Federal Judge Harold R. Medina for a 15-minute rebuttal of Stanton. Judge Medina said that the object of the hearings was the same as a judicial hearing—to sift evidence, determine facts, and administer justice. "Does the use of radio and television in any substantial sense affect the process of ascertaining the truth when examining the witnesses or considering other proofs?" he asked. "I say it does and that they constitute a psychological and very real barrier which, for all practical purposes, makes it impossible to get at the truth." When the participants perform before the microphones and the cameras, "knowing that perhaps ten millions of people or more are listening and watching their every move, the temptation to put on an act becomes irresistible," Medina said.[67]

The other networks joined CBS in protesting the ban, but Watkins remained firm, and there were no television cameras in the hearing room. Roy Cohn wrote later in his book *McCarthy* that if the senator had insisted he could have forced the committee to permit broadcasting the hearings but that he was persuaded by his attorney, Edward Bennett Williams, to agree to the exclusion.[68]

McCarthy made one last attempt to divert the committee from its grim adherence to its task. In an interview published March 12 in the *Denver Post*, Senator Edwin Johnson, a Colorado Democrat and member of the committee, had said that Democratic leaders in the Senate "loathed" McCarthy and that most Republicans were "disgusted" with him. McCarthy wanted to discuss this so as to discredit Johnson as a judge and raise doubts about the fairness of procedures; it was once again a case of defense by attack. But Watkins would have none of it. He gavelled McCarthy down and declared him out of order. "We are not going to be interrupted by these diversions and sidelines," he said. "We are going straight down the line." McCarthy rushed out to the TV cameras in the hall and made one of his most memorable public statements: "I think this is the most unheard-of thing I have ever heard of."[69] That was the liveliest event of the nine-day hearing. Reston commented in the September 1 *Times*, "As a television show this one would be approximately as exciting as a recitation from a New York telephone directory. ... The Watkins committee may not censure McCarthy, but it may bore him to death."

On September 24, the Senate voted to put off the McCarthy issue until after the election. Nearly all the Republicans and enough of the Democrats wanted to avoid making a vote on censure an issue in their campaigns. McCarthy went into eclipse almost at once. He announced that he had rejected hundreds of invitations to speak, and he canceled the few commitments he did have on the excuse that he had sinus trouble. "In any event," said the *New York Times* on September 26, "it is agreed that McCarthy can serve his party best by staying home. Republican strategists still think the 'Communist' issue is a good one, but they feel they can make political capital of it without him this time."

The one who carried the burden of exploiting the issue was Vice-President Nixon, and McCarthy said after the election that Nixon had done "a good job" on Communists-in-government. Nevertheless, both houses shifted back to Democratic control, ending McCarthy's career as a Communist-hunter by depriving him of his committee chairmanship.

On Wednesday, November 10, the day before the Watkins committee report was to go to the Senate, McCarthy showed a flash of his old form in the fight for publicity. He released a speech which he said he would give after the report was filed, so that his denunciation of the committee appeared in the papers before the story about the committee report. In it he said that the report was the work of the "Communist conspiracy" and that the Watkins committee was the "unwitting handmaiden" and the "involuntary agent" of the Communist party. He said that the committee had imitated Communist methods and that it had "distorted, misrepresented and omitted" in order to "accede to the clamor for my scalp."

McCarthy never bothered to give the speech, but it got into the papers and the *Congressional Record*. It had the effect of destroying the efforts of his friends to negotiate a compromise on the issue of censure, and it infuriated Senator Watkins. He proposed that an additional count of contempt of the Senate be added to the resolution, since the committee called a "handmaiden" had been set up by the Senate. The other Utah senator, Wallace Bennett, said that he would introduce such an amendment. McCarthy appeared on television once more to respond to this development: "Now they want to censure me because I am defending myself. That is getting to be so ridiculous it's beyond comprehension. . . . It they're going to bring up a new censure motion every time I defend myself it looks like we're going to be here indefinitely."[70]

Eventually the Senate adopted a resolution to "condemn" McCarthy by a vote of 67-22. Most of those who stood by McCarthy (all Republicans) were from states west of the Mississippi. It may be significant that the greatest support came from the part of the nation where McCarthy's activities had been given the least coverage in newspapers, and from the only part of the country that did not have access to live television coverage of the fateful Army-McCarthy hearings. In the election of 1952, McCarthy ran best in the parts of Wisconsin where people knew least about him, where he was not subject to newspaper criticism. In the Senate, his support came from representatives of the area where newspapers reported least and where the damaging televised hearings did not penetrate.

That was one of several ways in which the relationship between McCarthy and the press paralleled the relationship between McCarthy and broadcasters. For a time, McCarthy was able to get almost anything he wanted from either of the media; only a few individual broadcasters and a relatively small number of newspapers resisted him. Gradually the media stiffened, but it was not until 1954 that the networks and the mass of newspapers felt it safe to oppose him.

Resistance was more difficult for the broadcasters. The television networks were new, their policies unformed, and they lacked the tradition that helped sustain newspapers. They were subject to government regulation, and they suspected that McCarthy had influence among the regulators. They did not, and still do not, enjoy the protection under the First Amendment that newspapers do. They had been subjected to a campaign of Red-baiting and blacklisting that ruined the careers of many. The sponsor system, under which an advertiser was held responsible for the content of programs, weakened them. Their hesitation in standing up to McCarthy and his supporters was more understandable than that of the newspapers.

7.
Summing Up

THE DURABILITY of the term *McCarthyism* is a testament to the depth of the conflict that centered on McCarthy. Hardly a week goes by that some public official does not declare himself a victim of the dread "ism." The popular concept of McCarthy's activities has expanded so that the senator is given credit for the work of hundreds of less-well-remembered "Red-baiters," including the persecution of actors and writers on Broadway and in Hollywood, which was, of course, done by the House Committee on Un-American Activities before McCarthy entered the scene. So, too, have the myths about McCarthy and the press grown, and it has been a principal objective of this study to determine the validity of all the allegations about the part played by the media in the rise and fall of Joe McCarthy.

What is said most often is that McCarthy "used" the press, as well as the new medium of television, and of course he did. Under the conditions that prevailed, any politician clever enough and ruthless enough could maneuver the press into publishing such charges as his, especially when the accuser was a United States senator and for two years the chairman of a Senate committee. The television networks were already conditioned to be terrified of "Communist" charges, and it was a simple matter for McCarthy to bully them into giving him free time on almost any pretext. Eventually the networks developed enough confidence to stand up to McCarthy's demands, and the newspapers developed ways of reacting to McCarthy's accusations that guaranteed some measure of fair play for his victims, but both of these things took time. The implication of the charge that the press "created" McCarthy is that McCarthy was not really newsworthy and that the

214

[handwritten note: unable to substantiate his claims ✓]

press, by printing so much about him, gave substance to someone who was basically insignificant. This was Senator Benton's view, that McCarthy was "laughable," and that only the press took him seriously and made him someone whom politicians were forced to take seriously.

A popular theory in post-McCarthy years was that McCarthy was able to use the press because newspapers adhered too closely to the principle of "objectivity." The dictionary definition of objective is "expressing or involving the use of facts without distortion by personal feelings or prejudices." What was meant in the case of McCarthy was a little different; what people said the press was doing was reporting McCarthy's charges without attempting to determine the truth or falsity of the charges. To the extent that this criticism was just, it applied only to the wire services and the papers that sought to avoid controversy at all costs. *[handwritten margin note: # news has learned to decipher what's being said & really make news objective]*

For some time after McCarthy began issuing his accusations, no information was available against which to check his charges. Gradually this changed, as the State Department issued rebuttals and reporters and columnists tracked down the sources of McCarthy's information. Reporters accumulated files and spent long hours assembling the facts to explain the charges, as Murrey Marder did at the Washington Post. The wire service reporters could not do this immediately, working under the pressure of competition, but they often followed up with rebuttals a few hours later. Papers did not always wait for the rebuttals. *[handwritten margin note: ← go thru facts to get to truth]*

The wire services were further handicapped because they had to avoid offending clients. To an editor who was an all-out McCarthy supporter, even a factual explanation looked like anti-McCarthy prejudice; it suggested that the senator was lying. Explanations had to be carefully qualified. Newspapers that took sides on the McCarthy issue, however, did not pretend to be objective. Their reporters and editors schemed and conspired to discredit McCarthy or to promote him. Their headlines, as well as their editorials, their columns, and their cartoons, reflected their positions. Partisanship among newspapers was at a peak.   *[handwritten: denouncing/advocating up front will never...]* *[handwritten margin note: wire services were limited; newspapers w/ an agenda to report "news" that's really opinion; all of paper reflects position (NOT objective)]*

Alger Hiss, speaking at the San Francisco Press Club on 25 July 1975, answered in the affirmative when he was asked whether the press in the 1950s was "supine." "The press was not very good at wood-chopping in those days," he said, adding that it had gained in "vigor and courage" since that time. The implication was that the press had performed much better in its investigation of the Watergate scandal than in any investigation of McCarthy. But the Watergate affair was the unravelling of a mystery, a criminal case, not a conflict

over issues. Even though it involved courageous, dogged reporting by
the *Washington Post* and the *New York Times*, their investigations
might not have produced a conclusive result had it not been for the
unusual judicial behavior of Judge John Sirica and for President Nixon's folly—making and keeping the damning tape recordings. The
investigation of McCarthy's affairs was no less thorough, and no minor
wrongdoing was left undisclosed. But no one cared. McCarthy's character was not important; only his accusations were.

The *Washington Post* began its editorial campaign against McCarthy
just five days after the speech at Wheeling, and never let up. Moreover, the *Post* had been fighting this battle for several years before
the issue became known as McCarthyism, through Alan Barth's editorials warning of the danger to civil liberties posed by President
Truman's loyalty program. Most of the papers on McCarthy's "left-
wing press" list did much the same. The *Washington Post* deserves
at least as much credit for its long struggle against McCarthy as for
its Watergate triumph.

All politicians try to use the press and the other media. They say
or do things that they hope will produce favorable stories, headlines,
and editorials, or failing that, at least prominently displayed stories
and headlines. They ingratiate themselves with individual reporters
and editors. McCarthy did these things, too; for a while he successfully
maintained friendly relations with many individuals in the press, and
for a long time he was able to produce headlines almost at will. But
when reporters or editors did not handle the news to his satisfaction,
he tried to intimidate them. When this did not succeed, he tried to
discredit their newspapers in the eyes of the public, and while he
never succeeded in intimidating his most important critics in the press,
he did create such an atmosphere of fear that newspapermen were
very, very careful in what they wrote about him. No one knows how
well this campaign of intimidation worked; undoubtedly there were
many newspapers whose editors decided that opposition to McCarthy
was just not worth the risk. There was evidence of this in Wisconsin.

The effect of McCarthy's campaign against the press was described
succinctly by John B. Oakes, *New York Times* editorial writer, in a
memorandum to Lester Markel, Sunday editor, dated 23 December
1953. "It is my thought," Oakes wrote, "that while the United States
is in no sense in a 'wave of terror' and while there is no genuine
hysteria regarding spies and Communists, McCarthyism nevertheless
has had a profound effect on all of us—on our writing, our speaking
and even thinking. We are all very much more careful about what
we write, what we say, what we join, than we used to be because we
all start from the premise that whatever we do may be subject to

damaging criticism from the extreme right. Our takeoff point has moved without our even realizing it. Thus, if McCarthy should drop dead today, he would still have worked a fairly profound change in the American intellectual atmosphere that will take us a long time to recover from."[1]

But in the end, the persistence of McCarthy's critics in the media made it possible for the centrist politicians who dominated the Senate and the Eisenhower administration to act against him. While he used the press in the ordinary ways more effectively than anyone else, he was not, in the long run, able to use the press as he sought to. In the end, the press "used" him.

No other American politician in recent history has made such a determined campaign against the press, not even Richard Nixon, whose loathing of the press is well known. Yet many of the reporters who covered McCarthy compare him favorably to Nixon. They speak of his humor, his mischievous quality, his friendliness; they share, to a degree, his cynicism. They deplore his issue, his methods, and his insensitivity to his victims, but they also see him as an adventurer, an outlaw, a lone wolf who chose disgrace rather than compromise. It was deadly serious, but it was a game for McCarthy, and he enjoyed playing it; so did the reporters. They wanted to show him up as a fraud; he just wanted his name in the papers.

He was still playing the game in 1955 when he offered the *Milwaukee Journal* a copy of a speech in which he said, in effect, that his whole career as a Red-baiter had been a mistake.

McCarthy had not communicated directly with *Milwaukee Journal* reporters for a long time. The speech was brought to me one Saturday afternoon by Dion Henderson, an Associated Press outdoor writer and personal friend of McCarthy who spent a lot of time with him during the last three years of his life. McCarthy was bitter about his relegation to the back pages and his virtual elimination from most papers after his confrontation with the Eisenhower administration and his censure. Why, he kept asking Henderson, was an attack that was news in 1950 not news in 1955?

The speech, which was supposed to have been given that Saturday afternoon to a group of supporters, said that the right to dissent, the right to hold unpopular or even subversive opinions, was our most important right, and that no man should be persecuted for his beliefs. Henderson said McCarthy had told him that he had been reading Thomas Jefferson for the past two weeks and that Jefferson had influenced him in this direction. But Henderson also told me that McCarthy had wanted to say whatever the *Journal* would consider most out of character for him; he wondered whether the paper would consider it a story if he espoused the libertarian principles which the *Journal* had charged him with attempting to destroy.

Like other McCarthy stories, it was hard to know what to do with this. I wrote a story that tried to put it into perspective, to say that I did not know if this meant anything but that it was what McCarthy had said. I showed how it conflicted with McCarthy's previous statements and actions and I left it to the reader to make a judgment. I put the story on the desk of the city editor, who was out to dinner, and left for the night.

It didn't turn up in the paper on Sunday, and when I came back to work on Tuesday I couldn't find anyone who knew about the decision not to use it. I remember feeling annoyed, because Henderson said that McCarthy had offered to bet him that the *Journal* wouldn't use it, and I didn't like McCarthy to be proved right on anything about the *Journal*.

Henderson filed a brief story on the speech on the state AP wire, and he remembers that two or three papers used part of the story on Monday. No editor saw anything unusual in it, he said. He told me later that he thought McCarthy might have changed the direction of his career if the *Journal* had run the story. I think McCarthy was just playing games with the press again, but in retrospect I wish we had published the story.

One of the reasons that reporters turned so strongly against both McCarthy and Nixon was that they believed neither was telling the truth. But it was not enough to say, as Senator Benton and Palmer Hoyt, the *Denver Post* editor, had advocated, simply that McCarthy was lying; it was necessary to demonstrate the lie, and for a long time, as McCarthy shifted from one accusation to another, it was not possible to prove that he was lying. This was a source of great frustration, especially to the wire service reporters in Washington, at the key point in this dilemma.

What is most surprising in the examination of newspaper performance in the McCarthy period is not that so much news of McCarthy was published in some papers, but how little was published in many others, especially in the first years. The timidity of the wire services, the fear of controversy on the part of publishers, and an apparent lack of understanding of the importance of the issue by many editors worked to deprive many readers of full information. Equally deplorable was the presentation of the news in many papers. The editing of McCarthy stories seemed singularly inept. Wire service stories containing important news were often overlooked, and hoked-up overnight leads took the play; the few interpretive pieces by agency reporters were largely ignored by editors; headlines seemed to sub-stantiate McCarthy's charges and even to exaggerate them. It was no wonder that so many people were convinced that McCarthy was ex-posing Communists. The newspapers had said so. Another failure of newspapers in the McCarthy period was a failure to make judgments and to express opinions. At a time when the editorial page was the principal source of guidance to the understanding of the news, the majority of American editors took no stand at all, expressed no opin-ion. Even in Wisconsin, when McCarthy faced reelection in 1952, only 17 of the 39 daily newspapers in the state were clearly for or against his reelection. Of these, only five were against it.

McCarthy's tactics produced lasting changes in the media. News-paper people realized that it was not enough simply to tell what had happened or what was said, but that they had to tell what it meant and whether or not it was true. By 1954, interpretive reporting and news analysis had become standard practice; these functions were no longer left to the editorial writers. Television managers realized that they could stand up to demands for free time from even the boldest demagogues. Not everyone agrees that these changes were beneficial. Some believe that the prevalence of interpretive reporting and more personal styles of journalism have led to excesses. Reporting has be-come less disciplined, and the private lives and mores of public of-ficials are considered fair journalistic game; gossip becomes news, and issues are less important than personality and character. This, too, is one of the legacies of McCarthy, aggravated by the competition of television.

Was the opposition of the press to McCarthy effective? It was. The 1952 Wisconsin election proved conclusively that where the voters had been thoroughly informed about McCarthy's activities and where these activities had been examined critically, McCarthy's vote de-clined dramatically from his vote in 1946. Where this process had not taken place, McCarthy's share of the vote held firm or increased.

The primary function of a newspaper is to tell people what is hap-pening. It is not the duty of a newspaper to decide what is good for the people to know nor to be concerned about the effect of the news it publishes. Its duty is to furnish the information. In the case of McCarthy, the press did not properly fulfill this function. Nor does the press deserve credit for its final wolf-pack descent on McCarthy when it became apparent that he intended to go right on attacking the Republican Eisenhower administration with the same vigor and ven-om he had expended on Truman's Democrats. Criticism of McCarthy at this point was easy and unimportant.

But for those journalists who recognized the threat to American principles posed by McCarthyism, who took a stand when opposition to McCarthy rendered one's patriotism suspect, and who did it when it mattered, before the election of 1952—even though it put them in the position of seeming to defend a Democratic administration that many of them detested—it was a glorious time. History has given them too little credit.

Reference Material

Appendix

TABLE 1
McCarthy Coverage, 10 February–10 March 1950
(Editorial Performance, 129 Newspapers)

Newspaper	Circulation*	News Stories	Syndicated Columns	Total Inches	Page-One Stories	Editorials	Cartoons	Sources of News Stories†	
Appleton Post-Crescent	28,383 (e)	18 (235″)	5 anti‡ (112″)	347	16 (166″)	1 pro	1 pro	17 AP 1 na	(223″) (12″)
Arkansas Gazette (Little Rock)	97,847 (m) 111,617 (S)	7 (107″)	1 anti (13″)	120	6 (84″)	1 anti	0	7 AP	(107″)
Atlanta Constitution	180,948 (m) 216,956 (S)	6 (66″)	4 anti (58″)	124	2 (23″)	0	0	5 AP 1 INS	(61″) (5″)
Bakersfield Californian	30,881 (e)	12 (162″)	3 anti (50″)	212	3 (50″)	0	0	9 AP 2 UP	(139″) (23″)
Baltimore News-Post	226,538 (e) 353,510 (S)	13 (118″)	0	118	8 (81″)	0	0	7 INS 5 AP 1 Sp	(83″) (28″) (7″)
Baltimore Sun	172,456 (m) 305,825 (S)	15 (401″)	0	401	12 (379″)	0	1 neut.	11 WB 4 AP	(363″) (38″)
Baraboo News-Republic	5,367 (e)	7 (62″)	0	62	2 (16″)	0	0	7 UP	(62″)
Beloit Daily News	17,282 (e)	14 (144″)	0	144	7 (89″)	0	0	14 UP	(144″)
Berkshire Eagle (Pittsfield)	26,394 (e)	8 (120″)	2 anti (64″) 2 neut.	184	1 (20″)	2 anti	0	6 AP 2 UP	(87″) (33″)
Boston Globe	122,144 (m) 383,417 (S)	12 (115″)	0	115	5 (26″)	0	0	6 AP 2 UP 4 NYHT	(51″) (19″) (45″)
Boston Herald	132,300 (m) 245,637 (S)	11 (134″)	0	134	4 (26″)	0	0	7 AP 4 NYT	(55″) (79″)
Boston Post	330,456 (m)	11 (151″)	0	151	2 (19″)	1 pro	0	10 AP 1 Stf	(146″) (5″)
Boston Traveler	209,778 (e)	2 (22″)	4 anti (59″)	81	1 (6″)	0	0	2 AP	(22″)
Buffalo News	277,321 (e)	9 (114″)	3 anti (46″)	160	4 (36″)	0	1 pro	2 Stf	(35″)
Capital Times (Madison)	40,817 (e)	16 (331″)	4 anti (56″)	387	13 (128″)	10 anti	0	13 AP 1 NEA 1 UP 1 Stf	(195″) (124″) (5″) (7″)

*(e) evening; (m) morning; (S) Sunday.

†AP: Associated Press
  CDN: Chicago Daily News service
  INS: International News Service
  na: Not attributed, usually edited by that
    paper from several sources
  NEA: Newspaper Enterprise Association
  NYHT: New York Herald-Tribune service

NYT: New York Times service
S-H: Scripps-Howard
Stf: Local staff
Sp: "Special" to that paper
UP: United Press
WB: Washington Bureau of that paper

‡Designations *pro* and *anti* signify *pro-McCarthy* and *anti-McCarthy*.

Newspaper	Circulation*	News Stories	Syndicated Columns	Total Inches	Page-One Stories	Editorials	Cartoons	Sources of News Stories†
Charlotte Observer	134,754 (m) 141,575 (S)	8 (89")	1 anti (16")	105	6 (58")	2 neut.	0	7 AP (77") 1 NYT (12")
Chicago Daily News	514,266 (e)	12 (162")	2 anti (24")	186	2 (13")	1 neut. 1 pro	1 pro	6 AP (75") 3 UP (37") 3 WB (50")
Chicago Sun-Times	629,179 (m) 729,676 (S)	22 (263")	3 anti (51")	314	0	0	2 anti	8 AP (124") 3 WB (56") 7 na (18") 3 NYHT (61") 1 UP (4")
Chicago Tribune	957,448 (m) 1,535,495 (S)	19 (354")	0	354	6 (100")	1 pro	2 pro	13 WB (303") 6 AP (51")
Christian Science Monitor (Boston)	167,190 (e)	7 (187")	1 anti (30")	217	5 (126")	0	0	5 AP (103") 4 WB (84")
Cleveland Plain Dealer	285,393 (m) 494,590 (S)	11 (109")	1 anti (20")	129	1 (29")	3 pro	0	6 AP (56") 4 WB (50") 1 UP (3")
Columbus Dispatch	155,407 (e) 211,041 (S)	10 (85")	0	85	2 (2")	1 pro	0	9 AP (84") 1 INS (1")
Cumberland Times	12,236 (e)	11 (125")	3 anti (68")	193	11 (125")	0	0	11 AP (125")
Dallas News	157,525 (m) 170,362 (S)	8 (85")	2 anti (36")	121	5 (49")	1 pro	0	4 AP (34") 1 UP (11") 3 WB (40")
Denver Post	227,028 (e) 357,406 (S)	12 (105")	1 pro 4 anti (50")	155	1 (6")	1 pro	0	11 AP (93") 1 Stf (12")
Deseret News (Salt Lake City)	79,589 (e) 78,294 (S)	6 (53")	0	53	4 (34")	0	0	5 AP (40") 1 Stf (13")
Des Moines Register	217,711 (m) 520,338 (S)	14 (294")	3 anti (22")	316	5 (71")	1 neut.	0	7 WB (230") 3 AP (22") 3 NYT (42")
Detroit News	442,977 (e) 550,957 (S)	12 (161")	0	161	2 (15")	0	0	8 AP (71") 4 WB (90")
Duluth News-Tribune	46,612 (m)	10 (150")	1 pro 1 anti (28")	178	6 (57")	1 neut.	0	8 AP (111") 2 INS (39")
Eau Claire Leader	12,552 (m) 12,646 (S)	9 (107")	4 anti (36")	143	9 (95")	0	0	8 AP (102") 1 UP (5")
Eugene Register-Guard	27,360 (e)	8 (41")	1 anti (20")	61	3 (7")	0	0	3 AP (16") 5 UP (25")
Fall River Herald-News	39,053 (e)	8 (97")	0	97	6 (40")	0	0	8 AP (97")
Fitchburg Sentinel	13,912 (e)	8 (36")	1 anti (20")	56	5 (26")	0	0	6 AP (32") 2 na (4")
Fond du Lac Commonwealth-Reporter	16,620 (e)	9 (137")	3 anti (46")	183	7 (90")	2 neut.	0	9 AP (137")
Framingham News	10,287 (e)	2 (3")	0	3	2 (3")	1 neut.	1 neut.	2 INS (3")
Frederick News	6,912 (e)	8 (45")	1 pro 1 anti (36")	81	6 (34")	0	0	7 AP (45")
Green Bay Press-Gazette	34,446 (e)	20 (265")	0	265	9 (145")	0	1 pro	16 AP (244") 2 UP (13") 1 WB (6") 1 Stf (2")
Hagerstown Herald	7,263 (m)	10 (115")	2 anti (30")	145	6 (79")	0	1 pro	10 AP (115")

Table 1—*continued* 225

Newspaper	Circulation*	News Stories	Syndicated Columns	Total Inches	Page-One Stories	Editorials	Cartoons	Sources of News Stories†	
Hartford Courant	63,052 (m) 102,903 (S)	8 (144")	1 anti (24")	168	5 (66")	1 anti 1 neut.	0	6 WB 2 AP	(117") (27")
Haverhill Gazette	18,002 (e)	4 (42")	3 anti (124")	166	3 (32")	0	0	4 AP	(42")
Holyoke Telegram-Transcript	25,503 (e)	3 (8")	1 pro 1 anti (35")	46	1 (5")	0	0	1 AP 1 UP	(5") (3")
Honolulu Star-Bulletin	76,414 (e)	3 (15")	2 anti (56")	71	3 (15")	0	0	3 AP	(15")
Houston Post	164,129 (m) 177,656 (S)	6 (103")	0	103	2 (36")	2 pro	1 pro	6 AP	(103")
Humboldt Times (Eureka)	10,657 (e) 9,813 (S)	6 (43")	4 anti (55")	98	3 (17")	1 anti	0	6 AP	(43")
Huronite and Plainsman	10,849 (e) 11,031 (S)	8 (116")	4 pro 1 anti (27")	143	5 (90")	5 pro	0	6 AP 1 UP 1 Stf	(76") (6") (34")
Indianapolis Star	196,971 (m) 250,005 (S)	11 (138")	2 anti (17")	155	2 (36")	3 pro	0	11 AP	(138")
Jackson Clarion-Ledger	42,173 (m)	4 (36")	2 anti (26")	62	3 (18")	1 pro	1 anti	3 AP 1 INS	(18") (18")
Janesville Gazette	19,912 (e)	8 (111")	2 anti (45")	156	6 (81")	3 pro	0	8 AP	(111")
Kansas City Star	359,673 (e) 369,968 (S)	16 (218")	1 anti 1 pro (27") 1 neut.	245	5 (77")	2 neut. 1 pro	0	15 AP 1 WB	(202") (16")
Kenosha News	19,912 (e)	13 (97")	0	97	8 (58")	0	0	6 AP 7 UP	(59") (38")
La Crosse Tribune	28,498 (m) 28,331 (S)	14 (139")	3 anti (40")	179	10 (75")	1 pro	0	13 AP 1 Stf	(135") (4")
Los Angeles Daily News	251,232 (e)	8 (117")	1 pro 1 anti (64")	181	2 (28")	0	2 anti	8 UP 1 Stf	(109") (8")
Los Angeles Times	385,583 (m) 782,953 (S)	15 (198")	0	198	4 (36")	2 pro	2 pro	10 AP 3 UP 1 NYT 1 Stf	(112") (56") (14") (16")
Louisville Courier-Journal	170,205 (m) 265,926 (S)	11 (179")	3 anti (70")	249	3 (52")	0	1 anti	7 AP 1 UP 3 na	(94") (12") (73")
Lowell Sun	37,852 (e) 15,396 (S)	14 (196")	4 anti (64")	260	2 (9")	0	0	12 AP 1 UP 1 INS	(184") (4") (8")
Manchester Union	25,964 (m)	6 (65")	0	65	5 (33")	2 pro	0	5 UP 1 na	(52") (13")
Manitowoc Herald-Times	13,900 (e)	13 (185")	4 anti (53")	238	11 (131")	0	0	12 AP	(185")
Marinette Eagle-Star	8,224 (e)	16 (186")	2 anti (20")	206	7 (81")	1 neut.	0	16 AP	(186")
Memphis Commercial Appeal	185,104 (m)	11 (125")	1 pro 1 anti (49")	164	8 (85")	1 anti	0	9 AP 1 INS	(123") (2")
Miami Herald	186,166 (m) 185,182 (S)	5 (79")	3 anti (49")	128	2 (18")	3 pro	0	4 AP 1 UP	(51") (28")
Milwaukee Journal	318,881 (e) 413,087 (S)	25 (273")	0	273	7 (65")	4 anti	2 anti	14 AP 3 Stf 2 WB 2 UP 1 NYT 4 na	(168") (28") (26") (10") (12") (29")

Newspaper	Circulation*	News Stories	Syndicated Columns	Total Inches	Page-One Stories	Editorials	Cartoons	Sources of News Stories†	
Milwaukee Sentinel	175,658 (m) 297,783 (S)	15 (117″)	0	117	6 (35″)	0	0	3 AP 2 INS 7 na 1 Stf 1 Sp	(43″) (28″) (16″) (10″) (20″)
Minneapolis Star	295,035 (e)	13 (115″)	2 anti (30″)	145	2 (18″)	1 neut.	0	10 AP 1 UP 1 INS 1 DNS	(94″) (6″) (5″) (10″)
Montgomery Advertiser	54,653 (m) 67,133 (S)	10 (76″)	2 anti (31″)	107	7 (61″)	0	1 pro	7 AP	(76″)
Nashville Banner	85,161 (e)	5 (43″)	1 anti (6″)	49	3 (23″)	2 pro	0	4 AP 1 UP	(35″) (8″)
Nashville Tennessean	92,776 (m) 155,752 (S)	5 (58″)	4 anti (82″)	140	1 (6″)	1 anti	0	5 AP	(58″)
Nevada State Journal (Reno)	10,360 (m) 14,278 (S)	11 (115″)	2 anti (46″)	161	7 (65″)	1 anti	0	9 UP 2 Stf	(77″) (38″)
Newark News	246,074 (e) 192,227 (S)	12 (106″)	1 anti (14″)	120	3 (23″)	0	1 neut.	7 AP 4 INS	(65″) (25″)
New Orleans Times-Picayune	174,094 (m) 281,034 (S)	9 (126″)	0	126	3 (28″)	1 anti 1 pro	0	8 AP 1 INS	(112″) (14″)
New York Daily News	2,287,337 (m) 4,329,561 (S)	12 (80″)	0	80	0	2 pro	0	7 WB 4 UP 1 AP	(68″) (9″) (3″)
New York Herald-Tribune	323,661 (m) 662,370 (S)	12 (230″)	0	230	5 (29″)	1 anti	0	11 WB 1 na	(227″) (3″)
New York Journal-American	698,368 (e) 1,175,858 (S)	10 (82″)	0	82	2 (22″)	3 pro	2 pro	4 INS 3 AP 3 UP	(41″) (22″) (19″)
New York Post	284,335 (e) 265,625 (S)	9 (138″)	6 anti (70″)	208	2 (18″)	3 anti	3 anti	5 WB 2 AP 3 Stf 1 Sp	(91″) (15″) (19″) (13″)
New York Times	537,216 (m) 1,096,137 (S)	18 (333″)	0	333	1 (5″)	3 anti	0	17 WB 2 UP	(321″) (12″)
New York World-Telegram & Sun	365,864 (e)	11 (124″)	0	124	3 (33″)	0	0	5 UP 3 AP 1 WB 1 na 1 NEA	(61″) (19″) (22″) (10″) (12″)
Oakland Tribune	151,104 (e) 166,881 (S)	13 (194″)	3 pro 1 anti (65″) 1 neut.	259	10 (131″)	2 pro	1 pro 1 anti	12 AP 2 UP	(176″) (18″)
Omaha World-Herald	126,462 (m) 239,825 (S)	9 (86″)	1 pro (16″)	102	2 (30″)	0	0	5 AP 1 UP 1 INS 2 WB	(51″) (4″) (12″) (19″)
Oregon Statesman (Salem)	15,798 (m) 16,158 (S)	13 (113″)	1 anti (24″)	137	2 (12″)	1 neut.	1 pro	11 AP 2 na	(110″) (3″)
Oshkosh Northwestern	17,843 (e)	14 (196″)	1 anti (16″)	212	6 (68″)	2 pro	1 pro	12 AP 2 UP	(174″) (22″)
Philadelphia Bulletin	720,331 (e) 1,153,779 (S)	6 (103″)	2 anti (17″)	120	3 (16″)	1 neut.	1 anti	3 AP 3 Stf	(30″) (73″)
Phoenix Republic	63,016 (m) 80,016 (S)	7 (56″)	1 pro 1 anti (24″)	80	4 (30″)	0	0	3 AP 3 INS	(27″) (29″)
Pittsburgh Post-Gazette	289,000 (m)	1 (15″)	2 anti (40″)	55	1 (8″)	0	0	1 AP	(15″)

Table 1—*continued* 227

Newspaper	Circulation*	News Stories	Syndicated Columns	Total Inches	Page-One Stories	Editorials	Cartoons	Sources of News Stories†	
Portland Oregonian	214,916 (m) 270,049 (3)	10 (98″)	0	98	0	0	0	7 AP 3 INS	(81″) (17″)
Providence Journal	45,542 (m)	14 (243″)	1 anti (24″)	267	0	0	0	13 AP 1 WB	(221″) (22″)
Quincy Patriot-Ledger	30,654 (e)	2 (49″)	1 anti (29″) 4 neut.	78	1 (6″)	0	0	2 AP 2 NEA	(15″) (34″)
Racine Journal-Times	27,162 (e)	20 (364″)	3 anti (65″) 1 pro	429	5 (44″)	0	0	15 AP 4 UP	(199″) (33″)
Raleigh News & Observer	107,024 (m) 110,018 (S)	5 (99″)	1 anti (20″)	119	5 (32″)	3 anti	2 anti	3 AP 2 UP	(62″) (37″)
Redding Record-Searchlight	8,320 (e)	2 (26″)	3 anti (66″)	92	2 (26″)	0	2 anti	2 AP	(26″)
Redwood City Tribune	11,126 (e)	1 (12″)	2 anti (44″)	56	0	0	0	1 AP	(12″)
Reno Gazette	16,672 (e)	13 (216″)	0	216	10 (148″)	1 pro	1 pro	10 AP 3 Stf	(108″) (108″)
Rhinelander Daily News	4,054 (e)	10 (127″)	2 anti (34″)	161	10 (127″)	1 neut.	0	10 AP	(127″)
Richmond Independent	27,627 (e)	16 (66″)	0	66	3 (10″)	0	0	11 UP 5 INS	(42″) (22″)
Richmond News-Leader	96,186 (e)	13 (212″)	3 anti (50″)	262	5 (68″)	0	1 pro	13 AP	(212″)
Riverside Press	13,857 (e)	11 (104″)	3 anti (54″)	158	7 (61″)	0	0	11 UP	(104″)
Rochester Democrat & Chronicle	107,861 (m)	14 (144″)	1 anti (16″)	160	2 (28″)	0	0	14 AP	(144″)
Sacramento Bee	111,047 (e) 35,697 (S)	14 (116″)	0	116	1 (6″)	1 anti	0	14 AP	(116″)
St. Louis Globe-Democrat	293,404 (m) 371,711 (S)	7 (64″)	1 anti (20″)	84	0	2 anti	0	7 AP	(64″)
St. Louis Post-Dispatch	275,928 (e) 411,961 (S)	10 (163″)	1 anti (20″)	183	2 (33″)	3 anti	1 anti	10 AP	(163″)
St. Petersburg Times	41,802 (m) 38,713 (S)	11 (120″)	5 anti (84″)	204	4 (43″)	0	0	8 AP 2 UP 1 INS	(80″) (28″) (12″)
Salinas Californian	11,776 (e)	6 (21″)	0	21	6 (21″)	1 pro	0	6 UP	(21″)
Salisbury Times	15,354 (e)	9 (86″)	1 anti (20″)	106	9 (86″)	0	0	9 AP	(86″)
Salt Lake City Tribune	88,930 (m) 120,987 (S)	17 (204″)	0	204	10 (109″)	2 anti	0	14 AP 2 UP 1 Stf	(167″) (15″) (22″)
San Diego Union	61,643 (m) 114,313 (S)	12 (107″)	1 anti (14″)	121	7 (59″)	5 pro	0	9 AP 2 INS	(94″) (13″)
San Francisco Chronicle	160,477 (m) 267,318 (S)	11 (110″)	2 anti (34″)	144	1 (14″)	0	0	6 AP 5 UP	(36″) (74″)
San Francisco Examiner	219,842 (m) 581,172 (S)	13 (114″)	0	114	5 (41″)	0	0	5 AP 7 INS	(30″) (84″)
San Francisco News	132,476 (e)	9 (36″)	1 anti (22″)	58	0	0	0	8 UP 1 S-H	(35″) (1″)
San Jose Mercury-Herald	30,714 (m) 48,097 (S)	9 (76″)	1 pro (18″)	94	4 (31″)	1 pro	0	7 AP 1 UP 1 INS	(58″) (12″) (6″)
San Rafael Independent-Journal	11,708 (e)	1 (12″)	0	12	0	0	1 pro	1 AP	(12″)
Santa Barbara News-Press	20,924 (e) 20,972 (S)	7 (94″)	3 anti (118″) 1 pro	212	4 (40″)	0	2 anti	7 AP	(94″)

Newspaper	Circulation*	News Stories	Syndicated Columns	Total Inches	Page-One Stories	Editorials	Cartoons	Sources of News Stories†	
Seattle Post-Intelligencer	167,078 (m) 261,210 (S)	8 (72")	2 anti (32")	104	2 (28")	0	0	6 INS 2 AP	(58") (14")
Shawano Leader	5,440 (e)	9 (48")	0	48	9 (48")	0	0	9 UP	(48")
Sheboygan Press	24,715 (e)	11 (175")	5 anti (58")	233	4 (37")	2 anti	1 anti	8 AP 2 UP 1 Stf	(146") (23") (6")
Shreveport Times	69,983 (m) 76,858 (S)	12 (270")	0	220	9 (96")	4 pro	1 pro	10 AP 2 UP	(176") (44")
Springfield News	82,130 (e) 83,914 (S)	3 (18")	3 anti (43")	61	1 (2")	0	0	3 UP	(18")
Stevens Point Journal	8,028 (e)	17 (217")	0	217	8 (116")	0	1 pro	17 AP	(217")
Stockton Record	45,250 (e)	11 (166")	3 anti (60")	226	2 (44")	1 anti	1 anti	9 AP 1 UP 1 INS	(148") (10") (8")
Superior Telegram	22,235 (e)	7 (106")	3 anti (34")	140	6 (42")	0	0	7 AP	(106")
Tampa Tribune	49,600 (m)	11 (79")	3 anti (37")	116	7 (31")	2 anti	0	9 AP 2 UP	(56") (23")
Tulsa Tribune	63,533 (e)	11 (180")	2 anti (34")	214	7 (81")	0	0	11 AP	(180")
Wall Street Journal	142,527 (m)	8 (11")	0	11	8 (11")	0	0	8 na	(11")
Washington Daily News	120,079 (e)	9 (81")	2 pro 2 anti (38")	119	1 (15")	0	1 neut.	5 UP 4 Stf	(19") (62")
Washington Post	184,502 (m) 190,362 (S)	17 (324")	4 anti (64")	388	7 (68")	5 anti	2 anti	12 Stf 2 AP 3 NYHT	(229") (55") (40")
Washington Star	215,698 (e) 241,030 (S)	18 (341")	6 anti 2 pro (160")	501	7 (75")	1 anti	0	13 Stf 6 AP	(260") (81")
Washington Times-Herald	275,954 (e) 300,916 (S)	16 (249")	0	249	8 (83")	3 pro	1 pro	14 Stf 1 AP 1 UP	(279") (12") (8")
Wausau Record-Herald	16,132 (e)	16 (215")	0	215	4 (66")	1 pro	0	16 AP	(215")
Wichita Eagle	72,267 (m) 82,039 (S)	6 (85")	0	85	5 (53")	2 neut. 1 pro	0	4 AP 2 UP	(37") (48")
Willows Journal & Glen Transcript	1,902 (e)	0	0	0	0	0	0	0	
Wisconsin State Journal (Madison)	34,878 (m) 72,228 (S)	15 (244")	1 anti (10")	254	6 (109")	1 pro	1 pro 1 neut.	9 AP 6 UP 1 na	(140") (64") (40")
Worcester Telegram	51,147 (m) 100,170 (S)	8 (121")	1 pro (22")	143	1 (7")	2 anti	0	8 AP	(121")

TABLE 2
Apportionment of Headlines between Senatorial Candidates
by Dailies Circulating in Wisconsin during Last Week of 1952 Campaign

Newspaper	No. of Stories	McCarthy in Headline	McCarthy on Page One	Fairchild in Headline	Fairchild on Page One
Antigo Journal	15	14	7	0	0
Appleton Post-Crescent	29	25	4	2	1
Ashland Press	13	12	10	1	1
Baraboo News-Republic	8	7	2	0	0
Beaver Dam Citizen	6	6	5	0	0
Beloit Daily News	13	11	2	1	0
Capital Times (Madison)	*47*	*35*	*15*	*10*	*6*
Chicago Sun-Times	20	13	1	0	0
Chicago Tribune	18	15	2	0	0
Chippewa Falls Herald-Telegram	15	12	4	2	0
Eau Claire Leader	*14*	*13*	*5*	*2*	*0*
Eau Claire Telegram	*21*	*17*	*6*	*3*	*0*
Fond du Lac Commonwealth-Reporter	10	8	2	1	1
Green Bay Press-Gazette	20	15	5	2	0
Janesville Gazette	9	7	4	1	0
Jefferson County Union (Ft. Atkinson)	10	6	5	1	1
Kenosha News	11	10	4	0	0
La Crosse Tribune	13	12	6	2	0
Manitowoc Herald-Times	28	21	5	4	0
Marinette Eagle-Star	24	22	0	5	0
Marshfield News-Herald	22	20	8	2	1
Merrill Herald	14	11	3	2	0
Milwaukee Journal	*50*	*35*	*3*	*11*	*1*
Milwaukee Sentinel	16	14	3	0	0
Minneapolis Star	12	12	2	0	0
Monroe Times	24	18	9	2	1
Oshkosh Northwestern	27	20	5	4	0
Portage Register-Democrat	7	7	4	0	0
Racine Journal-Times	37	27	5	6	1
Rhinelander News	15	10	7	4	4
Shawano Leader	7	5	4	0	0
Sheboygan Press	*44*	*32*	*9*	*9*	*6*
Stevens Point Journal	23	17	4	4	0
Stoughton Courier-Hub	2	2	1	0	0
Superior Telegram	19	17	9	5	2
Twin Cities News-Record (Neenah)	14	12	3	3	0
Two Rivers Reporter	25	19	5	3	0
Watertown Times	13	13	5	0	0
Waukesha Freeman	24	21	7	4	3
Wausau Record-Herald	30	20	2	3	1
Wisconsin Rapids Tribune	22	17	4	4	0
Wisconsin State Journal (Madison)	41	35	8	9	0
Totals	832	665	209	112	30

Notes: Newspapers that endorsed Fairchild appear in italic type, those that endorsed McCarthy, in boldface.

In the above table, no significance should be placed on the preponderance of page-one stories in some of the smaller papers. All or nearly all of the state and national news automatically went on page one in small papers such as those in Ashland, Rhinelander, Monroe, and Stoughton. It does show a significant difference in the way the leading anti-McCarthy papers were playing the news, however; the Capital Times and the Sheboygan Press put a relatively high number of McCarthy-Fairchild stories on page one, while the Milwaukee Journal put only four out of fifty on that page.

Both candidates' names often appeared in the same headline; therefore the sum of the numbers of times the names of the two candidates appeared in headlines often exceeds the number of stories.

TABLE 3
Selection of News Stories Involving Senatorial Candidates
by Dailies Circulating in Wisconsin
during Last Week of the 1952 Campaign

	Number of Stories		
Newspaper	Favorable to McCarthy	Critical of McCarthy	Favorable to Fairchild*
Antigo Journal	12	0	0
Appleton Post-Crescent	17	5	1
Ashland Press	11	1	1
Baraboo News-Republic	4	3	0
Beaver Dam Citizen	4	1	0
Beloit Daily News	6	3	1
Capital Times (Madison)	1	21	8
Chicago Sun-Times	2	12	0
Chicago Tribune	9	5	0
Chippewa Falls Herald-Telegram	10	1	2
Eau Claire Leader	6	6	0
Eau Claire Telegram	7	10	2
Fond du Lac Commonwealth-Reporter	5	1	2
Green Bay Press-Gazette	9	4	0
Janesville Gazette	4	2	1
Jefferson County Union (Ft. Atkinson)	3	1	2
Kenosha News	6	1	0
La Crosse Tribune	5	3	1
Manitowoc Herald-Times	12	5	4
Marinette Eagle-Star	11	6	4
Marshfield News-Herald	10	8	2
Merrill Herald	6	4	1
Milwaukee Journal	9	22	4
Milwaukee Sentinel	9	2	0
Minneapolis Star	2	8	0
Monroe Times	9	7	2
Oshkosh Northwestern	20	5	3
Portage Register-Democrat	3	3	0
Racine Journal-Times	12	12	6
Rhinelander News	8	3	3
Shawano Leader	4	1	0
Sheboygan Press	5	20	8
Stevens Point Journal	10	6	4
Stoughton Courier-Hub	1	1	0
Superior Telegram	9	6	2
Twin Cities News-Record (Neenah)	3	6	2
Two Rivers Reporter	9	6	2
Watertown Times	2	10	1
Waukesha Freeman	11	8	2
Wausau Record-Herald	14	8	5
Wisconsin Rapids Tribune	13	5	3
Wisconsin State Journal (Madison)	14	18	4
Totals	317	263	83

Note: Newspapers that endorsed Fairchild appear in italic type, those that endorsed McCarthy, in boldface.
*There is no column for stories critical of Fairchild because there were no such stories.

TABLE 4
Vote Shifts in Milwaukee Journal Retail Trading Zone, 1948–52

County	Journal Evening Circulation	Circulation as % of Dwelling Units	Journal Sunday Circulation	Circulation as % of Dwelling Units	Shift in McCarthy % of Total Vote, 1946–52	Shift in McCarthy % c.w. GOP Average	Shift in Eisenhower % c.w. GOP Average	Shift in Kohler % c.w. GOP Average
Milwaukee (ABC City Zone)	232,848	100	221,031	100	−17	− 9	+4	+1
Waukesha	15,550	100	17,141	100	−20	− 9	+3	+1
Ozaukee	3,899	78	4,108	80	−13	− 9	+4	+3
Washington	4,504	61	5,319	72	−10	− 3	+6	+4
Walworth	3,480	37	5,616	59	− 8	− 3	+1	+4
Jefferson	3,535	33	6,285	59	− 8	− 3	+5	+6
Dodge	4,030	29	5,443	40	− 4	+ 2	+5	+6
Fond du Lac	3,235	20	8,228	50	0	+ 1	+6	+7
Racine	3,369	13.7	11,613	48	− 4	− 3	+4	+5
Sheboygan	1,776	9	7,972	39	− 9†	−10	+2	+6
Kenosha	1,255	8	7,454	44	− 5	0	+3	+5

*c.w.: compared with.

†The Milwaukee Journal influence in Sheboygan County was probably secondary to that of the Sheboygan Press, which also opposed McCarthy, and which accounts for the larger shift away from McCarthy than would be suggested by Journal circulation. In the city of Sheboygan, the shift was even greater, from 49.3 percent to 35 percent.

TABLE 5
Shifts in McCarthy Percentage of Total Vote Cast, 1948–52, in Circulation Zones of Wisconsin Dailies Opposing and Supporting McCarthy in 1952

Newspaper	Daily Circulation	ABC City Zone (City)	Retail Trade Zone (County)
Opposing McCarthy:			
Capital Times (Madison)	40,097	− 9.3	−10
Eau Claire Leader/Telegram	23,831	− 8	−10
Milwaukee Journal	327,944	−17	− 8.5
Sheboygan Press	25,621	−14.3	−10
Supporting McCarthy:			
Antigo Journal	5,270	+ 3	− 8*
Appleton Post-Crescent	30,462	+ 1	− 1
Beloit Daily News	18,379	− 5	− 6
Green Bay Press-Gazette	35,699	+ 4	+ 2
Janesville Gazette	20,988	+ 3	− 6
Marinette Eagle-Star	8,541	− 4	− 8*
Oshkosh Northwestern	18,147	− 6	− 2
Twin Cities News-Record (Neenah)	4,092	+ 0.5	− 2*

*It is questionable that the influence of newspapers this small made itself felt in an area as large as a county.

TABLE 6
Shifts in McCarthy Percentage of Total Vote Cast, 1946–52,
in Communities Served by Weekly Newspapers Opposing McCarthy

Newspaper	County	1946 % (City)	1952 % (City)	Vote Shift	1946 % (County)	1952 % (County)	Vote Shift	Kohler (Gub.) % 1952 (County)
Burlington Standard-Democrat	Racine	75	73	− 2	52	48	− 4	56
Darlington Republican-Journal	Lafayette	65	65	0	63	66	+ 3	72
Delavan Enterprise	Walworth	80.4	70	−10.4	80	72	− 8	79
Glenwood City Tribune	St. Croix	79	68	−11	64	57	− 7	68
Grant County Independent (Lancaster)	Grant	76	75.7	− 0.3	73	76.5	+ 3.5	82
Mauston Star	Juneau	83	77.8	− 5.2	75	72	− 3	77
Mellen Record	Ashland	47.9	43.6	− 4.3	57	52	− 5	59
Monroe County Democrat (Sparta)	Monroe	78.6	67	−11.6	69	68	− 1	76
Montello Tribune	Marquette	84.7	74	−10.7	82	77	− 5	83
New Richmond News	St. Croix	59	55	− 4	64	57	− 7	68
Plymouth Review	Sheboygan	64.7	57	− 7.7	56	47	− 8	63
Rice Lake Chronotype	Barron	70	63	− 7	65	63	− 2	73
Vernon County Censor (Viroqua)	Vernon	74	76	+ 2	66	63	− 3	71

TABLE 7
Shifts in McCarthy Percentage of Total Vote Cast, 1946–52,
in Communities Served by Weekly Newspapers Supporting McCarthy

Newspaper	County	1946 % (City)	1952 % (City)	Vote Shift	1946 % (County)	1952 % (County)	Vote Shift	Kohler (Gub.) % 1952 (County)
Chilton Times-Journal	Calumet	66	74	+ 8	72	76	+ 4	81
Hartford Times-Press	Washington*	72	57	−15	75	65	−10	72
Marion Advertiser	Waupaca	83.8	84.5	+ 0.7	79	81	+ 2	85
Mosinee Times	Marathon	63	59.5	− 3.5	56	56	0	62
New London Press-Republican	Outagamie	71	73.5	+ 2.5	71	70	− 1	77
Oconto County Reporter	Oconto	69	63.7	− 5.3	73	73	0	74
Peshtigo Times	Marinette	73	68	− 5	69	61	− 8	67
Richland Center Richland-Democrat, Republican-Observer	Richland	79	75.6	− 3.4	76	72	− 4	77
Vilas County News-Review (Eagle River)	Vilas	72	75	+ 3	67	70	+ 3	75
West Bend Pilot	Washington*	77	61	−16	75	65	−10	72

*Washington County is suburban to Milwaukee.

The U.S. Post Office bills McCarthy for improper use of his franking privilege, used for campaign mailings.

A group of 133 Methodist clergymen from Wisconsin issues a statement criticizing McCarthy.

Protests against McCarthy's attack flood the *New York Times* office in New York.

A well-known clergyman in Sheboygan says McCarthy's speech had helped the Communists.

At another McCarthy speech in Chicago, a Roosevelt College professor heckles McCarthy and is put in jail.

In Milwaukee, Tom Fairchild campaigns all day on Wisconsin Avenue, shaking hands in the cold and wind, getting mixed reactions.

Irv Kupcinet, a *Chicago Sun-Times* columnist, says he has examined McCarthy's documents and they don't back up his charges.

In New Jersey, a man named Tumulty, who said he was a Democrat, announces that he is convinced by McCarthy and will switch his vote to Eisenhower.

Senator Dirksen (Rep., Ill.) says he liked McCarthy's speech.

Willard Edwards, in the *Chicago Tribune*, "reveals" a plot by Harry Truman to "get" McCarthy.

In Connecticut, McCarthy says that Senator Benton is helping the Communists.

In Milwaukee, Fairchild campaigns at shopping centers, plant gates, and union meetings.

President Truman says McCarthy's charges against Stevenson are lies.

William T. Evjue, publisher of the *Capital Times*, denounces McCarthy in a speech in Chicago.

A former governor of Illinois and the former national commander of the American Legion says McCarthy told the truth about Stevenson.

McCarthy announces he will make another nationally broadcast speech about Stevenson on Monday, November 3.

Fairchild announces he will speak over a state radio network.

An Ohio television station cancels arrangements to broadcast McCarthy's Monday night speech.

Election day is designated "McCarthy Day" in Appleton, and chairmen of eight committees are appointed to plan a civic celebration and McCarthy "open house."

Senator Benton says McCarthy's charges are lies.

Hank Greenspun, editor and publisher of the *Las Vegas Sun*, withdraws his paper's announced support of Eisenhower because of McCarthy's speech.

Wisconsin's secretary of state says that the McCarthy campaign club failed to file its financial report at the required time.

Fairchild campaigns at Eau Claire and says he is encouraged.

Supporters announce McCarthy will speak at a south-side rally in Milwaukee.

Senator Sparkman (Dem., Ala.), nominee for vice-president, says that McCarthy's speech helped Stevenson.

A supreme court justice in Pennsylvania says McCarthy's charges against Stevenson are "devoid of sense."

A Republican committee in Meriden, Connecticut, cancels a scheduled McCarthy talk.

The owner of a television station in Toledo, Ohio, defends his decision not to broadcast McCarthy's Chicago speech.

A group calling itself the Committee for Farm Progress criticizes McCarthy, endorses Fairchild.

McCarthy declares that none of his critics have answered his charges.

In a mock election at the University of Wisconsin, students elect Eisenhower, Kohler, and Fairchild.

Fairchild is endorsed by the National Committee for an Effective Congress.

A woman fired by the government for leaking information from confidential loyalty files says she gave the data to McCarthy. McCarthy says he got nothing from her, didn't know her.

The *New York Times* announces its mail is running against McCarthy; the *Chicago Tribune* says its mail is pro-McCarthy.

McCarthy's speech in St. Louis, Missouri, is picketed.

Westbrook Pegler, the columnist, says that Democrats fear McCarthy most and that perhaps the senator can drag Eisenhower to victory on his coattails.

Hecklers invade McCarthy's Milwaukee south-side rally, delay a television broadcast. McCarthy says the *Milwaukee Journal* organized the disruption. J. D. Ferguson, *Journal* editor, denies this.

Edward Morgan, a former FBI inspector and Senate committee counsel, says in Milwaukee that McCarthy has found no Reds in government.

Fairchild, in Green Bay, says McCarthy's votes in the Senate have aided the Reds.

A group of Harvard professors announce they have raised $11,800 to use to defeat McCarthy.

In Buckhannon, West Virginia, McCarthy says his "documentation" of the charges against Stevenson has not been challenged.

In Appleton, Fairchild says that McCarthy dodges issues.

In straw votes at four Wisconsin colleges, students favor Eisenhower and Kohler, split on McCarthy and Fairchild.

Senator Wayne Morse of Oregon criticizes McCarthy and Eisenhower in a speech in Milwaukee.

George Haberman, a Wisconsin labor leader, charges McCarthy with "smearing" Stevenson.

A clergyman at Ogema, Wisconsin, preaches a sermon against McCarthy.

Morgan says McCarthy used false documents on the Senate floor.

A McCarthy group in Connecticut says the senator was never scheduled to speak in Meriden.

In Detroit, 179 citizens issue a statement that they are "disgusted" with McCarthy.

A former Wisconsin resident, 96, living in Denver, Colorado, sends a telegram to Democrats saying it would be a "disgrace" if McCarthy wins. (Reported in the *Capital Times.*)

Robert Hutchins and 19 other educators urge Eisenhower to repudiate McCarthy.

McCarthy says Stevenson would be "infinitely worse" than Truman.

Evjue charges the *Wisconsin State Journal* with slanting the news in favor of McCarthy and against Stevenson.

The McCarthy club files late, listing $90,000 as campaign expenditure.

A Unitarian minister in Madison says McCarthy uses the tactics of Hitler.

In a poll of state farmers, Eisenhower is two to one over Stevenson, and Kohler and McCarthy far ahead of Democratic opponents.

A poll of clergymen by the *Milwaukee Sentinel* says they like Eisenhower and McCarthy.

In his election eve speech, McCarthy repeats charges against Stevenson's "advisers," says that Stevenson is "even more dangerous" than Truman, and calls for a straight Republican vote.

Notes

Chapter 1

1 U.S. Congress, House, Committee on Un-American Activities, *Guide to Subversive Organizations and Publications*, 82d Cong., 1st sess., 3 March 1951, p. 1.
2 Ibid., p. 6.
3 California State Senate, *Fourth Report of the Senate Fact-Finding Committee on Un-American Activities*, 1948, p. 29.
4 Ibid., p. 91.
5 Edson, in *Manitowoc Herald-Times*, 14 February 1950.
6 Washington Post News Service, in the *Milwaukee Journal*, 25 April 1976.
7 Code of Federal Regulations, Executive Order 9835, 21 March 1947.
8 Ibid., p. 630.
9 Alan Barth, *The Loyalty of Free Men*, 2d ed. (New York: Viking Press, 1951), p. 138.
10 Roy Cohn, *McCarthy* (New York: New American Library, 1968), p. 8.
11 Torinus and Minahan interviews, 5 May 1976. All comments and reminiscences of Torinus and Minahan in the chapter are from these interviews.
12 Pusey interview, 7 January 1976. Observations and recollections of Pusey in the chapter are from this interview.
13 Wyngaard interview, 3 June 1976; all comments by Wyngaard in the chapter are from this interview.
14 Van Susteren interview, 5 May 1976.
15 McCarthy's reply to O'Hara from the Associated Press, in the *Appleton Post-Crescent*, 1 July 1953.
16 *Appleton Post-Crescent*, 1 July 1953.
17 Editorial, *Racine Journal-Times*, 3 July 1953.
18 Editorial, *Stevens Point Journal*, 2 July 1953.
19 Background on Minahan from Torinus interview, 5 May 1976.
20 Robert Griffith, *The Politics of Fear: Joseph R. McCarthy and the Senate* (Lexington: University Press of Kentucky, 1970), p. 10.
21 Wax interview, 1 February 1977.
22 Richard H. Rovere, *Senator Joe McCarthy* (New York: Harcourt Brace, 1959), p. 125.
23 *Milwaukee Journal*, 14 February 1956.
24 *Santa Barbara News-Press*, 5 April 1954.

25 Transcript in possession of author.
26 Olsen interview, 22 July 1976.
27 William F. Buckley, Jr., and L. Brent Bozell, *McCarthy and His Enemies: The Record and Its Meaning* (Chicago: Henry Regnery, 1954), pp. 41–61.
28 Henderson interview, 17 May 1976.
29 Reedy interview, 15 May 1976.
30 Olsen interview, 22 July 1976. All comments and reminiscences of Olsen in the chapter are from this interview.
31 McCulloch interview, 22 July 1976.
32 *Milwaukee Journal,* 17 February 1950.
33 Ringler to Bayley, 3 March 1976.
34 Fairfield interview, 28 February 1976.

Chapter 2

1 Agronsky interview, 8 July 1980.
2 *Quincy Patriot-Ledger,* 1 March 1950.

Chapter 3

1 Arrowsmith interview, 25 March 1976. This interview and the others cited below were the sources for this chapter's comments and reminiscences of those interviewed, unless otherwise indicated.
2 Steele interview, 26 March 1976.
3 Theis interview, 25 March 1976.
4 Reedy interview, 15 May 1976.
5 Seib interview, 26 March 1976.
6 Hanley interview, 17 May 1976.
7 Marder interview, 12–13 June 1979.
8 Alexander to Alfred Friendly, 28 February 1977 (letter in the possession of the author).
9 Undated Fleming memorandum, Fleming Papers, State Historical Society of Wisconsin.
10 Chadwick interview, 26 March 1976.
11 Henderson interview, 17 May 1976.
12 *New York Times,* 26 August 1952.
13 Louis Lyons, *Newspaper Story: One Hundred Years of the Boston Globe* (Cambridge, Mass.: Harvard Belknap Press, 1971), pp. 317–18.
14 Elmer H. Davis, *But We Were Born Free* (New York: Bobbs-Merrill, 1953), p. 159.
15 Rovere, *Senator Joe McCarthy,* pp. 165–66.
16 Griffith, *The Politics of Fear,* p. 140.
17 Joseph R. McCarthy, *McCarthyism, the Fight for America: Documented Answers to Questions Asked by Friend and Foe* (New York: Devin-Adair, 1952), p. 3.

18 Information on the Hazen controversy from *Associated Press Managing Editors' Red Book*, 1950, pp. 63–79, and from *Editor & Publisher*, 18 and 25 November 1950.

19 *APME Red Book*, 1952, pp. 199–200, 227.

20 For an account of the debate, see *APME Red Book*, 1953, pp. 49–57.

21 *New York Times*, 27 April 1955.

22 Relman Morin, 4 April 1954, *St. Paul Pioneer Press*.

23 *The AP McCarthy Series* (New York: Associated Press, 1954).

Chapter 4

1 Griffith, *The Politics of Fear*, p. 9.

2 Ringler to Philip Potter, 23 February 1979.

3 My source was Davis.

4 Ringler to Bayley, 3 March 1980.

5 Potter to Laurence C. Eklund, 2 February 1979.

6 Ringler to Potter, 23 February 1979.

7 Ringler to Bayley, 3 March 1980.

8 *Milwaukee Journal*, 25 February 1953.

9 Ibid., 15 September 1951.

10 Ibid., 27 August 1952.

11 Ibid., 4 September 1952.

12 Associated Press story from *Sheboygan Press*, 10 September 1952.

13 The author was the correspondent for these publications.

14 *Janesville Gazette*, 30 October 1952.

15 *Seattle Times*, 24 October 1952.

16 *Milwaukee Journal*, 21 September 1952.

17 Associated Press, 15 October 1952.

18 See Percy H. Tannenbaum, "The Effect of Headlines on the Interpretation of News Stories," *Journalism Quarterly*, Spring 1953, pp. 189–97.

19 *New York Times* story, as printed in the *San Francisco Chronicle*, 28 October 1957.

20 Associated Press story in the *Sacramento Bee*, 28 October 1952.

21 Willard H. Pedrick, "Senator McCarthy and the Law of Libel: A Study of Two Campaign Speeches," *Northwestern University Law Review* 48.2 (May–June 1953): 177–78.

22 Louis H. Bean, *Influences in the 1954 Mid-Term Elections: War, Jobs, Parity, McCarthy* (Washington, D.C.: Public Affairs Institute, 1954), p. 36.

23 *Grant County Independent* (Lancaster, Wis.), 16 October 1952.

24 Fairchild to Bayley, 7 May 1976.

25 O'Brien interview, 19 September 1977.

26 Circulation figures used were taken from the Audit Report on the *Milwaukee Journal* for 1950 made by the Audit Bureau of Circulations, Chicago.

27 Ben H. Bagdikian, *The Effete Conspiracy, and Other Crimes by the Press* (New York: Harper & Row, 1972), p. 55.
28 *Capital Times*, 16 September 1952.
29 Clapp interview, 23 April 1976.

Chapter 5

"Camp-following," "mocking-bird," "bleeding-heart," and "left-wing" were adjectives used by McCarthy to describe opposition newspapers, during the pretrial examination in his libel suit against the *Syracuse* (N.Y.) *Post-Standard.*

1 Van Susteren interview, 5 May 1976.
2 Ringler interview, 14 June 1976. This interview is also the source for other comments and reminiscences of Ringler in the chapter, unless otherwise cited.
3 Hunter interview, 25 April 1976.
4 *Sheboygan Press*, 21 May 1951.
5 *Milwaukee Journal*, 13 September 1950.
6 Daniel Bell, "Interpretations of American Politics," in Daniel Bell, ed., *The Radical Right: The New American Right Expanded and Updated* (Garden City, N.J.: Doubleday Anchor Books, 1963), p. 68.
7 Story from Washington, D.C., by Laurence C. Eklund, in the *Milwaukee Journal*, 9 November 1949.
8 Associated Press story in *Janesville Gazette*, 10 November 1949.
9 *Capital Times*, 10 November 1949.
10 *Milwaukee Journal*, 11 November 1949.
11 *Milwaukee Journal*, 10 November 1949.
12 McMillin interview, 25 April 1976. This interview is also the source for the comments and reminiscences of McMillin that follow.
13 *Milwaukee Journal* editorial in the possession of the author.
14 *Milwaukee Journal*, 31 July 1950.
15 Ibid., 13 September 1950.
16 Ibid., 12 April 1951.
17 Memorandum, 7 April 1951, Fleming Papers, State Historical Society of Wisconsin.
18 Memorandum, 23 April 1951, Fleming Papers.
19 *Milwaukee Journal*, 8 June 1952.
20 Edwin R. Bayley, in the *Milwaukee Journal*, 20 December 1953.
21 Memorandum, 1–6 January 1952, Fleming Papers.
22 George Dixon columns, *San Francisco Examiner*, 9–10 September 1952.
23 *Milwaukee Journal*, 13 September 1950.
24 Memorandum, 6 August 1950, Fleming Papers.
25 Associated Press, in the *New York Times*, 9 May 1954.
26 *New York Times*, 1 December 1954.

27 Ringler to Bayley, 3 March 1976.

28 *New York Times*, 5 March 1954.

29 A tape recording sent to the author by Johnston and dated 27 September 1976 is the source for this and the following passage.

30 Turner Catledge, *My Life and The Times* (New York: Harper & Row, 1971), pp. 227–30.

31 *New York Times*, 20 April 1956.

32 See memoranda in the Joseph Pulitzer II Papers, Library of Congress. These memoranda are also the source for subsequent references to Pulitzer's exchanges with his staff.

33 *New York Post*, 21 September 1951.

34 Information about Wechsler's appearances before the subcommittee is taken from the transcript of the hearings printed in the *New York Times* of 8 May 1953.

35 Dooley interview, 20 October 1977, for this and subsequent quotations of Dooley in the chapter.

36 Hoyt memorandum, Pulitzer II Papers, Library of Congress.

37 Malin to Joseph Pulitzer II, 19 October 1953, Pulitzer II Papers.

38 *New York Times*, 22 November 1954.

39 McCarthy, *McCarthyism, the Fight for America*, p. 284.

40 Strout interview, 10 March 1976.

41 *Washington Post*, 13 February 1977.

42 Marder interview, 12–13 June 1979. All comments and reminiscences of Marder that follow are from this interview.

43 Edwards interview, 27 June 1977, also the source for the comments and reminiscences of Edwards that follow.

44 *Chicago Tribune*, 17 November 1950.

45 *Washington Times-Herald*, 6 April 1951.

46 Potter declined to be interviewed about his coverage of McCarthy, when asked in 1976.

47 Griffin to Bayley, 7 July 1976.

48 Rubin interview, 23 April 1976.

49 McGrory interview, 2 July 1977.

50 Hibbs to McCarthy, 10 August 1950, and Alsop to Hibbs, 25 August 1950, Alsop Papers, Library of Congress.

51 McCarthy to Hibbs, 25 August 1950, Alsop Papers.

52 Hibbs to McCarthy, 11 September 1950, Alsop Papers.

53 Jones to Alsop, 7 November 1952, Alsop Papers.

54 *Houston Post*, 19 September 1950.

55 *Milwaukee Journal*, 14 February 1952.

56 *Milwaukee Journal*, 2 March 1952.

57 *New York Times*, 21 May 1950.

58 *Milwaukee Journal*, 25 October 1952.

59 Alsop letter, 11 March 1976.

60 Information on Pearson's fight with McCarthy from the *New York Times* (Associated Press), 13 and 15 December 1950; *Washington Post* (United Press), 14 December 1950, and (staff), 15 December 1950; and *New York Post*, 15 and 17 December 1950.

61 *Washington Post*, 27 and 28 September 1951; *Milwaukee Journal*, 27 September 1951.

62 *New York Times*, 30 December 1951.

63 *New York Times* (Associated Press), 3 March 1951.

64 *Capital Times*, 6 May 1957.

65 Bauer interview, 30 April 1976.

66 A. Robert Smith to Bayley, 29 March 1977.

67 McArdle interview, 24 October 1979.

68 *Grant County Independent*, 26 October 1951.

69 Original press release in possession of the author.

70 Luce letter and subsequent material on this exchange in the *New York Times* morgue.

71 *Business Week*, 16 February 1952.

72 *New York Times*, 28 January 1952.

73 *Milwaukee Journal*, 17 June 1952.

74 Information about the 29 March 1952 pretrial examination of McCarthy in his libel suit against the Post-Standard Co., held in the Onondaga Supreme Court, Syracuse, N.Y., is taken from a copy of the transcript in the possession of the author.

75 *New York Times* (Associated Press), 15 March 1953. Amount of settlement from *Editor & Publisher*, 4 April 1953.

76 Ferguson telephone interview, 17 November 1977.

77 *New York World-Telegram*, 12 July 1954.

Chapter 6

1 See the 1950 and 1956 volumes of *World Communications: Press, Radio, Film*, published yearly in Paris by the Division of Free Flow of Information, Department of Mass Communications, United Nations Educational, Scientific and Cultural Organization.

2 The following passage on the institutionalization of the blacklist is based primarily on three sources: John Cogley, *Report on Blacklisting*, vol. 2, *Radio-Television* (New York: Fund for the Republic, 1954), esp. pp. 246–82; Merle Miller, *The Judges and the Judged* (New York: Doubleday and Company, 1952); and Erik Barnouw, *The Golden Web: A History of Broadcasting in the United States*, 3 vols. (New York: Oxford University Press, 1968), vol. 2, *1933–1953*.

3 *Broadcasting-Telecasting*, 26 May 1952.

4 Ibid., 14 July 1952.

5 Ibid., 17 November 1952.

6 Ibid., 8 December 1952.

7 Ibid., 20 April 1953.

8 *New York Times*, 16-17 August 1951.

9 Copy of transcript in possession of the author. The original was destroyed by the American Broadcasting Company in 1953.

10 Phonograph record in possession of the author.

11 The account of the hearings that follows is based on newspaper reports, particularly daily coverage in the *New York Times*.

12 *New York Times*, 5 March 1953.

13 Bagdikian interview, 4 January 1976.

14 *New York Times*, 7 November 1953.

15 Ibid., 15 November 1953.

16 Associated Press in the *New York Times*, 24 November 1953.

17 *New York Times*, 25 November 1953.

18 Ibid., 25 November 1953.

19 *Washington Post*, 26 November 1953.

20 *New York Herald-Tribune*, 26 November 1953.

21 Childs column in *Appleton Post-Crescent*, 1 December 1953.

22 Speculation about administration tactics based upon columns by Marquis Childs (*Appleton Post-Crescent*, 1 December 1953), Jay G. Hayden (*Montreal Star*, 3 November 1953), and Drew Middleton (*New York Times*, 21 November 1953).

23 *New York Times*, 29 November 1953.

24 Ibid., 20 February 1954.

25 Pearson column in *Washington Post*, 8 March 1954.

26 This and subsequent quotations from Reston column, *New York Times*, 4 March 1954.

27 *New York Times*, 3 March 1954.

28 Edwards interview, 27 June 1977.

29 *Capital Times*, 1 March 1954.

30 *New York Times*, 10 March 1954.

31 *Memphis Commercial Appeal*, 11 March 1954.

32 *New York Times*, 10 March 1954.

33 Friendly, *Due to Circumstances*, pp. 23-67; Alexander Kendrick, *Prime Time: The Life of Edward R. Murrow* (Boston: Little, Brown, 1969), pp. 46-71.

34 Friendly, *Due to Circumstances*, p. 41.

35 *Broadcasting*, 9 January 1978.

36 Agronsky interview, 8 July 1980. All comments and reminiscences of Agronsky are from this interview.

37 Gould interview, 24 September 1976.

38 *New York Times*, 11 March 1954.

39 Ibid., 7 April 1954.

40 *Washington Post*, 7 April 1954.

41 International News Service in *Washington Post*, 7 April 1954.

42 *New York Times,* 9 April 1954.

43 Ibid., 9 May 1954.

44 Ibid., 15 May 1954.

45 Ibid., 13 May 1954.

46 *New York Post,* 11 March 1954.

47 *Commonweal,* 26 March 1954.

48 Friendly, *Due to Circumstances,* p. 52.

49 *New York Times,* 14 March 1954.

50 John E. O'Connor, "Film Study and the History Classroom," *Newsletter of the American Historical Association,* March 1977, pp. 7–15.

51 Associated Press in the *Capital Times,* 6 May 1952.

52 *New York Times,* 22 April 1954.

53 Ibid., 23 April 1954.

54 Ibid., 26 April 1954.

55 Ibid., 27 April 1954.

56 *Editor & Publisher,* 24 April 1954.

57 *New York Times,* 2 May 1954.

58 Ibid., 2 May 1954.

59 Ibid., 13 June 1954.

60 Quotations from the hearing are from Michael Straight, *Trial by Television* (Boston: Beacon Press, 1954), pp. 246–54; and from U.S. Congress, Senate, *Hearing before the Special Committee on Investigations of the Committee on Government Operations: Pursuant to S. Res. 189,* 83d Cong., 2d sess., 9 June 1954, pt. 59: 2424–30.

61 Roy Cohn, *McCarthy,* p. 204.

62 Gould interview, 24 September 1976.

63 *Editor & Publisher,* 22 May 1954.

64 Ibid., 22 May 1954.

65 Ibid., 26 June 1954.

66 *New York Times,* 27 August 1954.

67 Ibid., 3 September 1954.

68 Cohn, *McCarthy,* p. 220.

69 *New York Times,* 1 September 1954.

70 Associated Press in the *Milwaukee Journal,* 17 November 1954.

Chapter 7

1 John B. Oakes Papers, State Historical Society of Wisconsin, Madison, Wisconsin.

Sources

Newspapers

10 February–10 March 1950

Appleton Post-Crescent
Arkansas Gazette (Little Rock)
Atlanta Constitution
Bakersfield Californian
Baltimore News-Post
Baltimore Sun
Baraboo News-Republic
Beloit Daily News
Berkshire Eagle (Pittsfield)
Boston Globe
Boston Herald
Boston Post
Boston Traveler
Buffalo News
Capital Times (Madison)
Charlotte Observer
Chicago Daily News
Chicago Sun-Times
Chicago Tribune
Christian Science Monitor (Boston)
Cleveland Plain Dealer
Columbus Dispatch
Cumberland Times
Dallas News
Denver Post
Deseret News (Salt Lake City)
Des Moines Register
Detroit News
Duluth News-Tribune
Eau Claire Leader
Eugene Register-Guard
Fall River Herald-News
Fitchburg Sentinel
Fond du Lac Commonwealth-
  Reporter

Framingham News
Frederick News
Green Bay Press-Gazette
Hagerstown Herald
Hartford Courant
Haverhill Gazette
Holyoke Telegram-Transcript
Honolulu Star-Bulletin
Houston Post
Humboldt Times (Eureka)
Huronite and Plainsman
Indianapolis Star
Jackson Clarion-Ledger
Janesville Gazette
Kansas City Star
Kenosha News
La Crosse Tribune
Los Angeles Daily News
Los Angeles Times
Louisville Courier-Journal
Lowell Sun
Manchester Union
Manitowoc Herald-Times
Marinette Eagle-Star
Memphis Commercial Appeal
Miami Herald
Milwaukee Journal
Milwaukee Sentinel
Minneapolis Star
Montgomery Advertiser
Nashville Banner
Nashville Tennessean
Nevada State Journal
Newark News
New Orleans Times-Picayune

New York Daily News
New York Herald-Tribune
New York Journal-American
New York Post
New York Times
New York World-Telegram & Sun
Oakland Tribune
Omaha World-Herald
Oregon Statesman
Oshkosh Northwestern
Philadelphia Bulletin
Phoenix Republic
Pittsburgh Post-Gazette
Portland Oregonian
Providence Journal
Quincy Patriot-Ledger
Racine Journal-Times
Raleigh News & Observer
Redding Record-Searchlight
Redwood City Tribune
Reno Gazette
Rhinelander Daily News
Richmond Independent
Richmond News-Leader
Riverside Press
Rochester Democrat & Chronicle
Sacramento Bee
St. Louis Globe-Democrat
St. Louis Post-Dispatch
St. Petersburg Times

Salinas Californian
Salisbury Times
Salt Lake City Tribune
San Diego Union
San Francisco Chronicle
San Francisco Examiner
San Francisco News
San Jose Mercury-Herald
San Rafael Independent-Journal
Santa Barbara News-Press
Seattle Post-Intelligencer
Shawano Leader
Sheboygan Press
Shreveport Times
Springfield Daily News
Stevens Point Journal
Stockton Record
Superior Telegram
Tampa Tribune
Tulsa Tribune
Wall Street Journal
Washington Daily News
Washington Post
Washington Star
Washington Times-Herald
Wausau Record-Herald
Wichita Eagle
Willows Journal & Glen Transcript
Wisconsin State Journal
Worcester Telegram

28 October–4 November 1952

Antigo Journal
Appleton Post-Crescent
Baraboo News-Republic
Beaver Dam Citizen
Beloit Daily News
Capital Times (Madison)
Chicago Sun-Times
Chicago Tribune
Chippewa Falls Herald-Telegram
Eau Claire Leader
Eau Claire Telegram
Fond du Lac Commonwealth-
   Reporter
Green Bay Press-Gazette

Janesville Gazette
Kenosha News
La Crosse Tribune
Manitowoc Herald-Times
Marinette Eagle-Star
Marshfield News-Herald
Merrill Herald
Milwaukee Journal
Milwaukee Sentinel
Minneapolis Star
Monroe Times
Oshkosh Northwestern
Racine Journal-Times
Rhinelander News

Shawano Leader
Sheboygan Press
Stevens Point Journal
Stoughton Courier-Hub
Superior Telegram
Twin Cities News-Record (Neenah)

Two Rivers Reporter
Watertown Times
Waukesha Freeman
Wausau Record-Herald
Wisconsin Rapids Tribune
Wisconsin State Journal (Madison)

1 October–4 November 1952 (Wisconsin Weeklies)

Algoma Record-Herald
Ashland County Record (Mellen)
Black River Falls Banner-Journal
Burlington Standard-Democrat
Clark County Press (Neillsville)
DePere Journal-Democrat
Door County Advocate
  (Sturgeon Bay)
Grant County Independent
  (Lancaster)
Iron County Miner (Hurley)
Kewaunee Enterprise
Kickapoo Scout (Soldiers Grove)
Lafayette County News (Darlington)
Mauston Star
Medford Star News

New London Press-Republican
Oconto County Reporter
Peshtigo Times
Plymouth Review
Prairie du Chien Courier
Rice Lake Chronotype
Richland Center
  Republican-Observer
Richland Center
  Richland-Democrat
Sparta Herald
Tomahawk Leader
Waupaca County Post
West Bend News
Whitewater Register

11 March 1954

Appleton Post-Crescent
Arkansas Gazette (Little Rock)
Atlanta Constitution
Baltimore News-Post
Baltimore Sun
Beloit Daily News
Berkshire Eagle (Pittsfield)
Boston Globe
Boston Herald
Buffalo News
Capital Times (Madison)
Chicago Sun-Times
Chicago Tribune
Columbus Dispatch
Cumberland Times
Dallas News
Denver Post
Duluth News-Tribune

Eau Claire Leader
Frederick News
Green Bay Press-Gazette
Hagerstown Herald
Hartford Courant
Houston Post
Indianapolis Star
Janesville Gazette
Kansas City Star
Louisville Courier-Journal
Lowell Sun
Memphis Commercial Appeal
Miami Herald
Milwaukee Journal
Minneapolis Star
Montgomery Advertiser
Nevada State Journal (Reno)
New Orleans Times-Picayune

New York Daily News
New York Herald-Tribune
New York Journal-American
New York Post
New York Times
New York World-Telegram & Sun
Oregon Statesman (Salem)
Oshkosh Northwestern
Philadelphia Bulletin
Pittsburgh Post-Gazette
Portland Oregonian
Racine Journal-Times
Rochester Democrat & Chronicle

St. Louis Post-Dispatch
Salisbury Times
Salt Lake City Tribune
Sheboygan Press
Springfield News
Washington Daily News
Washington Post
Washington Star
Washington Times-Herald
Wichita Eagle
Wisconsin State Journal (Madison)
Worcester Telegram

8–10 March 1956

Baltimore News-Post
Baltimore Sun
Capital Times (Madison)
Chicago Tribune
Cumberland Times
Dallas News
Hagerstown Herald
Houston Post
Indianapolis Star
Memphis Commercial Appeal
Milwaukee Journal
Miami Herald
Montgomery Advertiser
New Orleans Times-Picayune
New York Daily News

New York Herald-Tribune
New York Journal-American
New York Post
New York Times
New York World-Telegram & Sun
Philadelphia Bulletin
Pittsburgh Post-Gazette
Racine Journal-Times
St. Louis Post-Dispatch
Salisbury Times
Washington Post
Washington Star
Wichita Eagle
Wisconsin State Journal (Madison)

Interviews and Correspondence

Agronsky, Martin. 8 July 1980, Washington, D.C.
Alexander, Allen. 15 April 1977, Cabin John, Maryland.
Alsop, Joseph. 11 March 1976, Washington, D.C. Letter, 29 April 1976.
Arrowsmith, Marvin. 25 March 1976, Washington, D.C.
Bagdikian, Ben H. 4 January 1976, New York, N.Y.
Bechtel, William. 20 April 1976, Madison, Wisconsin.
Chadwick, John. 26 March 1976, Washington, D.C.
Clapp, Norman. 23 April 1976, Madison, Wisconsin.
Dooley, Edward. 20 October 1977, Redwood City, California.
Edwards, Willard. 27 June 1977, Washington, D.C.
Eklund, Laurence C. 23 March 1976, Bethesda, Maryland.
Fairchild, Thomas E. 7 May 1976, letter from Chicago, Illinois.
Fairfield, William S. 28 February 1976. New York, N.Y.

Gould, Jack. 24 September 1976, Kensington, California. Letter, 14 April 1977.

Griffin, Gerald. 7 July 1976, letter from Emmitsburg, Maryland.

Hanley, Dan. 17 May 1976, Milwaukee, Wisconsin.

Henderson, Dion. 17 May 1976, Milwaukee, Wisconsin.

Hunter, John Patrick. 23 April 1976, Madison, Wisconsin.

Johnston, Richard J. H. 28 September 1977, letter and audiotape from Columbia, South Carolina.

Lewis, Anthony. 25 January 1976, Cambridge, Massachusetts.

Loeb, Lewis. 2 August 1976, La Jolla, California.

Marder, Murrey. 12–13 June 1979, Washington, D.C.

McMillin, Miles. 25 April 1976, Madison, Wisconsin.

McArdle, Kenneth. 24 October 1979, Berkeley, California.

McCulloch, Frank. 22 July 1976, Sacramento, California.

McGrory, Mary. 2 July 1977, Washington, D.C.

Miller, Lawrence K. 16 January 1976, Pittsfield, Massachusetts.

Minahan, Victor I., Jr. 5 May 1976, Appleton, Wisconsin.

Oakes, John. 21 December 1975, New York, N.Y.

O'Brien, James. 19 September 1977, Wilmington, Delaware.

Olsen, Edward. 22 July 1976, Reno, Nevada.

Potter, J. Philip. 29 April 1980, letter from Sonoma, California.

Pusey, Nathan Marsh. 7 January 1976, New York, N.Y.

Reedy, George. 15 May 1976, Milwaukee, Wisconsin.

Ringler, H. Paul. 14 June 1976, Solana Beach, California. Letter, 3 March 1976.

Rubin, Morris. 23 April 1976, Madison, Wisconsin.

Schorr, Daniel. 27 April 1977, Berkeley, California.

Seib, Charles. 26 March 1976, Washington, D.C.

Smith, A. Robert. 29 March 1977, letter from Washington, D.C.

Steele, John L. 26 March 1976, Washington, D.C.

Strout, Richard L. 10 March 1976, Washington, D.C.

Theis, William. 25 March 1976, Washington, D.C.

Torinus, John. 5 May 1976, Appleton, Wisconsin.

Van Susteren, Urban. 5 May 1976, Appleton, Wisconsin.

Wax, Melvin. 1 February 1977, San Francisco, California.

Wyngaard, John. 3 June 1976, Madison, Wisconsin.

Manuscript Collections

Joseph and Stuart Alsop Papers. Library of Congress, Washington, D.C.

Americans for Democratic Action Papers. State Historical Society of Wisconsin, Manuscripts Division. Madison, Wisconsin.

Edwin R. Bayley Papers. State Historical Society of Wisconsin, Manuscripts Division. Madison, Wisconsin.

William Benton Papers. State Historical Society of Wisconsin, Manuscripts Division. Madison, Wisconsin.

Marquis Childs Papers. State Historical Society of Wisconsin, Manuscripts Division. Madison, Wisconsin.

William T. Evjue Papers. State Historical Society of Wisconsin, Manuscripts Division. Madison, Wisconsin.
Robert H. Fleming Papers, 1950–52. State Historical Society of Wisconsin, Manuscripts Division. Madison, Wisconsin.
John B. Oakes Papers. State Historical Society of Wisconsin, Manuscripts Division. Madison, Wisconsin.
Precinct returns, 1946 and 1952. State Historical Society of Wisconsin, Wisconsin State Archives. Madison, Wisconsin.
Joseph Pulitzer II Papers. Library of Congress. Washington, D.C.
Helen Reid Papers. Library of Congress. Washington, D.C.
Eric Sevareid Papers. Library of Congress. Washington, D.C.
Walter Trohan Papers. State Historical Society of Wisconsin, Manuscripts Division. Madison, Wisconsin.

Books and Articles

Anderson, Jack, and Ronald W. May. McCarthy: The Man, the Senator, the "Ism." Boston: Beacon Press, 1952.
Aronson, James. The Press and the Cold War. Indianapolis: Bobbs-Merrill Company, 1970.
Bagdikian, Ben H. The Effete Conspiracy, and Other Crimes by the Press. New York: Harper & Row, 1972.
Barnouw, Erik. The Golden Web: A History of Broadcasting in the United States. Vol. 2. 1933–1953. New York: Oxford University Press, 1968.
Barth, Alan. The Loyalty of Free Men. 2d ed. New York: Viking Press, 1951.
Bayley, Edwin R. "Joe McCarthy: His Last, Lost Try for a Headline." New Republic, 16 May 1960, p. 16.
Bayley, Edwin R. [E. B. Richards]. "McCarthy in Wisconsin: Down But Not Out." New Republic, 26 September 1955, p. 7.
Beale, William, ed. The AP McCarthy Series. New York: Associated Press, 1954.
Bean, Louis H. Influences in the 1954 Mid-Term Elections: War, Jobs, Parity, McCarthy. Washington, D.C.: Public Affairs Institute, 1954.
Bell, Daniel, ed. The Radical Right: The New American Right Expanded and Updated. Garden City, N.J.: Doubleday & Company, Anchor Books, 1963.
Buckley, William F., Jr. "McCarthy to the Rescue." National Review, 30 January 1970, pp. 804–5.
Buckley, William F., Jr., and L. Brent Bozell. McCarthy and His Enemies: The Record and Its Meaning. Chicago: Henry Regnery Company, 1954.
Burns, James McGregor. The Deadlock of Democracy: Four-Party Politics in America. Englewood Cliffs, N.J.: Prentice-Hall, 1963.
Cater, Douglass. "The Captive Press." The Reporter, 6 June 1950, pp. 17–20.
Catledge, Turner. My Life and The Times. New York: Harper & Row, 1971.
Chambers, Whittaker. "Odyssey of a Friend: Letters to William F. Buckley, Jr." National Review, 1 January 1970, pp. 22–32.
Code, Dozier C. "Witch-Hunting, 1952: The Role of the Press." Journalism Quarterly, December 1952, pp. 397–407.
Cogley, John. "The Murrow Show." Commonweal, 26 March 1954, p. 618.

Cogley, John. *Report on Blacklisting*. Vol. 2. *Radio-Television*. New York: The Fund for the Republic, 1954.

Cohn, Roy. *McCarthy*. New York: New American Library, 1968.

Commonweal. "The McCarthy Question." Unsigned editorial. 16 November 1973, pp. 172–73.

Cook, Fred. J. *The Nightmare Decade: The Life and Times of Senator Joe McCarthy*. New York: Random House, 1971.

Davis, Elmer H. *But We Were Born Free*. New York: Bobbs-Merrill Company, 1953.

Davis, Elmer H. "Giving Wolves an Appetite." *Nation*, 24 January 1953, p. 78.

Donoghue, James R. *How Wisconsin Voted, 1848–1954*. Madison: University of Wisconsin Extension Division Bureau of Government, 1956.

Epstein, Leon D. *Politics in Wisconsin*. Madison: University of Wisconsin Press, 1958.

Ferguson, LeRoy C., and Ralph H. Smuckler. *Politics in the Press: An Analysis of Press Content in 1952 Senatorial Campaigns*. East Lansing: Michigan State College, Governmental Research Bureau, 1954.

Feuerlicht, Roberta Strauss. *Joe McCarthy and McCarthyism: The Hate That Haunts America*. New York: McGraw-Hill, 1972.

Fiedler, Leslie A. "McCarthy as Populist." In *An End to Innocence: Essays on Culture and Politics*, edited by Leslie A. Fiedler. Boston: Beacon Press, 1955.

Ford, Sherman, Jr. *The McCarthy Menace: An Evaluation of the Facts and an Interpretation of the Evidence*. New York: William-Frederick Press, 1954.

Freeland, Richard M. *The Truman Doctrine and Origins of McCarthyism: Foreign Policy, Domestic Politics, and Internal Security, 1946–1948*. New York: Alfred A. Knopf, 1975.

Fremont-Smith, Eliot. "I. F. Stone: His Own Pygmalion." *Columbia Journalism Review*, January–February 1974.

Fried, Richard M. *Men Against McCarthy*. New York: Columbia University Press, 1976.

Friendly, Alfred. "The Noble Crusade of Senator McCarthy." *Harper's*, August 1950, pp. 34–42.

Friendly, Fred W. *Due to Circumstances Beyond Our Control*. New York: Random House, 1967.

Goldston, Robert C. *The American Nightmare: Senator Joseph R. McCarthy and the Politics of Hate*. New York: Bobbs-Merrill Company, 1973.

Gore, Leroy. *Joe Must Go*. New York: Julian Messner, 1954.

Greenspun, Hank. "A Few Columns on McCarthy." Anonymous reprint, 1954.

Greenspun, Hank, with Alex Pello. *Where I Stand: The Record of a Reckless Man*. New York: David McKay Company, 1966.

Griffith, Robert. *The Politics of Fear: Joseph R. McCarthy and the Senate*. Lexington: University Press of Kentucky, 1970.

Hughes, Emmett John. *The Ordeal of Power: A Political Memoir of the Eisenhower Years*. New York: Atheneum Publishers, 1963.

Hulten, Charles M. "The Impact of Senator Joseph McCarthy on the Press of the United States." *Gazette* (Netherlands) 4 (1958): 11–20.

Johnson, Gerald W. "Murrow, McCarthy and the 'Booboisie.'" *New Republic*, 19 April 1954, p. 3.

Kendrick, Alexander. *Prime Time: The Life of Edward R. Murrow*. Boston: Little, Brown and Company, 1969.

Latham, Earl, ed. *The Meaning of McCarthyism*. Boston: D. C. Heath and Company, 1973.

Lattimore, Owen. *Ordeal By Slander*. Boston: Little, Brown and Company, 1950.

Lubell, Samuel. *The Future of American Politics*. New York: Harper and Brothers, 1951.

Luthin, Reinhard H. *American Demagogues: Twentieth Century*. Boston: Beacon Press, 1954.

McCarthy, Joseph R. *America's Retreat from Victory: The Story of George Catlett Marshall*. New York: Devin-Adair Company, 1951.

McCarthy, Joseph R. *McCarthyism, the Fight for America: Documented Answers to Questions Asked by Friend and Foe*. New York: Devin-Adair Company, 1952.

Manly, Chesly. "Sulzbergerism." *American Mercury*, July 1979, pp. 17–23.

Mannes, Marya. "Comments on TV." *Reporter*, 31 March 1953, pp. 34–35.

March, James G. "McCarthy Can Still Be Beaten." *Reporter*, 28 October 1952, pp. 17–19.

Matusow, Allen J., ed. *Joseph R. McCarthy*. Englewood Cliffs, N.J.: Prentice-Hall, 1970.

May, Ronald. "Is the Press Unfair to McCarthy?" *New Republic*, 20 April 1954, pp. 10–14.

Miller, Merle. *The Judges and the Judged*. Garden City, N.Y.: Doubleday and Company, 1952.

Nation. "The Press Meets McCarthy." Unsigned article. 9 May 1953, pp. 387–88.

Nesbit, Robert C. *Wisconsin: A History*. Madison: University of Wisconsin Press, 1973.

O'Connor, John E. "Film Study and the History Classroom." *Newsletter of the American Historical Association*, March 1977.

Pearson, Drew. *Diaries, 1949–1959*. Edited by Tyler Abell. New York: Holt, Rinehart and Winston, 1974.

Pedrick, Willard H. "Senator McCarthy and the Law of Libel: A Study of Two Campaign Speeches." *Northwestern University Law Review* 48 (1953): 135–84.

Pilat, Oliver. *Pegler, Angry Man of the Press*. Boston: Beacon Press, 1963.

Polsby, Nelson. "Toward an Explanation of McCarthyism." *Political Studies* (1960): 250–71.

Polsby, Nelson, and Aaron Wildavsky. *Presidential Elections*. 3rd ed. New York: Charles Scribner's Sons, 1954.

Potter, Charles E. *Days of Shame*. New York: Coward-McCann, 1965.

Riggs, Robert. Untitled. *New Republic*. 24 May 1954, pp. 10–11.

Rogin, Michael Paul. *The Intellectuals and McCarthy: The Radical Specter*. Cambridge, Mass.: The M.I.T. Press, 1967.

Rorty, James, and Moshe Decter. *McCarthy and the Communists*. Boston: Beacon Press, 1954.

Rovere, Richard H. "The Last Days of Joe McCarthy." *Esquire*, August 1958, pp. 29–34.

Rovere, Richard H. *Senator Joe McCarthy*. New York: Harcourt Brace, 1959.

Rubin, Morris H., ed. "McCarthy: A Documented Record." *The Progressive*, 1954.

Rubin, Morris, ed. *The McCarthy Record*. Madison: The Wisconsin Citizens' Committee on McCarthy's Record, 1952.

Seldes, George. "New War on the Press." *Nation*, 5 February 1955, pp. 113–16.

Siebert, Fred S., Theodore Peterson, and Wilbur Schramm. *Four Theories of the Press*. Urbana: University of Illinois Press, 1956.

Stevens, David H. "Letter from Wisconsin: McCarthy on the Home Front." *Pacific Spectator* (1950): 275–278.

Stormer, John A. *None Dare Call It Treason*. Florissant, Mo.: Liberty Bell Press, 1964.

Straight, Michael. *Trial by Television*. Boston: Beacon Press, 1954.

Tannenbaum, Percy H. "The Effect of Headlines on the Interpretations of News Stories." *Journalism Quarterly*, Spring 1953, pp. 189–97.

Thomas, Lately. *When Even Angels Wept: The Senator Joe McCarthy Affair, a Story without a Hero*. New York: Morrow and Co., 1973.

Thomas, Lately. Transcript of pretrial examination of McCarthy, 29 October 1952, in libel suit against the Post-Standard Co. in the Onondaga Supreme Court, Syracuse, N.Y.

UNESCO. *World Communications: Press, Radio, Film*. Paris, 1950 and 1956.

U.S. Congress, Senate, Subcommittee on Privileges and Elections of the Committee on Rules and Administration, *Maryland Senatorial Election of 1950*. Hearing on S. Res 250, 81st Cong., 2d session, 20 February–11 April 1951.

U.S. Congress, Senate, Subcommittee on Privileges and Elections of the Committee on Rules and Administration, *Investigation of Senator Joseph R. McCarthy, Hearing on S. Res. 187*, 82d Congress, 1st and 2d sessions, 28 September 1951–16 May 1952.

U.S. Congress, Senate, Subcommittee on Privileges and Elections to the Committee on Rules and Administration: *Investigations of Senators Joseph R. McCarthy and William Benton, S. Res. 187 and 304*, 82d Cong., 2d sess., 1952.

Watkins, Arthur V. *Enough Rope*. Englewood Cliffs, N.J.: Prentice-Hall and the University of Utah Press, 1969.

Wechsler, James A. *The Age of Suspicion*. New York: Random House, 1953.

Weinstein, Allen. *Perjury: The Hiss-Chambers Case*. New York: Alfred A. Knopf, 1978.

Wendt, Lloyd. *Chicago Tribune: The Rise of a Great American Newspaper*. Chicago: Rand McNally and Company, 1979.

Williams, Edward Bennett. "The Final Irony of Joe McCarthy." *Saturday Evening Post*, 9 June 1962, pp. 21–29.

Wisconsin Legislative Reference Bureau. *The Blue Book*. Madison: State of Wisconsin, 1948, 1950, 1952, and 1954.

Index

source of news, 66; and interpretive reporting, 80–85; charged with left-wing bias, 82, 154; publishes analysis of McCarthy career, 86; polls editors, 98; rebuttal to Chicago speech, 106; accused of "going easy" on McCarthy, 130; story on Murrow, 196; gets complaints about hearing coverage, 209; mentioned, 8n, 19n, 20–36 passim, 42, 43, 44, 46, 67, 70, 71, 72, 74, 79, 81, 84, 87, 107, 130, 133, 142, 189, 209, 217, 218

Associated Press Managing Editors Association (APME): considers bias charges, 82–84

Association for Education in Journalism, 17

Atkins, Ollie, 162

Atkins clothing store, 168

Atlanta Constitution: coverage of Army-McCarthy hearings, 210; mentioned, 3, 27, 31, 47, 60, 62

Atomic Energy Commission, 60

Attorney General's list of subversive organizations, 5, 177

Author Meets the Critics, 180

Bagdikian, Ben H.: on influence of small newspapers, 119; on McCarthy's use of television, 184

Bakersfield Californian, 45

Baltimore News-Post, 18n

Baltimore Sun: first-month coverage, 61; sees crossover vote, 96; on Chicago speech, 112–13; on "left-wing" press list, 127; read by Truman, 155; coverage of McCarthy, 157–58; mentioned, 30, 48, 64, 72, 73, 77, 90, 150, 172

Baraboo News-Republic, 108

Barkley, Alben, 83

Bartell Broadcasters: application for TV license, 178

Barth, Alan: blames Truman for McCarthyism, 7; on objectivity, 76–77; called "pinko," 154; mentioned, 148, 150, 216

Bass, Mrs. Charlotta, 108

Bauer, Malcolm, 167

Beale, William, Jr.: defends reporting McCarthy as news, 84

Bean, Louis H.: on effect of newspaper opposition to McCarthy, 114; mentioned, 118

Bechtel, William R., 125

Bell, Daniel, 127–28

Bell, Jack: explains Republicans use of McCarthy, 44–45; mentioned, 86

Beloit Daily News: news bias, 105; endorses McCarthy, 116; mentioned, 26, 41

Bennett, Wallace, 212

Bentley, Elizabeth, 110

Benton, William: charges perjury, 23; opposed by McCarthy, 102; explains tape editing, 201; says press created McCarthy, 215; mentioned, 17, 106, 134, 171, 218

Berkshire Eagle, 40, 41, 45, 50

Bernays, Edward L.: 1952 list of best newspapers, 127

Bernstein, Carl, 159

Big Pay-Off, 204

Blaine, Reed, 60

Block, Herbert. See Herblock

Bloomer, John, 84

Bloor, Mother, 103

Bonner, Artemas, 98

Boston Globe: misleading headline, 37; appraised by Lyons, 77; mentioned, 45, 62, 95, 157

Boston Herald, 21, 31

Boston Post: coverage of hearings, 209; mentioned, 15, 31, 43

Boston Traveler, 11

Boycott attempts: against *Capital Times*, 128; against *Milwaukee Journal*, 131; against *Time*, 170

Bozell, L. Brent, 19n, 23, 24

Brewster, Owen, 45, 46

Bricker, John, 69

Broadcasting media: exploited by Red-baiters, 176–77

Broadcasting-Telecasting: accuses McCarthy of censorship, 178; criticizes McCarthy reply to Murrow, 198; mentioned, 177

Browder, Earl, 171

Brown, Constantine, 60, 160

Brownell, Herbert: says Truman promoted White, 184; as strategist, 186

Buckley, William F., Jr.: proposed as substitute for McCarthy, 197; mentioned, 19n, 23, 24

Budenz, Louis, 110, 177, 179

Buffalo News, 18n, 37, 56, 62

Business Week, 170

Butler, John, 171

But We Were Born Free, 77

Byrnes, James F.: author of McCarthy's "list," 20; mentioned, 20, 22, 24, 35

Bystrom, Arthur, 25, 130

Cain, Harry, 102

California State Senate Committee on Un-American Activities: defines

Communist fronts, 5; lists ACLU as subversive, 196

Canham, Erwin D., 147n

Capital Times: praises AP, 31; leads in opposition to McCarthy, 50; supports La Follette in 1946 primary, 90; endorses Schmitt, 93; news bias, 105; endorses Fairchild, 114; influence on voting, 117; on "left-wing" press list, 127; relations with McCarthy, 128–31; mentioned, 10n, 18n, 31, 32, 43, 45, 62, 80, 81, 83, 93, 105, 115, 118, 126, 132, 134, 142, 148, 154, 170, 172, 173, 180

Cargill, Jesse, 56

Carr, Francis, 202

Cartoonists, 55–56

Cater, Douglass: on "straight" reporting, 76

Catledge, Turner, 138

Central Intelligence Agency (CIA), 202

Chadwick, John: scolded by McCarthy, 72–73

Chamberlain, William Henry, 147n

Chambers, Whittaker, 4, 44, 110, 144

Chapple, John B., 98

Charlotte Observer: reverses its stand on McCarthy, 51

Chiang Kai-Shek, 4, 34, 54

Chicago Daily News, 48, 51, 56

Chicago Daily News Service, 66

Chicago speech attacking Stevenson (103–13): reaction to, 105–7; analyses of, 106–12; examined for libel, 111–12; effects of, 112–13; mentioned, 123, 180, 184

Chicago Sun-Times: criticizes McCarthy, 115; mentioned, 30, 42, 56n, 59, 63, 83, 106, 127, 192

Chicago Tribune: isolationist influence in Wisconsin, 15; influence on McCarthy, 16; editorial support, 54; sees crossover vote, 96; says McCarthy smeared, 97; challenges Stevenson, 107; supports Eisenhower, 111; endorses McCarthy, 115; attacks on other newspapers, 152–55; called McCarthy's "stoutest supporter," 155; criticizes McCarthy, 193; coverage of hearings, 209; mentioned, 18n, 19, 25, 31, 41, 43, 51, 55, 63, 64, 94, 104, 105, 106, 110, 135, 151, 174, 179, 189

Chicago Tribune (history), 19n

Childs, Marquis: early criticism, 57; called "left-wing," 155; says McCarthy forming new party, 186; mentioned, 58

Chilton Times-Journal: endorses McCarthy, 122

China, People's Republic of. *See* Communist China

Christian Science Monitor: on "left-wing" list, 127; relations with McCarthy, 147–48; mentioned, 37, 48, 60, 75, 113, 155, 172, 173, 198

Christoffel, Harold, 90

CIO News: supports McCarthy, 90

Clapp, Norman, 120–21

Claremont Daily Eagle, 16

Clark, Tom, 7n

Cleveland News, 87, 153

Cleveland Plain Dealer: says McCarthy unconvincing, 112; mentioned, 50, 62, 64, 153

Cleveland Press, 153

Coe, Frank, 107

Cogley, John: says Murrow program unfair, 200

Cohen, Octavus Roy, 161

Cohn, Roy: view of press, 8; accused by army, 202; questioned by Welch, 206; says McCarthy was damaged, 208; mentioned, 19n, 135, 160, 203, 205, 207, 211

Coleman, Thomas E., 106

Collins, Frederic W.: describes McCarthy technique, 60

Columbia Broadcasting System (CBS): offers McCarthy free radio time, 178; offers free television time, 185; refuses McCarthy free time, 190; reaction to Murrow program, 195; nightly summary of hearings, 204; asks to cover censure hearings, 210; time to Medina, 210–11; mentioned, 178, 192, 193, 198, 199, 200

Columbia University, 142, 143, 182

Columbus Dispatch, 51, 96

Columbus Ledger, 84

Columnists, 56–61

Commonweal, 172, 173, 198

Communist China, 4

Communist fronts: defined, 5; redefined, 176–77; mentioned, 42, 46

Communist party (in America): use of fronts, 5; in Wheeling speech, 18; in 1946 primary, 90; mentioned, 11, 12, 20, 21, 22, 23, 107, 108, 109, 128, 138, 166, 179, 207, 212

Compton, Wilson M., 181

Congressional Record, 21, 22, 44, 82, 170, 212

Conrad, Will C.: and La Follette, 91

Considine, Bob, 191

Cook, Fred J., 19n, 24n

Coplon, Judith, 52, 160

Vernon County Censor, 98
Veterans of Future Wars, 15n
Vietnam War: basis for intervention laid,
   6; compared with Korean War, 06 07;
   mentioned, 15n, 151
Vilas County News-Review, 123
Vincent, John Carter: accused by
   Thompson, 59; cited as McCarthy
   "success," 140; mentioned, 171
Voice of America: investigated by
   McCarthy, 180-84; charged with
   subversion, accused employes fired,
   181

Wallace, Henry, 144
Walters, Basil L., 144
War Production Board, 153
Washington Book Shop, 42
Washington Daily News, 107n
Washington Guild Reporter, 76
Washington Post: first editorial, 32;
   identifies "Case No. 9," 42; ranked in
   opposition, 50; vote analysis, 95-96;
   asks Eisenhower repudiate Chicago
   speech, 112; among 10 best, 127; on
   "left-wing" list, 131; relations with
   McCarthy, 148-52; merged with
   Times-Herald, 151; read by Truman,
   155; says McCarthy trying to dictate,
   186; campaign against McCarthy, 216;
   and Watergate, 216; mentioned, 6, 7,
   30, 38, 40, 41, 43, 48, 55, 56n, 62, 68,
   70, 72, 73, 76, 77, 80, 84, 113, 128, 134,
   135, 144, 152-59 passim, 172, 179, 196,
   198, 215
Washington Post-Los Angeles Times
   News Service, 86
Washington Star: criticizes Chicago
   speech, 112; second in circulation, 151;
   coverage of McCarthy, 160; read by
   McCarthy, 172; coverage of hearings,
   209; mentioned, 21, 37, 41, 45, 50, 60,
   62, 157, 198
Washington State Press Club, 102-3
Washington Times-Herald: "spy ring"
   lead, 38; largest circulation, 54;
   purchased by Meyer, 151-52; read by
   McCarthy, 172; mentioned, 19, 41, 50,
   64, 154
Watergate, 134, 137, 159, 165, 215-16
Waters, George, 19
Watertown Times, 117
Watkins, Arthur V.: bans television, 210;
   chairman, censure committee, 210;
   rules McCarthy out of order, 211;
   denounced by McCarthy, 212;
   mentioned, 159

Watkins committee: hearings, 210-13;
   mentioned, 160
Watson, L.R., 13
Waukesha Freeman: endorses
   McCarthy, 116; effect on vote, 118
Wausau Record-Herald, 18n, 43, 51, 97,
   105, 117
Wauwatosa Republican Club, 127, 132,
   135
Wax, Melvin: on withholding news,
   16-17
WBEV (radio), 179
Weadock, J.F., 83
Wechsler, James A.: attacked in Chicago
   speech, 104, 110; rebuttal, 110-11;
   called before McCarthy, 142;
   questioned about editorial policy,
   143-44; as "Bennie Wexler," 172
Weiss, Louis: linked by McCarthy to
   Hiss and Milwaukee Journal, 132-33
Welch, Joseph: clash with McCarthy,
   206-8; mentioned, 55, 202
Wendt, Lloyd, 19n
Wheeling speech: newspaper use, 16-20;
   arguments about numbers, 21-24;
   mentioned, 31, 32, 49, 54, 66, 126, 139,
   142
Wheeling Intelligencer, 17, 18, 19n, 23
Wherry, Kenneth: threatens to sue
   Acheson, 40; quoted on "perverts,"
   161; mentioned, 31, 41, 53, 162
White, Bob, 179
White, Harry Dexter: accused of spying,
   184; mentioned, 185, 186
White, Lincoln, 32, 33
White, William S., 41, 86, 158, 182
Whitehead, Don: vote analysis, 95;
   mentioned, 86
Wichita Eagle, 47, 51
Wiggins, J. Russell: and space given
   McCarthy, 84; chairs ASNE committee
   on Wechsler incident, 144-45
Wiley, Alexander: reelected, 89; and
   "atheistic Communism," 122;
   mentioned, 18, 92, 116
Williams, Edward Bennett, 156, 211
Williams, Gladstone, 60
Willkie, Wendell, 153
Winchell, Walter, 155
Wire service reporters, 215, 218
Wire services: as source of news, 66;
   status of reporters, 67; competition, 68;
   praised by McCarthy, 80; and
   objectivity, 215; mentioned, 25, 32, 40,
   43, 46, 157, 189-90, 218. See also
   specific agencies

DESIGNED BY GARY G. GORE
COMPOSED BY IMPRESSIONS, INC., MADISON, WISCONSIN
MANUFACTURED BY BANTA COMPANY, MENASHA, WISCONSIN
TEXT IS SET IN MELIOR
DISPLAY LINES ARE SET IN CRAW CLARENDON AND BULLETIN TYPEWRITER

Library of Congress Cataloging in Publication Data
Bayley, Edwin R.
Joe McCarthy and the press.
Bibliography: pp. 245-254
Includes index.
1. McCarthy, Joseph, 1908-1957—Relations with
journalists. 2. Press and politics—United States.
3. Journalists—United States. I. Title.
E748.M143B34   973.918′092′4   81-50824
ISBN 0-299-08620-8   AACR2